The

PRIMAL FORCE
in
SYMBOL

UNDERSTANDING THE
LANGUAGE OF
HIGHER CONSCIOUSNESS

RENÉ ALLEAU

TRANSLATED BY ARIEL GODWIN

Inner Traditions
Rochester, Vermont

Inner Traditions
One Park Street
Rochester, Vermont 05767
www.InnerTraditions.com

Originally published in French under the title *La science des symbols* by Éditions
    Payot, Paris
First U.S. edition published in 2009 by Inner Traditions

Library of Congress Cataloging-in-Publication Data

Alleau, René.
   [Science des symbols. English]
   The primal force in symbol : understanding the language of higher consciousness /
René Alleau ; translated by Ariel Godwin.—1st U.S. ed.
      p. cm.
   Includes bibliographical references and index.
   ISBN 978-1-59477-249-8 (pbk.)
   1. Symbolism. I. Title.

   BL600.A4413 2009
   302.2'223—dc22

                                                                    2008037991

Printed and bound in the United States by Lake Book Manufacturing

10 9 8 7 6 5 4 3 2 1

Text design and layout by Priscilla Baker

This book was typeset in Garamond Premier Pro with Copperplate used as a display
typeface

Inner Traditions wishes to express its appreciation for assistance given by the
government of France through the National Book Office of the Ministère de la
Culture in the preparation of this translation.

Nous tenons à exprimer nos plus vifs remerciements au government de la France
et le ministère de la Culture, Centre National du Livre, pour leur concours dans le
préparation de la traduction de cet ouvrage.

CONTENTS

ACKNOWLEDGMENTS

Having no illusion of being the only author of this book, I must at least address all my thanks to the specialists, French and foreign, who informed me of their work in the area of symbolism during these last years, whether by letters or in private interviews or by sending me their publications. I cannot name them all; I ask that they excuse me for this, and know that I have followed the progress of their research with great attention.

Among them, I mention those whose persevering efforts succeeded in clearing the first paths of access to general symbology. First I thank Dr. Moïse Engelson of Geneva and Ms. Claire Lejeune of the University of Mons (Belgium). Since 1950, their role has been decisive in the organization of the first interdisciplinary conferences in this area of study and, since 1962, in the publication of *Cahiers Internationaux de Symbolisme,* a source of documentation of major importance for the progress of research in this subject. I suggest readers take in Claire Lejeune's letter in appendix 1, which she has authorized me to publish integrally in this book. In it, readers will find a historical overview of these important initiatives and a highly accurate analysis of the spirit that animated the pioneers of the interdisciplinary study of symbolism.

Next, I must render particular homage to my professor at the Sorbonne, Gaston Bachelard, under whose auspices the first conference on the subject, "The Foundations of Symbolism in Light of Multiple Disciplines," was organized at the UNESCO palace in June 1962. At this time (as Ms. Claire Lejeune recalls in her letter), courage and high ideals of the freedom of spirit were required in order to dare to ignore the prohibition that still hindered academic circles in the study of symbols and also to combat certain excessively conservative and dogmatic theological and pseudo-traditional tendencies.

Among the young academics who then counted themselves among these pioneers of the study of symbols and defenders of the rights of imagination, most had been through the French Resistance, and were not inclined to submit to the bourgeois cultural police or its hierarchy of values. If we read the texts of this first conference in 1962, we find already developed the principal revolutionary themes of 1968. In the significative sense, there is a convergence between questioning the rationalist ideas of scientism and contesting consumer society and the mythology of "production at any price," which have blended together into the alienation of humans and the destruction of their intimate and profound relationships to the poetry of the world and nature.

The main representative of these contesters of 1962 was Gilbert Durand (also a former student of Gaston Bachelard), who is now the moderator of the Center for Research on the Imaginary (C.R.I.) in Chambéry, and one of the world's greatest specialists on symbolism.

Among other correspondents and friends, I cannot forget my debt to the writing and work of Dr. Durand de Bousingen, Raymond Ruyer, Marie-Madeleine Davy, and Prince Constantin Andronikoff (one of the most profound theologians of the present day), as well as to the documents on the Aristotelian and scholastic logic of analogy that were kindly sent to me by Mr. François Chenique, professor at the School of Political Sciences.

I also express my thanks to Ms. Marguerite-Marie de Schloezer, Ms. Élizabeth de Farcy, Ms. Anne Forgeot, and Mr. Yves Chalas, who made invaluable contributions to my bibliographic and iconographic research, as well as to the presentation of this book.

INTRODUCTION

*And the vision of all is become unto you as the words of a book
that is sealed, which men deliver to one that is learned, saying,
Read this, I pray thee: and he saith, I cannot; for it is sealed:
And the book is delivered to him that is not learned, saying,
Read this, I pray thee: and he saith, I am not learned.*

ISAIAH 29:11–12, KING JAMES VERSION

The methodological approach to the symbol is no less important than the analysis of its anthropological and theological functions. In epistemological terms, no domain of knowledge is more difficult to define because the process of symbolization takes place on multiple levels of experience, from the complex function of our perceptions to the highest degrees of development and systematization of our depiction of the world. In an era when a whole lifetime of research is barely sufficient to tackle the increasingly overwhelming challenges of information—even when highly specialized—any attempt to study all the aspects of a subject as vast as symbolism would be an interminable undertaking, fruitless and impossible to complete individually.

This is not the intent of this book, whose boundaries are defined by its definition as "a contribution to the study of the problems posed

1

by the methods and principles of general symbology (the science of symbols)."

First of all, this relatively new discipline must not be confused with *symbolism,* a term referring to the *usage* of symbols, which goes back to prehistoric times. The first attempts at coherent classification, systematic comparison, and interpretation of ancient symbols occurred no earlier than the sixteenth century, in the erudite works of Renaissance iconologists and mythologists. These investigations were extended in the eighteenth and nineteenth centuries alongside the considerable progress of archaeology and other historical sciences.

But above all, it has been in modern times, in the last fifty years or so, with the development of linguistics, psychology, ethnology, the history of religion, and art history, that questions have really been posed concerning signs, symbols, and myths in relation to the methods and principles of their various interpretations. Profound divergences have appeared among specialists; Paul Ricoeur justly called this the "conflict of hermeneutics."[1] An example is the violent controversy among Freudian and Jungian psychoanalysts, "phenomenologists," and "structuralists," as well as many other schools and groups, including those that oppose each other in the name of the same initiatory or religious tradition.

Thus, here I have cautiously chosen to dwell initially upon the importance of a terminology of general symbology. Readers might judge as excessive the development given here to the researching of definitions and to the study of synonyms and the often subtle nuances that distinguish them. Therefore, I have devoted the first chapter of this book solely to the study of the etymological origin and semantics of the word *symbol.* Likewise, I have insisted upon the necessity of choosing the word *syntheme* over *symbol* in the vocabulary of science and logic. Herein lies an issue that goes beyond the rules of usage and the propriety of words to the truth of the notions that the words express and the validity of reasoning and its methods. An impropriety that is tolerable in other areas of knowledge is not tolerable in the language of mathematics and axiomatics. Their coherence is at stake, and I hope that logicians will understand the need for reforming their vocabulary.

Readers should not expect to find in this book a dictionary of symbols that would allow them, with little effort, to understand an obscure and veiled language through the translation and interpretation of signs. There are already numerous examples, both ancient and modern, of this encyclopedic genre. I have listed principal examples in the bibliography. Their usefulness is no less certain than their didactic insufficiency. In fact, nothing is closer to the language of symbols than the language of music. To learn this language truly, we must resign ourselves to the patient, thankless task of learning its theoretic principles. If we do not know the notes, the scales, the chords, and the rules of harmony, then just as if we were to refuse to learn the grammar of a language, the best dictionary in the world cannot teach us really to understand, much less to speak.

Moreover, in the realm of symbology, there is no *general* code for deciphering, but only *specific* codes, which themselves require interpretation. A symbol does not signify; it evokes and focuses, assembles and concentrates, in an analogically versatile manner, a multiplicity of meanings that cannot be reduced to one or many single meanings. Nor does a musical note have a meaning determined once and for all, whatever that meaning might be. A note's meaning depends as directly on its rhythmic and sonorous context as a symbol depends on the mythical and ritual context associated with it.

To penetrate the world of symbols is to try to perceive harmonic vibrations and, in a way, to divine a music of the universe. This requires not only intuition but also an innate sense of analogy, a gift that can be developed through exercise but that cannot be acquired. There is a "symbolic ear" just as there is a "musical ear," and it is partially independent from an individual's degree of cultural development. The symbolic ear of the Australian Aborigine, for example, is incomparably more developed than that of the modern "civilized" person.

This phenomenon is generally attributed to the "archaic" nature of the unconscious, which, being more active in primitive people, is more easily expressed by an immediate and spontaneous symbolic language. We may question the value of this explanation, however. Someone who studies closely the mythic and religious life of Australian Aborigines will be astounded not by the simplicity of their analogical and symbolic structures, but rather by the extraordinary complexity of their forms and expressions. If the unconscious alone is capable of developing and distinguishing so many subtle and varied nuances in the relationship of humans to their interior and exterior environments, we may well ask why "evolved" consciousness and intelligence have become incapable of this.

In our assessment, however, we should not erroneously confuse two distinct phenomena: first, that which arises from a life that is still very close to animal life because of the many obstacles presented by the natural environment and an almost complete lack of technological development, a state that is truly "archaic" when compared to ours; and second, the development of a language intended for interpreting and supporting these conditions, as well as adapting to them. From this perspective, it is natural for primitive people to gain more from myths and symbols than we do, because the everyday obstacles the Aborigine must confront are more difficult to overcome. Yet not everything is unconscious in this response of the human "logosphere" to the pressures of the "biosphere": A great number of Australian religions and initiations appear to be organized voluntarily and planned logically. The symbolic ear of primitive people, although probably innate, like the nose of a hunting dog, is nonetheless developed and refined by the exercise of its functions. Therefore, it also exists, in a latent state, in civilized people—and in them it is less used because it is atrophied; it no longer appears necessary for everyday internal and external life.

Another example of this phenomenon of the atrophy of the sources of analogical and symbolic intuition by technological development can be found in regional styles of architecture. When the industrial production and transport of materials were still problematic, peasant houses were constructed using local resources—through the borrowing of mineral and vegetable materials from the terrain. In this way, the human habitat was adapted to the natural landscape, to its colors and its forms. The pleasant analogy of structures, their harmonic correspondences to the environment, the personal style expressed in the least wall, and the overall achievement of the beauty of symbolic harmonies did not result solely from the builders' patience and sense of good proportion. They also followed from the lack of any means of production other than those of the artisan. When it became easier to use concrete rather than cut stone, sheet metal rather than thatch or slate, peasant dwellings became uniform and regional styles disappeared. Because the intuition of adaptation to the landscape was no longer necessary, it was no longer exercised, and therefore it atrophied.

We should not separate humans, as symbolizing animals, from our concrete, corporeal, and material conditions, our daily existence. Too often, attempts are made to forget these connections; we consider only the relationship of symbolism to cultural, artistic, religious, and initiatory life, or even to individual and collective psychology. Although we should not deny the obvious importance of these relationships, they are not the first, original conditions of the analogical process—which comes from a far-off and profound source that is purely experiential and common to all living beings. This source is not just sexuality, as Freud believed; it is *nutrition,* or, to be more exact, *the assimilation of the living by the living,* of which reproduction is only one of the consequences. The logic of analogy has been imposed on us since prehistoric times by the concrete conditions of the hunting economy and by techniques of mimicry and trapping. This analogical process, moreover, is not exclusively human; Here in this book, I have given numerous examples of its importance in animal life. Therefore, we may rightly consider it universal. This is why analogy is the key to general symbology. My research has been focused on this point rather than on the symbol itself.

FOUNDATIONS OF GENERAL SYMBOLOGY

All science, including the science of history, has the logical obligation to operate using a certain number of concepts that cannot be justified by deduction or induction, because they constitute the foundations of the operations of that science. When a physicist assures us that he has defined force as a quantity proportional to the product of mass and acceleration, he is stating nothing more than a formal operative rule, allowing us to observe, in an experiential case, whether the phenomenon in question is present or absent: whether it is produced, under what conditions, and to what degree.

General symbology must likewise allow for initial assumptions that cannot be proved, even though they are imposed by their constant relationships to all the operations of this discipline. The first of these is the idea of the *existence of order in the universe.* In reality, this order cannot be demonstrated because our systems of reference are more specific than their object. Yet all our sciences admit this hypothesis and verify it partially by discovering laws. Therefore, we may give symbology that which we give to all other physical and human sciences.

The second postulate seems more easily contestable: the *probability of the analogy or homology of structures between a partial order and a total order.* This notion is less obvious than the first postulate. Yet the observation of nature does not contradict it. In fact, we observe that in a succession of ordered systems, the probability that they resemble one another is greater than the probablility that they differ. For example, we might expect to find chemical elements in outer space having no resemblance to carbon, the basis of terrestrial life. But astronomers continually discover objects made up of carbon, rather than from the other elements, which, theoretically, could just as easily be formed in that immense laboratory of outer space. Bioastronomy has other still-undreamed analogies of this kind in store for us. The ancients claimed that nature loves to imitate her most complex operations in the simplest ways. If analogy is never proof, then at least it encourages us to explore similarities in all areas. Its role in the science of symbols is fundamental.

Once accepted, these two initial hypotheses—the *existence of order in the universe* and the *logic of analogy*—are sufficient for establishing general symbology and studying its various forms. They are the foundations of this book, which endeavors to isolate the principles and methods of a new science based on an immemorial usage. Just as arithmetic was founded on the "art of counting" after millennia of experience, so we can hope that after lengthy interdisciplinary research, *symbology* will be founded, little by little, upon the study of *symbolism*—that is, the "art of symbolizing," the usage and experience of symbols.

There is nothing surprising in this: the initial object of usage is always the final object of a science. Arithmetic proves it to us. The nature of the whole number still poses problems, even after the minds of illustrious mathematicians have made vain efforts to solve them. What we know least about in each thing is that thing's beginning.

SYMBOLOGY AND TYPOLOGY

In an important work that constitutes an introduction to "general archetypology" and that consequently forms part of the foundation for the future development of the science of symbols—*Les structures anthropologiques de l'imaginaire*[2]—Gilbert Durand writes of the "extreme confusion" that reigns in the "overly rich terminology" of general symbology: "Signs, images, symbols, allegories, emblems, archetypes, schemata, schemes, illustrations, schematic representations, diagrams, and synepies are the terms employed indifferently by the analysts of the imagination. Sartre, Dumas, and Jung all devoted several pages to explaining their vocabularies. This is what we in our turn will attempt to do."[3]

Gilbert Durand sets aside everything relating only to pure semiology. When he uses the word *sign,* it is only in a very general sense and with no intention to give it its precise meaning of "arbitrary algorithm" or "signal contingent on a signification." Yet he does not use the term *emblem,* although Dumas admits that emblems can "attain symbolic life."[4] Likewise, Durand avoids allegory, "frosty and cold"[5] in Hegel's words, "semantics desiccated into semiology, having value only as a conventional and academic sign."[6]

This exclusion is explained from Durand's typological perspective. What appears most important is the scheme, the "dynamic and affective generalization of the image,"[7] Piaget's functional symbol, Bachelard's motor symbol. These are the schemes that form "the dynamic and structured drive of the imagination."[8] Archetypes constitute the substantifications of schemes. Sartre had already observed that the scheme appeared as the presentifier of unconscious gestures and impulses. Jung substantified this notion based on Jacob Burckhardt, and made it the synonym of primordial image, engram, original image, archetype. The primordial image, according to Jung, must incontestably be connected to certain perceptible processes in nature that reproduce unceasingly and are always active, and is also connected "to certain inner conditions of the life of the mind and of life in general."[9] Durand emphasizes the essential role of the archetypes that "constitute the junction between the imagination and the rational processes."[10]

Archetypes, however, are equally linked to images differentiated culturally by social groups and civilizations. I will give only one example: alchemical symbolism. We may assume the archaic existence of a sacred metallurgy whose discovery—that of fire—was common to humanity in its relationship to nature. Yet this was not an *original image,* but a *concrete primordial experience* that, in a later phase, was the material for a very complex development of images and symbols whose system varied not only among the different areas of civilization, but also within each individual area, between their epochs and their dominant cultures. Thus there is not one alchemical symbolism but many, although initially they all had the same archaic experiential basis. This is why Chinese, Indian, Greek, Arabic, and medieval alchemists required so many specialists in each of these cultural arenas in order to interpret precisely their distinct forms of symbolization.

Under these conditions, when Jung writes of alchemical archetypes, to what alchemy does he refer and in what epoch? If he is referring to images "in connection with certain perceptible processes of nature that reproduce unceasingly and are always active,"[11] then these images have been modified by the historical process of culture in such a constant and profound manner that we can consider them as original and immutable models of the inner conditions of the life of the mind.

On the other hand, we can accept the idea of an archaism of the human psyche because neither biology nor physiology refutes this experientially verifiable hypothesis. We must not forget, however, that there is no image of the primordial at this level, because the primordial cannot be represented or imagined. It can only be experienced in its massive opacity in which the image is no longer distinguished from the object—one has the same value as the other—and the inability to imagine is precisely one of the clinical signs of psychical regression. If an original typical imagination existed, this pathological phenomenon would not exist.

Certainly, the symbol appears to lose its polyvalence in an unequivocal or conventional sense—for example, when the archetype of the wheel changes into a cruciform symbol, then becomes the sign of the syntheme of an abstract operation of addition or multiplication. Struck by this process of reduction of the initial polyvalence of a symbol, I initially thought that the starting point of general symbology was the type and that the termination of this increasing degradation was the syntheme[12] because, like all other specialists, I had a tendency to "substantify" the primordial scheme or type—that is, to consider it as a model or a pattern determined by its structure.[13]

It seems that at present we have not attached enough importance to the fact that these structures respond to the operations and logic of analogy, as well as to archaic experiential origins, while on the other hand we have concentrated all our analytical means on consequences and results, forms and products, assigning them their own internal power of determination. But where does the *isomorphism* of the schemes, archetypes, and symbols in mythical systems come from if not from the eternal power of analogy?

ANALOGICAL PROCESS AND
TAUTOLOGICAL PROCESS

This is why, in this book, the logic of analogy, the *analogical process* itself, rather than the symbol itself, is considered as the principal basis of general symbology, just as the logic of identity, the *tautological process* itself, and not the number, is the basis of mathematics and axiomatics. Léon Brunschvicg* writes,

> Just as the number has been considered an object in itself, so the philosophy of arithmetic oscillates continually between the primacy of the *cardinal* and the primacy of the *ordinal,* much as the philosophy of logic was incapable of putting an end to the debate of comprehension and extension. Here and there, the confusion has disappeared when the *static realism of the concept* has given way to the *dynamic idealism of judgment.* A number is constituted by the intelligence of the operation, which makes a new and progressive image of *collection* correspond to each of the successive actions of *seriation.* But this was recognized clearly and definitively only after Georg Cantor, in light of his set theory.[14]

Thus, from the general perspective that I propose, this is a matter of "desubstantifying" the symbol, of no longer making it a substrate, a reality in itself, no longer confusing a product with its producer, a consequence with its cause, but instead restoring the dialectic reality of its operations to the dynamics of the life of nature, the mind, imagination, and reason. These operations, furthermore, are not divided between two logics absolutely separated from one another—those of analogy and identity—because every number can also be a symbol and every sym-

---

*[Léon Brunschvicg (1869–1944) was a French philosopher of idealism. —*Ed.*]

bol a number. Moreover, if analogy does not take part in the methods of mathematical science as an instrument of proof, its role is no less considerable as an instrument of discovery. History offers numerous examples of this.

Thus, Kepler was able to deduce the laws of the movements of the planets from Tycho Brahé's observations, connecting them analogically to the geometric properties of the ellipse studied by ancient Greek mathematicians. Likewise, Henri Poincaré traced his discovery of Fuchsian functions to an analogical intuition whereby, while taking a walk one day, he realized that the transformations his researches had just achieved corresponded exactly to those of non-Euclidean geometry.

Moreover, mathematical ideas present examples of all the degrees of analogy, from the literal identity of two polynomials having no dissimilar character between them to the equality of two geometric figures, different from one another only in their position on a plane or in space, to the close analogical correspondence between two figures as different in appearance as a straight line in space and the sphere associated with that line by Sophus Lie's transformation. Analogical exploration, Robert Deltheil writes, also leads in certain arenas to perspectives of the whole in which harmony constitutes an essential element of the beauty of mathematics.[15]

Further, because analogy is of experiential and concrete origin, it cannot be sufficient for the abstract proof, which, in axiomatic and mathematical logic, achieves above all an economy of thought through the tautological process—that is, operating on the coherence of the *same* and its noncontradictory consequences rather than on the correspondences of the *similar,* which can achieve only the determination of the pure identity of the object of thought or the idea. Nevertheless, notions of the isomorphism of structures also play a major role in axiomatics, and from this point of view, we can compare this situation with what we observe in the realm of general symbology with regard to schemes and types.

Here, however, we must watch out for the substantification of models. If mathematics appears as an immense reservoir of abstract structures or symbology as an inexhaustible source of analogical and concrete structures, we must recall that these forms do not exist in themselves or by themselves independently from the dynamics of the logical process that constitutes them in the languages of mathematics and symbology. Nor do they exist without certain initial experiential and intuitive content.

Under these conditions, if we want to assume that all our knowledge rests upon two logics—the logics of analogy and identity—we could perhaps finally understand their equal epistemological dignity. Civilization cannot be built on a single pillar or with only one instrument of knowledge. Ancient and medieval civilizations developed the powers of symbology and abusively neglected the mathematical tool. In an inverse excess, modern civilization, essentially mathematical, scientific, and technological, has rejected the symbolic tool as insignificant and has thus condemned not only religion but also the arts to inevitable disappearance. One of the most obvious testimonies to this misunderstanding is the scarcely believable fact that the science of symbols, general symbology, which is so necessary for all disciplines, is not even considered teaching material, and is not found in the program of any university.

Certainly, general symbology has not yet been truly established. Further, because of the immense extent of its domain, one individual work is not enough to constitute it. This new science, essentially interdisciplinary but still confused and embryonic, will perhaps become the metascience of the twenty-first century, because it is able to show the close solidarity among all hermeneutics in their common task of interpreting nature, humans, and the universe.

The nonhuman appears to surround us on all sides in the cosmos, and our infrahuman machines, capable of opposing us with their own technological determinations, are unceasingly and increasingly reducing our freedom of choice and decision. Our world has been profoundly transformed, and to change it, we must first eliminate interpretations that have become hollow and sterile. Once we have done this, we must reinterpret.

Our new knowledge will clarify the old knowledge taught to us before; what is new will deepen what is old. It is not impossible to unify knowledge if we start out truly wanting to do so and if we understand that tolerance not only is a moral requirement but also is, above all, an epistemological necessity.

In the realm of general symbology, ideological and religious conflicts have run free, and the time taken to justify their arguments has been time lost for the general progress of this discipline. It appears people have forgotten that all hermeneutics, considered both individually and together, are simultaneously necessary and insufficient. If humans are archetypal symbolizing animals, it is because the very character of the symbolic function implies the impossibility of being satisfied with a "proper" meaning for things and beings and the capacity to add to these further meanings that can transfigure them. Malebranche writes: "We always have movement to go elsewhere,"[16] and it is precisely this experiential addition that calls to all hermeneutics and condemns them to turn into pillars of salt as soon as they look back at it, hoping to halt this addition and define it.

The sealed book of the universe does not allow itself to be read aloud. Nature flees from the violation of evidence: She confides her mysteries only in murmurs, in half-light. Her landscapes reveal their depths only at dawn and dusk, through vapors and mist. Knowing is not understanding; it is only savoring what we have glimpsed along the way. Reality does not require us to reduce the symbol to the limits of our thought. Instead, it invites us to immerse ourselves in the absence of its limits. Thus, the veiled speech of the symbol can protect us from the worst error: the discovery of a definitive and ultimate meaning of things and beings—for no one is more in error than he who knows all the answers . . . except, perhaps, he who knows only one answer.

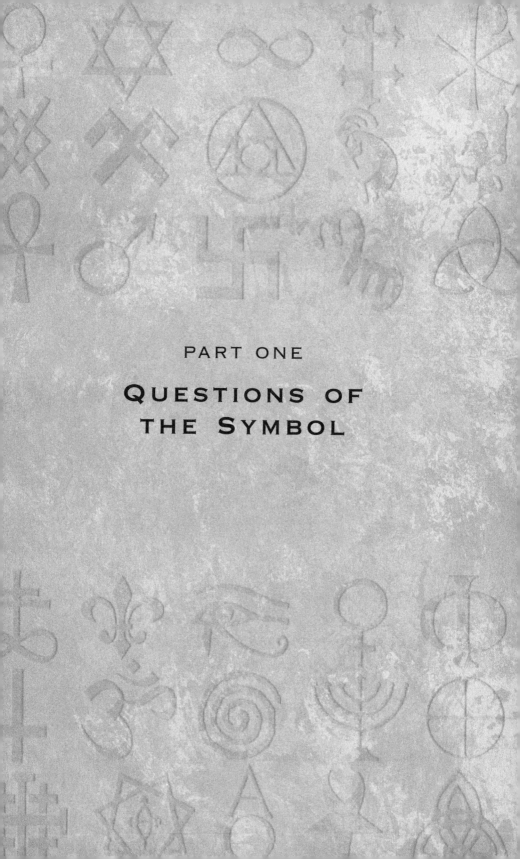

PART ONE

QUESTIONS OF
THE SYMBOL

1 ORIGIN AND SEMANTICS OF THE WORD *SYMBOL*

The semantics of the *symbol*—the study of the various modifications of the meaning of this term and its alterations throughout time—allows us to isolate certain aspects of the eternal questions posed by symbolism in various epochs of culture, and to analyze their answers and various interpretations on this subject.

THE SEMIC DISPERSION OF THE SYMBOL

One of the most significant examples of the semic dispersion of *symbol* appears, in my view, to be Trévoux's famous *Dictionnaire universel,* whose characteristic expressions I italicize: "Symbol: *Sign, type of emblem,* or *representation of some moral thing,* through images or representations of *natural things. Symbolum, signum, typus, emblematis species.* The lion is the *symbol* of bravery; the ball, of fickleness; the pelican, of paternal love . . ."[1]

I believe this example describes not a *symbol,* but an *allegory.* "Among the Egyptians, symbols were highly esteemed and concealed most of the *mysteries of morals.* The hieroglyphs of Pierius passed for symbols."[2] Here, the Trévoux dictionary mentions *Hiéroglyphiques* by Jean-Pierre Valerian, known as Pierius, published in 1615 and divided into fifty-eight books. This work is historically important but is principally allegorical and iconological. The Trévoux dictionary goes on: "The letters of the Chinese are, for the most part, significative *symbols*. Medalists use the term *symbols* for certain *marks* or *attributes* peculiar to certain *persons* or *deities*. . . . Provinces and cities also have their various symbols on their medals."[3] Here the author of the article is no longer confusing *symbol* with *allegory*, but instead confuses it with *emblem*. The Trévoux dictionary also categorizes *fables* under *symbols*. In the same category, "in terms of religion, the exterior signs of the Sacraments are called *symbols* and *sacred symbols*. . . . *Symbol* is also a term used among Christians for a certain *formula* that contains the principal articles of faith."[4]

Quite a remarkable detail: The Trévoux dictionary uses the word *symbolologie* to refer to what is later called *séméiologie* ("the part of pathology that deals with the signs and symptoms of maladies").[5]

The Encyclopaedia Britannica, published in Edinburgh in 1771 (the same year as the Trévoux *Dictionnaire*) by a certain Society of Gentlemen in Scotland, summarizes the previous information with exemplary concision: "Symbol, a sign or representation of something moral, by the figures or properties of natural things. Hence symbols are of various kinds, as hieroglyphics, types, oenigmas, parables, fables, etc. Among Christians, the term symbol denotes the Apostles' creed."[6]

This combining of the symbol and allegory in the eighteenth century is very important because it inspired Kant's conceptions of symbolism, reduced anthropologically to a "hypotyposis."[7] Moreover, starting in the seventeenth century, in books of rhetoric there was no longer a distinction between allegory and symbol; they were both considered tropes or figures. The confusion between them actually began in the fifteenth century, as we will see later. On the other hand, Romanticism (not without some exaggeration) contrasted the allegory (considered a continued metaphor without value) with the symbol (bearer of eternally profound meanings)—which is not the case for all symbols.

The entry "Symbole" in the "Table analytique et raisonnée" listing the contents of the thirty-three in-folio volumes of Diderot and d'Alembert's *Encyclopédie,* published in 1780 (see vol. 2, pages 726–27), seems to have inspired Trévoux's definitions more or less word for word, but also includes an interesting reference to the word *mystery:* "Symbol: Mystery spoken of in the symbols of Christians and in volume 10, 921.9 and 922."[8] There, after the interpretation of the Christian mysteries, we find this significant passage: "The secrets of religion [in paganism] were called the mysteries not because they were *incomprehensible* or elevated *above reason,* but *only* because they were covered and *disguised* beneath *types* and *figures* in order to excite the veneration of the people with this *obscurity.* The mysteries of paganism were celebrated in grottoes more suitable for hiding *crimes* than for celebrating the mysteries of religion."[9]

In this article, the correspondence of sign, sacrament, and mystery goes further: "This word *mystery* is also used for *sacrament, figure, sign,* which are terms of the *same meaning,* as M. Rigault has demonstrated and proved." Moreover, according to the author of the article, in scripture, mystery always designates a "parabolic sentence" that contains "a hidden meaning," a mystical action representing another meaning and action. Thus *parable* and *mystery* are confounded with *allegory.*[10]

The most interesting article on this subject is found in the supplement to the *Encyclopédie* (3, 132) under the entry "Freemasons" (Modern History): "The society or order of the Freemasons is a union of chosen persons who are linked by an obligation to love one another as brothers, to aid one another in need, and to keep an inviolable silence about all that concerns their order . . ."[11] On the subject of their symbols, the author adds:

Among the Greeks there were similar customs. The initiates to the mysteries of Ceres or the Good Goddess also had words and signs to recognize each other, as one can see in Arnobius and Clement of Alexandria. Those sacred words, essential for the recognition of initiates, were called *symbols* or *collations. From here comes the name of the symbol given to the profession of faith that characterizes Christians.*[12]

The author of the article proposes a curious interpretation of the origin of Masonic signs and words of "recognition": They were first used by Christian knights dispersed among the infidels as a means for communicating secretly and meeting to rebuild the destroyed Christian temples. The French term *francs-maçons* also evoked the importance of the role of French knights in the conquest of the Holy Land.

Semantically, we can see that the word *symbol* is understood here with the fairly narrow meaning of "sign of recognition" of a conventional and cryptic type. The etymology proposed for the word *mystery* is no less singular: "This word comes from the Greek *muserion,* which is said to be formed from *muo,* Latin *claudo, taceo* ('I close, I keep silent') and *soma* ('mouth') But where does the letter *r* come from in *mystery*? *This word is therefore originally Hebrew:* It comes from *sator,* which means 'hidden'—thus *mystar,* 'a hidden thing.'"[13]

We must concede that this etymology is no less mysterious or incomprehensible than the word itself. In all the previously cited encyclopedia articles, we may notice that the etymological origin of the word *symbol* itself is never mentioned. We might hope to find some necessary explanation in Du Cange's[14] monumental work, *Glossarium mediae et infimae latinitatis.*

THE LATIN AND GREEK ETYMOLOGY
OF THE WORD *SYMBOL*

Symbola, Du Cange tells us, designated the *ciborium* or the *pyxide* (*pyxis*) in which the consecrated hosts were preserved. A decree of the Parliament of Paris from 1354 mentions those who, through "a diabolical impulse" (*instinctu diabolico*), pierced the "symbol" in which the body of Christ had been placed. *Symbolae* corresponds to the Greek *agapai,* meaning "public banquet."

Du Cange indicates, with great precision, the various usages of the word *symbolum* in the sense of "sum of the Catholic faith" and "collation," and mentions that it refers to the apostolic *assembly* to which each of the Apostles brought a part of the general confession of the faith. This, moreover, is what St. Augustine states on the subject: *"Quod Graecae symbolum dicitur, latine collatio nominatur. Collatio ideo, quia in unum collata Catholicae legis fides . . . Petrus dixit: Credo in unum Patrem, etc. Joannes dixit: Creatorem coeli et terrae. Jacobus dixit . . . etc."**

"To violate the symbol"—*Symbolum violare*—Du Cange teaches us, is to "sin." Only incidentally, and without indication of their Greek etymology, do we find mention in this dictionary of two important words: *symbolum,* in the sense of "tessera," and *vexillum,* in the sense of "ensign," "standard."

But this investigation, as we can see, cannot sufficiently explain the problem of the exact meaning of the word *symbol* itself. The various encyclopedias consulted are no more precise on this point. Albert Dauzat's *Dictionnaire étymologique de la langue français* tells us only that it is "derived from the Christian Latin *symbolum* (properly, 'mark, sign'), from the Greek *sumbolon,* 'sign,' and from *sumballein,* 'to throw together, assemble.'"[15] Thus, it appears necessary to find some elements of information on this point that may be useful to researchers.

The first Greek meaning is topological. It is the meaning for *sumbola* found in Pausanias (VIII, 54). It specifically designates "the *assembly* of the waters," the place where they assemble, where they are thrown together and "flow together."[16] This essentially dynamic, verbal meaning of *sumballein* has been used with the same meaning since Homer's time: hence the name Sumbola, a place located at the border between Laconia and the territory of Tegea, the result of the "assembly" of many waterways at this point.

Sumbola was also a word in the Greek technical language of navigation; it referred to the central part of the yard, because the two halves of the yard, once assembled (*sumballein*), overlapped high up on the mast and were then linked by belts.

In these two cases, the concrete, natural, and dynamic meaning of the word is evident enough. It describes the evoking of a movement that

---

*St. Augustine, Sermon 115, *De tempore.*

"brings together" and "assembles" elements previously separate from each other, and it designates the results. Consequently, this "bringing together" is an act of assembly that legally joins contracting parties, and in writing, the person who drew it up—a professional notary—was called the *sumbolai graphos,* literally "he who writes the juridic symbol." This is why, in Justinian legal terminology, documents drawn up by private notaries were called *sumbolaia* or, to be more exact, *sumbolaia agoraia.* Justinian's dispensatories used the term *sumbolai graphos,* "notary," in keeping with its Latin equivalent, *tabellio.*

Ancient Greek law had no generic term expressing the concept of a "contract," but in private law, the word *sumbolaion* quickly emerged in cases of legally acceptable contestation. Two more associated words appear by "convention": *sunalagma* and *sunteke,* much closer than *sumballein* (which is essentially dynamic) to verbs indicating an action of linking together and evoking a link. It should be noted that the idea of assembling, bringing together, is also inherent in the notion of the *sumbolaion* as a "contract," because its homologation was obtained by the assembly of a specific number of witnesses or jurors.

The "thing written" and its authority were certainly imposed in Greece: Evidence has been found in Sparta suggesting the debtor would write out his contract in the presence of two witnesses. Originally, a copy of a document was merely material proof of it, but starting in the fourth century BC in Athens, it served for establishing patterns of legal responsibility. We may wonder whether some noticed the formation of two distinct directions in one word: One was primary and concrete, evoking a movement that assembles and unites, and the other was secondary and abstract, evoking the consequence of this action—that is, the mutual link between the parties assembled. The first meaning was dynamic and causal, the other static and effectual. The verb *sumballein,* moreover, initially presents a transitive usage: "to throw or cast together, to place together," hence "combine in bulk," "assemble," "connect," and, by extension, "to exchange words with someone," according to Plato, for example, in the *Republic—sumballein sumbolaia pros allelous*" (425 c) and even "to throw one against the other," in the sense of "pit against one another," as in a cockfight (*sumballein alectruonas;* Xenophon, *Banquet* [*Convivium*], 4, 9). In this transitive sense, we move from "assembling" and "connecting" to "comparing" one thing or person to another, then to "conjecturing," "interpreting," "assessing," and "evaluating." For example, in *Cratylus,* Plato uses *sumballein manteian* in the sense of "explaining a prediction," and Aristotle uses *sumballein kresmon* in the sense of "interpreting an oracle."

This same verb in its intransitive usage relates to meanings that are no longer dynamic and causal, but static and effectual. While the action of "throwing together" achieved the same point, *sumballein* now designates this consequence as a "meeting—for example, by various routes— or as a "relationship" between people, hence the meanings "to meet with" and "to enter into relations with."

All these verbal ideas are evoked by the nouns derived from *sumballein*. The meaning of an "exchange" is confirmed, for example, in an economic usage: *sumbolateuo* applied to the action of "making a deal," "trafficking." Likewise, the verb *sumbolikos* was used in a dynamic sense, to designate "that which explains with the aid of a sign" (that which is "symbolic"—for example, by Theon of Alexandria) and in the sense of the result of this property of the symbol—that is, the "symbolic character" itself (*"to sumbolikon,"* according to Plutarch)—or even in the sense of the "conventional" by the grammarian Apollonius Dyscolus of Alexandria (mid-second century AD), in his treatise on conjunctions and adverbs.

From here we arrive at *sumbolon,* a "sign of recognition." What exactly is the meaning of the example often cited, the object cut in half as a sign of a "link of hospitality," for example, where each of the two parties keeps half in order to recognize the link by reuniting the two halves? First, we must remember that this is not the only meaning of the verb *sumballein*—far from it, as we have seen. This is an action comparable on all points with the action evoked by *sumbola,* which was previously defined as a term in maritime vocabulary that concerned the union of the two halves of the yard.

The object that became the sign of the "mutual link" was passed on to the children, and by joining the two halves, the bearers recognized each other and proved the reality of the links of hospitality contracted earlier by the parents. Euripides used the word *sumbolon* in this sense in the tragedy of Medea. Thus, in short, people separated for a long time had at their disposal what I have called a *mnemotechnical syntheme:* a simple, conventional sign rather than a "symbol" of an initiatory or religious type. *Sumbolon* most often is used with this elementary synthematic meaning. The tokens that the Athenian judges received upon entering the tribunal, which they remitted for their earnings, were also designated by this word—which was also applied to residence permits for foreign travelers, as well as to all sorts of commercial and political conventions.

Yet we must observe an important point regarding the *sumbolon.* The word was not applied solely to a convention allowing a mutual connection to be identified upon the meeting of the parties who had dealings with each other based on this link. This synthematic aspect was joined with a specifically symbolic aspect in that it was not applied to an "object," such as a broken stick or jeton, but rather was designated by what permitted the subjects to meet under the sign of a belief or a value. It was less of a social contract and more of a sacred alliance or an alliance held as sacred.

THE SYMBOLIC MEANING OF
SACRED ENSIGNS

Sumbolon, according to Dionysius of Halicarnassus (*Roman Antiquities,* ca. 30 BC, book 8, chapter 38), indicates the insignia of God. According to the historian Herodian of Alexandria (AD 170–240), it is what "brings together" soldiers around a rallying sign: for example, a flag. In this sense, Constantine's *labarum* and the *oriflamme* of French medieval tradition are not purely social and profane conventions. These "ensigns" had magical and religious significance because they were charged with a mysterious power that was believed capable of assuring victory in the field to those who deployed such sacred symbols. Likewise, in Islam, the "Prophet's standard" played an essential role in the "holy war" and in Muslim conquests. Above all, we must not forget the archaic tradition of shamanism, in which vanquishing and killing an individual's enemy, following certain rites, commits that individual to the service of the person *in whose name the enemy was killed.*

This is also why the "hunting circle," *nerge* in the Mongol language, had a meaning that was not solely technical. The Mongol standard, which bore an animal effigy—often the blue wolf or horse hairs, a horse's mane, or an animal's tail—gave the war circle its magical value as a hunting circle, in keeping with the theme of the sacred animal-guide. The standard was placed at the head of the army. On the field and at stopping points, it was placed before the door of the sovereign. The texts tell us that it received worship addressed to the "spirit" that inhabited it. This was because the khan himself was born from the blue wolf,[17] and therefore his warriors, who magically became wolves due to the sacred presence of the standard, encircled their enemies, who were slaughtered like sheep. One of the powers most often attributed to shamans is transformation from human into animal. To display the standard of the blue wolf was to announce the presence of a formidable magical metamorphosing power whose purpose was to terrify the adversary.

Pennants, standards, and pennons were of great importance among Altaic peoples. According to E. H. Minns, the Scythians also used banners.[18] The custom of attaching nine yak or horse tails to the standard was widespread among the Turko-Mongols. Marco Polo wrote of the standards of the Mongol empire, describing the great khan's banner as showing the image of the sun and moon.[19] The image of the clan, its emblem, has been always sacred. Here we must distinguish two distinct functions of the symbol: the *sociological* function of a clan's emblem or sign of recognition, necessary for distinguishing the tribal group, and the *typological* function of this same emblem as a birth sign or a magical or religious reference to the ancestral lineage. This function is specifically symbolic because it evokes a sacred alliance with either infrahuman forces or suprahuman powers. The dynamics of the clan gathering around the sign of the origins come not from the conventional and social meaning of the syntheme chosen, but from the sign's reference to the nonhuman and to the energy of its primordial model or type. Only on this level of sacral interpretation can we consider the sign as a symbol in the proper sense of the term.

ALLIANCE AND TOTEMISM

An alliance with numinous or sacred powers, whatever they might be, is a *pact,* not a *contract.* Any can exchange goods, wives, objects, or services contractually, as a function of certain structures of social relations defined by their logical operations and by a determined code. But this function of exchange cannot be extrapolated to relations between humans and the nonhuman because this would involve other ritual and sacrificial structures and operations.

Moreover, the totem is not merely the animal or vegetable species, natural object, or mythical being with which a clan is connected. The totem, forever a bearer of multiple meanings, is also the plastic or graphic representation of this species, object, or being.

Totemism is extraordinarily complex, and in order to try to understand it, we must examine not just some but all the aspects of the life of the indigenous people in question—the social ones, of course, but also the magical and religious ones. The current definition of *totemism* is a relationship between a person or group and a species or object belonging to the natural world; the sign of the relationship is the name of the totem, borne by the person or group. This approach is useful, but still unanswered is the question of the nature of the relationship examined. Is this relationship a social and physiological one, or is it religious, ceremonial, magical? "Does the totem merely exist to give a name to a group, and so provide a symbol of the common relationship of its members one to another, and incidentally serve as a method of classifying and denoting members of the tribe?"[20] And when this totem performs its functions of assisting, warning, and acting as a name, does it do so in waking life only, in dream life only, or in both? These questions, posed by one of the greatest modern specialists—A. P. Elkin, director of the Institute of Anthropology at the University of Sydney—give some idea of the difficulty of the problems presented by totemism, which are still quite far from being resolved.

A. P. Elkin classified the "function and meaning of totemic phenomena" into six distinct categories: "Social, cult, conception, dream, classificatory, and assistant."[21] The most important difference is between social and cult totemism: "The former is concerned with human relationships and marriage, whereas the latter has *little if any concern with these matters;* it has to do with mythology, ritual and the sacred side of tribal life."[22]

I have emphasized Elkin's expression because in my view, most modern ethnologists, psychologists, and sociologists have perpetuated constant confusion and misunderstanding in this area, having neglected to make this crucial distinction. A. P. Elkin mentions, for example, that Australian cult totemism is local and patrilineal, whereas in social totemism, the transmission of totems nearly always or perhaps always takes place through the maternal line. This matrilineal relationship of flesh and blood is also expressed by the term for the social totem: *flesh*. For example, if we ask an Australian Aborigine what his flesh is, he will respond with the name of his matrilineal totem (e.g., kangaroo or emu). This is the symbol of the common flesh shared by all the members of his clan, who, as a result, consider themselves relations. Thus, they will not injure, kill, or eat the animal, their own flesh, nor will they marry someone who has the same totem, which would amount to incest because all the people who are in the same social clan are mothers and children, brothers and sisters.

A. P. Elkin explains that sex totemism is merely a variety of social totemism that points to the solidarity between individuals of the same gender: "a solidarity which is expressed in ritual quarrels and marriage preliminaries and is symbolized by each sex possessing a bird or plant totem."[23] Moreover, on the gender level, the totem's function is not merely to provide a name or serve as an emblem, which is a purely synthematic function of social classification by a sign. The relationship between men and women, with their respective natural genders, is quasi-biological, because these are living communities that are experienced as such. The men, for example, are all "brothers" and the women all "sisters," and the totem animal is itself the brother or sister of the group with which it is associated. Another important detail is that the totem can even be a man or woman who has undergone a transformation. Although Elkin himself does not say so, this circumstance can be compared to shamanistic experiences or to possession by the spirit of the totem. From this analysis, we should remember that "sex totemism is social in nature because it functions as a social grouping and also because it symbolizes and expresses social and kinship relationships in much the same way as does social clan totemism."[24]

CULT TOTEMISM

Cult totemism, Elkin explains, is very different from the other types we have examined:

> Over the greater part of Australia, perhaps formerly over all of it, there has existed a variety of totemism, which may best be described as a secret religious or cult organization. In each tribe there are a number of cult societies or cult groups or lodges, each of which consists of a number of fully initiated male members whose affiliations were designated by right of birth. Each group exists to take care of and hand on a prescribed portion of the sacred totemic mythology and ritual of the tribe.[25]

In Australia we also find a new level of meaning for the symbol, which I previously deduced from the etymology of the Greek verb *sumballein:* its topological meaning, generally unnoticed by specialists. The gods are profoundly linked to places. From the beginning, all geography is sacred, because walking re-creates the path and commemorates the primordial opening of the way of the earth and of men by the acts of the gods, following the mythical primordial trails.

Thus, each Australian cult group must care for the sacred totemic sites and celebrate certain ritual ceremonies, in keeping with the journeys made and the exploits accomplished by the tribe's heroes when they planned out the subdivisions of the tribal territory belonging to the group in question. A pile of rocks, a standing stone, a pond, or any other feature of the terrain may mark the place where a hero rested or transformed himself or the place where he is expected to reappear. There he has placed the spirits of the children existing in these collective residences or, by his ritual powers, he has charged certain places with vital principles and the spirits of natural species, both animal and vegetable. Therefore, this is where the people must celebrate the ceremonies thanks to which these species can be multiplied.

These cult paths, which are intergroupal and intertribal in nature, traverse the territories of local clans and tribes. The members of a lodge or a society of mysteries who must perform the rites associated with the heroic and mythical journey can therefore move without fearing hostile reactions from the clans. To search for red chalk, for example, the Aborigines of lower northeast Australia had to travel nearly five hundred miles to the clay deposits of Parachilna. The mythical theme of this journey was the commemoration of the journey of the emu and the dogs whose blood supposedly formed these red ocher deposits.

It is important to note that among Australian Aborigines, the cult totem has not the least connection to the sexual totem or to marriage. Sometimes it appears to play this latter role, but this illusion comes from the fact that the totems are distributed among the local exogamous groups of the tribe.

TOTEMIC SUPERPOSITION AND
ETERNAL DREAMTIME

What begins to appear is a fact of considerable anthropological importance: *totemic superposition*. This phenomenon may explain the essentially
polyvalent nature of the symbol, justifying the necessity for the plurality
of hermeneutics and a multidisciplinary approach to general symbology.
For example, in the tribes of lower northeast Australia, an indigenous
person receives not one totem but five: The first is a cult totem, local, and
patrilineal; the second is a cult totem inherited from his mother's brother;
the third is social, carnal, and matrilineal; the fourth is social and halfway, because the tribe is split into two groups; and the fifth is sexual.

This superposition or accumulation poses some major questions
in the realm of the study of structures and codes. But what should
be the observer's reference system: the waking state or the dreaming
state? In most of the great regions of totemic worship among aboriginal
Australians, the cult totem is identified by some with the Dreamtime
totem; for others, the Dreamtime totem is the social totem. The importance of the dream is such that the Aborigines often repeat the maxim
He who loses his dream is lost. To what dream does this refer? The most
important sacred symbols of the Aborigines are the *tjurunga* (or *churinga*). These are various objects that are not only the concrete and sensory signs of Dreamtime (*alcheringa,* according to the Aranda term used
by Spencer and Gillen [1899], from *altjiranga*), but are also themselves
of that nature on which depend the life and force that they contain.
Thus, passing a churinga over the body of a sick person will supposedly
restore his vigor. When the neophyte is rubbed with these objects or
when he is authorized to look at what he is shown for the first time,
he knows that he is entering into contact with what Elkin calls eternal
Dreamtime.

We can wonder, though, whether Dreamtime is really the most
accurate name for this fundamental category of Australian mythic
thought. Undoubtedly, it is different from mythical time, because it

relates directly to the experience of the dream—as Elkin verified in the field, starting in 1927 in the south, center, northwest, and north of the continent. We may note, however, that while the Aranda word for "dream" is *altjira,* and in other regions *djugur, bugari, ungud,* or *wongar,* there is also a religious clan among the Wongkonguru (a tribe living northeast of Lake Eyre) whose name, or Dream, is *fire,* obtained by a rapid movement of friction accompanied by rotation. Proceeding thus for its successful operation, the rite requires a song of Dreamtime handed down by those descended from the Dreamfire, their father.

The creator of fire was a Yigauara, a man with the appearance of a wildcat. Among the Wongkonguru, fire is named *maka* and the Dream, the time and nature of the Dream as mythical categories, corresponds to the name Ularaga.[26]

We may well question our own modern interpretation of myth and the mythical categories of this kind, for according to our logic, what is viewed as real opposes what is fictitious, imaginary, or dream. In fact, we separate the images of our perceptions in the waking state from the images of our perceptions in other states of consciousness, all of which we reduce to a single category: the dreaming state. This is an abusive and summary opposition and simplification. In the lives of those who suffer from hunger and thirst, as is often the case for primitive peoples, hallucinatory states occur much more frequently than among civilized people. Moreover, the use of poisonous vegetable intoxicants is often part of magical and religious rites, for example among Siberian shamans and certain Amerindian groups. Finally, the mystical life itself plays a considerable role in the daily experience of primitive people, and this encourages—at least for some of them—the emergence of paranormal faculties, especially phenomena of telepathy, premonition, and clairvoyance.

As Elkin mentions:

[M]any white folk who have known their native employees well, give remarkable examples of the Aborigine's power for knowing what is happening at a distance, even hundreds of miles away. A man may be away with his employer on a big stock trip, and will suddenly announce one day that his father is dead, that his wife has given birth to a child, or that there is some trouble in his own country. He is so sure of his facts that he would return at once if he could, and the strange thing is, as these employers ascertained later, the Aborigine was quite correct.[27]

It is important to observe that at these times, the indigenous man fell into a state of receptivity and meditation lasting several minutes. In many tribes, the various parts of the body are considered as each giving information regarding specific relatives or groups of relatives. Thus, meditation, in its progression, is based upon symbols or conventional reference points. For example, if the Aborigine sees a totemic animal belonging to his group or to that of a close relative, he sets about deciphering the "message" thus transmitted in order to understand its content.

I myself have observed similar "paranormal" phenomena among the Pygmies of the Cameroon, and these have also been noted in other reliable testimonies. We may wonder whether certain functions of the rhinencephalon that are exercised by people in primitive societies—most of all by women—may have become obsolete in "civilized" people due to the environment in which all our physical and mental activity takes place. In short, these phenomena are rarely observed because the conditions in which they used to occur have changed profoundly. Yet this is not sufficient reason for denying that they are anthropologically possible and real in societies other than our own.

Moreover, these phenomena result from the perception or *cenesthesia* of the primitive person—that is, the individual's true existential experience—rather than from the dream state that it doubtless resembles, as it is experienced but not as we know it. This is why the Aborigine seems to associate this dream not with a lesser degree of reality, but with a higher intensity of perception of beings and things; for this is where he sees the very source of force and life. The symbol thus gives him an assembly of inner powers of a purely experiential order, and not an intellectual and abstract conception of the world.

What is perceived in this particular state is felt as eminently real because it is felt more profoundly than in other states—and thus it is understandable that the heroic types and ancestral models should have operated in this way, in an exemplary fashion, in the same state corresponding to a privileged time, an eternally present vision that can be accessed through the initiatory imitation of the original action. The symbol thus leads back to their inner state separate concrete concepts from various levels of reality, which allows them to be unified in their primordial splendor. For those of vision, the symbol restores the spectacle of a universe in the nascent state—that universe which has become crystallized, solidified, opaque, and closed or off-limits to those of thought.

2 Sign and Symbol

DEFINITIONS AND SEMIOLOGICAL
APPROACHES TO THE SYMBOL

The symbol has often been defined as a sign "of recognition formed by two halves of a broken object that are rejoined; later, some sign, token, seal, insignia, watchword," according to Lalande[1]; a conventional sign, like the signs used by logicians and mathematicians or in various scientific disciplines; or an analogical sign, capable of evoking a relationship between a concrete image and an abstract idea (such as the scepter, a symbol of royalty).

This is the sense in which Ferdinand de Saussure, defining language as "a system of signs expressing ideas," compared the sign to

> writing, the deaf-and-dumb alphabet, symbolic rites, forms of politeness, military signals, and so on. It is simply the most important of such systems. It is therefore possible to conceive of a science *which studies the role of signs as part of social life.* It would form part of social psychology, and hence of general psychology. We shall call it *semiology* (from the Greek *sēmeîon*, "sign"). It would investigate the nature of signs and the laws governing them.[2]

Semiology, notably, assumes that the explicit forms of symbolism are "signals" associated with tacit "significations"[3] on the model of the relationship between sound and meaning in language. Under these conditions, in order to interpret a symbol, we must decode it and integrate it into the symbolic systems of a specific culture, according to Claude Lévi-Strauss's conception, which extended this method from structural anthropology to matrimonial rules, economic dealings, art, science, and religion.

Concerning the initial definitions of the symbol cited, comparing them to the preceding discussion of the origin and semantics of the word itself would be enough to see that they are quite far from covering all the complexity of its true meaning.

Saussure's "semiological scheme" is much more important, so it must be explained first. The sign, in Saussure's sense, is not simply one thing that is substituted for or replaces another. It is a link and relationship of union between them. "A linguistic sign," he writes, is a link "between a concept and a sound pattern"—that is, a "signification" and a "signal."[4] Moreover, the sign presents two essential characteristics: the *arbitrariness*[5] and the *linear character*[6] of the signal. Essentially, the vocal signs of language are produced and perceived successively, whereas graphic or pictorial signs, for example, are produced in the same manner but can be perceived globally or in any kind of order.

Moreover, in Saussure's sense, signs are not abstractions. Instead, they are "concrete entities" studied by linguistics, and they oppose each other in the mechanism of language. The concept of language, for Saussure, is one of form and not substance. It presents no positive term, only differences.[7] Hence this clear definition: "What distinguishes a sign is what constitutes it."[8] Could the same be said for a symbol?

Saussure himself answers this question. He states that "signs which are entirely arbitrary convey better than others the ideal semiological process." He observes:

> [T]he word *symbol* is sometimes used to designate the linguistic sign,
> or more exactly that part of the linguistic sign, which we are call-

ing the signal. This use of the word *symbol* is awkward, for reasons connected with our first principle. For it is characteristic of symbols that they are never entirely arbitrary. They are not empty configurations. They show at least a vestige of natural connection between the signal and its signification. For instance, our symbol of justice, the scales, could hardly be replaced by a chariot.[9]

Here, we must also remember that Saussure understood the word *arbitrary* not in the sense of a signal depending on the "free choice of the speaker," but in the sense of the signal being "unmotivated"—that is, "arbitrary in relation to its signification, with which it has no natural connection in reality."[10]

Saussure had already used the term *symbol* in 1894, in his article commemorating W. D. Whitney.[11] This text is interesting in that it shows us the characteristic oscillation of Saussure's analytical process in this area: "Philosophers, logicians, and psychologists have been able to illuminate us as to the nature of the basic contract between the idea and the symbol [in the first draft, which was later corrected, we find "between a conventional symbol and *the mind*"], and in particular the contract between an independent symbol and the idea it represents."[12]

Saussure's teachings were divulged in three general linguistics courses taught in 1906–07, 1908–09, and 1910–11, and the notes taken by various students were combined and published by C. Bailly and A. Sechehaye in 1916 under the title *Cours de linguistique générale.* This book has had a profound influence on the development of modern linguistics, especially linguistic structuralism. We should therefore repeat the classic distinctions that Saussure proposed; some of them have extended far beyond the realm of their specialized applications.

The first relates to the difference between language and speech. In order to understand this better, we must first situate Saussure's thought historically. It developed within the framework of a Western cultural situation dominated by academic positivism, but also from the perspective of sociological problematics, leading up to the end of the nineteenth century, marked by the opposition between Durkheim's and Tarde's perspectives concerning the dominance of the factors of the "collective consciousness of the social group" or the factors of "individual initiative." W. Doroszewski pointed out connections between sociology and linguistics,[13] but perhaps did not place enough emphasis on a little-known text published in 1902 by Tarde, who was probably not unfamiliar with Saussurean "dichotomies," to use G. C. Lepschy's expression: "All is symmetrical, dualistic, antithetical, in matters of combination, as in matters of struggle—all is dual or coupling . . ."[14] In his *Sémantique,* Bréal observed an entirely spontaneous application of this general truth in linguistics. "Whatever may be the length of a compound," he writes, "it only ever contains two terms. This rule is not arbitrary; it is part of the nature of our spirit, which associates its ideas in pairs."[15]

In Saussure's sense, speech designates the individual element, the basis of linguistic change, which in a way constitutes a polarity opposed to language as an institution. This, however, is not a neo-idealist concept on the level of intuition-expression, opposing communication formalized and rationalized by social institutions. Rather, it is a contrast between the psychophysical reality of a particular linguistic action, an "act of speech" that is necessarily variable and a system external to the individual, the social aspect of language—that is, the language itself—which "is not a function of the speaker" but "the product passively registered by the individual."[16] In short—as Saussure emphasizes—this is a matter of distinguishing "between the language itself and speech," thus distinguishing "at the same time: (1) what is social from what is individual, and (2) what is essential from what is ancillary and more or less accidental."[17]

Saussure's semiological scheme is therefore no less clearly "positivist" than its inspiration: "By considering *rites,* customs, etc., as *signs,* it will be possible, we believe, to see them in a *new perspective.* The need will be felt to consider them as semiological phenomena and to *explain them in terms of the laws of semiology.*"[18] I have italicized the expressions characteristic of this conclusion relative to semiology. This explains, to a great extent, the general tendency of contemporary linguistic structuralism and its rationalist and scientific orientation.

Saussure's distinction between *synchrony* and *diachrony* is based on the preceding, according to the principle that "everything which is *diachronic* in language is so only through speech," as is confirmed in the scheme proposed by Saussure himself for "a rational structure for the pursuit of linguistic studies."[19]

The following diagram appears in *Course in General Linguistics,* trans. Roy Harris (Chicago: Open Court, 1986), 97.

$$
\text{Language} \left\{ \begin{array}{l} \text{tongue} \left\{ \begin{array}{l} \text{synchrony} \\[1em] \text{diachrony} \end{array} \right. \\[2em] \text{speech} \end{array} \right.
$$

Synchronic linguistics studies the "facts which constitute any linguistic state," the "logical and psychological connections between coexisting items constituting a system, as perceived by the same collective consciousness."[20]

"Synchrony" is located on the "axis of simultaneity," which "concerns relations between things which coexist, relations from which the passage of time is entirely excluded." Diachrony is connected to the "axis of succession," on which "one may consider only one thing at a time. But here we find all the things situated along the first axis, together with the changes they undergo."[21] All that relates to the static aspect or to a state of language is synchronic; all that relates to evolutions or to a phase of evolution is diachronic.

One of the fundamental points of Saussure's teaching is his constant affirmation of the arbitrary nature of sign and language. We can notice, however, that in this sense Saussure clearly distinguishes languages from systems of symbols: "One could likewise discuss the pros and cons of a system of symbols, because the symbol has a rational connection with what it symbolizes. But for a language, as a system of arbitrary signs, any such basis is lacking, and consequently there is no firm ground for discussion. No reason can be given for preferring *soeur* to *sister, Ochs* to *boeuf,* etc."[22]

Here, we can see a fairly obvious contradiction of the semiological scheme mentioned previously, wherein rites, which are incontestably symbolic, are considered as signs. The American structuralist Edward Sapir likewise places continual emphasis on the fundamentally symbolic character of language, which he considered "a vocal manifestation of the tendency to see reality *in a symbolic manner,* and it is precisely this quality that makes it an instrument suited for communication."[23]

These contradictions and difficulties are not the only ones presented by the study of semiological and linguistic approaches to symbols. It is perhaps appropriate first to seek their causes in an important fact recalled by Saussure himself: "We retain the term *sign* because current usage suggests no alternative by which it might be replaced."[24]

NECESSITY FOR THE WORD *SYNTHEME*

It appears important to recommend the use of the word *syntheme*[25] to designate, in general, any arbitrary and conventional sign whose unequivocal and constant meaning is voluntarily established by parties communicating on this subject. I will explain its etymology and definition later. Essentially, in this way, we can more easily distinguish the syntheme from the symbol, on the one hand, and the syntheme from the strictly linguistic sign, in the Saussurean sense, on the other hand. In fact, this linguistic sign is arbitrary not in the sense of a free choice of the signal by the speaker, but in the unmotivated sense in relation to the signification, having no real connection to it. The use of the word *syntheme* thus adds the ideas of free choice and convention to the notion of the arbitrary, which no other word in common language expresses.

Yet an essential difference exists between a sign linked to a thing or an idea by a convention, which can be modified by an initial decision by the parties who decide on it at their will, and a sign linked to a thing or idea by a relationship independent from any such convention. We could decide, for example, to designate oxygen with the letter *O,* but we could just as well have chosen the letter *G* and given the sign *G* the intended meaning in chemical reactions. This is why Jean Piaget justly notes that a symbol

> . . . is to be defined as a link of resemblance between the signal and the signification, whereas the "sign" is "arbitrary" and is necessarily based on a convention. The sign therefore requires *social life* for it to be constituted, whereas the symbol can be developed by the individual alone, as in the games of little children. It goes without saying, furthermore, that symbols can be socialized, a collective symbol then being in general my sign, my symbol; a pure sign, on the other hand, is always collective.[26]

It is therefore by an unjustifiable extension of meaning that logicians and mathematicians speak of symbolic logic, given that according to the intention of Gottlob Fregge, its actual inventor, this is a typically "ideographic" and purely conventional logic, implying no intuitive or subjective "residue." Thus, in 1958, I proposed to restore to the Greek word *synthema,* from the verb *sundesmeo* ("I link together"), a methodical usage for designating all conventional signs, calling them synthemes, the object of a new, specific discipline: *synthematics.* I will return to this subject later, but it seems indispensable to emphasize its importance from here on. It allows symbolics to be clearly separated from synthematics, and synthematics from linguistics. I have dedicated some chapters specifically to the study of these relationships and concepts.

THE STRUCTURALIST INTERPRETATION
OF SYMBOLS

The structuralist anthropological conception of symbols assimilates these signs and their various associations to a sociocultural language and, in short, situates them in the universe of discourse. An initial problem is posed in this regard: Can we observe the specificity of the elements of this language, their articulation, and their mutual relationships? At first glance, it does not seem so. In fact, if we accept that military signals, forms of politeness, signs of recognition, conventional signs, and the deaf-mute alphabet belong to categories of signs analogous to those of religious rites and myths, then we cannot see what differences may separate the elements of the language of symbols from the other signs of the language.

We may recall that in ancient Greek civilization, the reduction of the *mythos* to the *logos* by the rationalist critics constituted a fairly characteristic condition of cultural evolution. Xenophanes not only openly attacked the Homeric pantheon and Hesiod's mythology, but also scoffed at mortals who "consider that the gods are born, and that they *have clothes and speech and bodies like their own.*"[27]

In the time of Thucydides, the term *mythodes* meant "exaggerated fancies," in contrast with any given truth or reality.[28] The Alexandrian rhetoricians such as Aelius Theon carried out a devastating criticism of myths, just like modern positivists. Theon demonstrated the impossibility of a myth, using an analysis of the contradictions and implausibilities in the myth of Medea. The reverse allegorism of Euhemerus's "Sacred Story" from the early third century BC was used by Christian apologists to demonstrate the humanity and therefore the unreality of the Greek gods. This reductive criticism of the language of the gods, assimilating it to the language of culture and viewing symbols only as signs of human language, is thus not a "modern" discovery. It is a phenomenon characteristic of all desacralized culture and consequently of our own civilization, which has been profoundly subject to the influence of the experience of written tradition (the transmission of meaning through signs and of beliefs through books).

Mircea Eliade observed, on this subject:

[W]e do not have any Greek myth transmitted with its *cultural* context. We know the myths in the form of literary and artistic "documents," and not as sources or expressions of a religious experience in connection with a rite. An entire *living,* popular region of the Greek religion escapes us, simply because it has not been described in a systematic manner by writing.[29]

We must therefore choose between two possible attitudes toward symbols and symbolism or else consider both as belonging to the universe of discourse—that is, the sociocultural logos. In this case, the symbolic and mythical meaning has no particular criterion relative to the other signs of language. It is distinguished solely on the level of descriptive and interpretative methods on the one hand and on the other the level of the categories and classifications it defines. Alternatively, we can admit that symbols go beyond the cultural logos, because they are linked to the nonhuman logos through the intermediary of myths and rites. In this case, they must necessarily be distinguished from all other profane signs, because they constitute the archetypal sacred language that, to the chagrin of Xenophanes and modern critics, has been recognized by all the traditions of ancient civilizations and primitive societies as the language of the gods. This is why it seems necessary to avoid confusion between signs that arise from semiological analysis and its interpretations and signs that can be understood only through initiatory and religious experiences and their traditions.

Certainly, we may consider initiation and religion as cultural facts in societies in which the culture itself is linked to the experience of the sacred in the majority of its expressions. But insofar as these traditions are expressed culturally on the level at which ethnologists study them, they always require an interpretation of their hidden meanings for the profane or unbelievers. How can this meaning be reducible to a discourse or to one thought when its elements, their articulations, and their mutual relations are neither clearly explained nor taught indifferently to all the members of a group? If, as Rudolf Otto rightly wrote, the experience of the sacred or the numinous is that of the "wholly other" and the "quite different,"[30] then we can deduce that its symbolic, mythical, and ritual expressions as a whole constitute a system that is "wholly other" than the system of the signs of language or the elements of discourse: namely, the system of social synthemes.

The science of symbols, unlike structural anthropology, does not consider it sufficient to reconstitute the functioning of a "structure in order to understand its formation—that is, the passage from an absence of structure to the presence of structure. If we want to study myths, rites, and symbols without betraying the experiences upon which they have been built, then we must participate actively in their existential genesis and not analyze them as if they were examples of pure linguistic mechanisms or conceptual categories.

This mechanical aspect of structural anthropology appeared clearly enough in Claude Lévi-Strauss's declaration: "If the final goal of anthropology is to contribute to a better knowledge of objective thought and its mechanisms, this comes down to saying that in this book, the thought of indigenous South Americans takes form in the operation of my thought, or my thought in the operation of theirs."[31] Certainly, if the aim is a better knowledge of the functioning of symbolic discourse, then Lévi-Strauss's position is scientifically valid. The structural knowledge of a function does not require a decision of the philosophical order concerning reality in itself or the "what?" of the phenomenon—its noumenal aspect. The shadow of the dog trotting on its four paws behind its master could likewise be described precisely as the dog's model in terms of the mode of locomotion. For a structure constituting a closed group of operations, in mathematics and in other realms such as a sphere, it is enough to know the group of operations of the sphere in order to define its structure by its rotation. Thus, by means of a given function, we can always fabricate or imagine an automaton of structure and functioning equivalent to the phenomenon studied, within the limits of a certain threshold of complexity.

Yet the incontestable scientific validity of the study of structures considered in terms of their semiological interpretation—or, if we prefer, their linguistic functioning—remains limited to a purely descriptive

approach to these phenomena. If we want to understand the formation—
the specific genetic nature—then the problem changes.

In other words, semiology by itself cannot resolve the problem of
the nature of the symbol because it reaches the symbol only on the level
where it is already constituted and codified. Under these conditions, the
decoding in fact amounts to an essentially analytical method using a collection of signs that are assumed to be initially closed or shut, whereas
the central problem of general symbology consists instead of investigat-
ing the causes and conditions of the occurrence of this closing and shut-
ting. What's more, these causes and conditions may be either apparent
or real. Psychoanalytically, if (as the Freudian school, along with Ernest
Jones, assumes) "only what is repressed is symbolized, and only what is
repressed needs to be symbolized,"[32] then this touchstone of the theory
of symbolism presents immediately a fundamental question: What is
the origin of the repression that has determined the unconscious associations symbolized?

Thus it seems that the first methodical approach required by general symbology consists of noting how civilizations of the "traditional"
type have themselves understood this nature of the symbol—a historical question that requires us, to a great extent, to try to forget our own
ideological systems in this area.

The decontamination of our modern mentality is required just as
much in relation to general symbology as in relation to the economy of
primitive societies and civilizations of the "traditional" type. In 1957, a
group of researchers from Columbia University, under the leadership of
Karl Polanyi, published an important book on this subject: *Trade and
Market in the Early Empires*. In this text they tell us that in order to
describe and explain systems of production in ancient societies, ethnologists and archaeologists hardly ever use anything other than the economic concepts taught in modern universities, which reflect the practice
of capitalism. For Karl Polanyi, "The market envelopment of our own
economy and society was seen as the major obstacle to understanding
the economy in early societies."[33]

An attentive and minute study of the facts shows that what modern specialists generally consider a *market* in antiquity—for example, the market in Mesopotamia during the time of Hammurabi or currently in Kabylia—conceals a reality radically different from the *market* in the modern sense of the term. Of course, wood, grains, perfumes, and metals were traded by the merchants of the Assyrian markets, but as traders, statutorily they could not take any economic risks. Assuming a principally technical function, in particular the transport and stocking of the foodstuffs necessary for cities, the exercise of their profession was strictly regulated by the state, and in practical terms they experienced neither the insolvency of debtors nor the problems of loss through prices and speculation. In the trading ports of the Hittite era, as well as in commerce between the Aztecs and Maya, the team of researchers directed by Polanyi found economic conditions analogous to those still found today in the analysis of markets in Kabylia, Guinea, and India, which showed the need for studying the often considerable variations in the manner in which the economic process is conceived and institutionalized depending on time and place. The same conditions apply to the study and logic of signs as to all systems of exchange and communication.

A semiology of meaning can be validly founded upon only its principle—that is, on the communication that first proceeds from intentional factors. L. P. Prieto rightly states: "The semiology of meaning must find a much more appropriate model in the semiology of communication than what linguistics offers. If, up to the present, it has used concepts borrowed from linguistics for beginning its researches, this is exclusively because of the nonexistence of a sufficiently developed semiology of communication."[34]

Under these conditions, it is important to remember that both in primitive civilizations and in ancient societies of the "traditional" type, symbols were not abbreviations of a statement arising from a discourse or a concept, but rather global expressions evoking a situation of verbal communication (as through the intermediary of ritual gestures). This communication that forms the basis of symbolic meaning depends in turn on a drive of intention, and not a drive of narration—an essentially sacral behavior, orienting the human toward the nonhuman. Thus, the symbolic process as a whole, as it is experienced and perceived in these civilizations, does not correspond to symbolic concepts as they are currently understood and taught in our universities to ethnologists, linguists, psychologists, and various other specialists in the humanities in such a profoundly desacralized and rationalized society as our own. We must therefore try in some manner to forget what we believe we know in order not to project unconsciously our own ideological systems and their cultural codes onto circumstances that are the result neither of our logical criteria of knowledge nor of our psychological and physical conceptions of experience.

THE TRADITIONAL CONCEPTION OF THE SYMBOL'S NONHUMAN ORIGIN

If there is one point on which the various early societies and traditional civilizations all agree, it is surely the nonhuman origin of symbols, particularly in magical and religious mysteries, myths, and initiation rites. In the archaic levels of culture, however, the human world and the signs that express it did not constitute a system closed to the nonhuman, whether infrahuman or suprahuman. The world of the divine beings or mythical ancestors, for the transcendent on the level of the "wholly other" (implying the experience of the sacred), remained no less accessible, thanks to rites and symbols that did not allegorically or conceptually represent this nonhuman world, but instead dynamically reactualized it.

The existence of a nonhuman model that seemed certain to paralyze human initiative with its intangible character, by contrast, guaranteed, through its mythical, ritual, and symbolic commemoration, the existence of a primordial and transhistorical order capable of legitimizing all new endeavors to organize space and time. In fact, it contributed to unconsciously dispelling human doubts concerning the results of the predicted action. Facing an unknown and formidable territory, for example, it was enough to repeat the cosmogonic ritual revealed by the gods in order that this chaos, changed into cosmos, might become an area conforming to the original image of the world—to the will of the gods—and consequently might be habitable and open to humans who possessed it and transformed it in their name. The imitation of the exemplary gestures of gods, heroes, and mythical ancestors thus implied a link not only of significative resemblance and a drive of narration but also a drive of intention.

On first sight, it appears that ritually and symbolically repeating and commemorating a primordial act would assume an orientation of the consciousness toward the most distant past. But when we judge things in this way, we are viewing a mentality different from our own as having a historicism that is in fact wholly foreign to it. Because the fundamental relationship of human to nonhuman is genetic, original, and transhistorical, this relationship instead corresponds to a movement of ritualized intent that becomes a means of communication analogous to those observed among certain social insects.

Bees communicate with each other via movements, in which individuals must participate in order to understand them. This behavior resembles that of the ant excitement centers described by D. W. Morley. Tinbergen and Armstrong discovered many other examples throughout the area of instinct and animal behavior. The "mood language" described by Konrad Lorenz among flocks of jackdaws allows for a progressive stimulation of the individuals, the cry *kia* meaning "I am in the mood to stay away from the nest" and *kiaw* meaning "I am in the mood to go back." These calls, at first contradictory, become oriented little by little in the direction of an increasing unanimity, finally expressed in the action chosen by the entire flock of birds.[35]

All other things being equal, the essentially dynamic communication implied by the reactualization of the ritual and symbolic model is no more understandable solely on the level of human discourse than the jackdaws' cries of *kia* and *kiaw*, if we separate this communication from the drive of intention of the individuals and collective in question—

that is, separate it from a sacral orientation, beyond which the symbol has no autonomous meaning or any specific signification.

This is why the drive of narration by itself does not allow us to consider a grouping of symbols and, for example, a myth as significative of a symbolic thought describing the relationships between the categories based on a certain number of propositions regarding the world. Symbolism—the use of symbols—is not a conceptual process. Therefore, we cannot apply our criteria of pertinence and rationality to it. A symbol does not mean something predetermined for someone. It is simultaneously a center of accumulation and concentration of images and their affective and emotional charges; a vector of the analogical orientation of intuition; and a field of magnetization of the anthropological, cosmological, and theological similitudes evoked.

Here, the intention is not separated from a certain tension of the individual or the group, which, moreover, is always present in very diverse forms in ritualized behaviors and in frequent mythical dramatizations. The symbol concentrates this tension and makes it converge at its center, preserving its latent evocative power. This is different from the relationship of the signal and signification because symbolic relationships imply an endlessly possible accumulation of analogical relationships that are always new. The signification, at every moment, can be considered as incomplete, as a single element in an endless process of symbolization in which the signal itself participates. As Iamblichus said: "The soul is made so that it understands symbolically that which is present in a symbolic form."[36] Lévi-Strauss himself observed that symbolic relationships can just as well be founded upon contiguity as upon resemblance, that they can be close or distant, sensible or intelligible, synchronic or diachronic, and that, in fact, the link is more important than the actual nature of what is linked.[37]

That which archetypally constitutes *symbolic magnetization* proceeds from a simultaneously logical and psychological power: that of analogy, which (unlike the logic of identity, which is principally conscious and present in all the processes of abstraction of thought) is characterized by its concrete archaism, its unconscious thematic organization, and the affective and emotional charge that it is capable of projecting onto all objects of existential experience. Symbols, myths, and rites therefore cannot be understood if we reduce their systems to one of their principal consequences—to their classifying properties, their categories and hierarchies, even if these are epistemologically and socially important. We must go further and inquire into the functions of analogy to the process of symbolization, both in human understanding and in its possible relationship to the nonhuman.

In this respect, we should remember that the expression *nonhuman* does not always mean "divine" or "suprahuman." There are examples of rites and symbols of the magical type through which, in an archaic perspective of conquest and possession of efficacious vital powers, humans are linked to the infrahuman by conscious and voluntary ceremonies and pacts because these latter require a certain number of crimes and violations of taboos in order to be considered real. This is the case in certain types of initiations into African secret societies, notably the panther men who specifically seek an intimate and profound relationship of behavior between man and panther. This, however, does not imply the exclusion of an experience of the sacred—the "wholly other"—as proved by the analysis of these strange myths. *Demonology* is connected in great measure to these primitive practices. Here again, the linguistic and sociological approach to these rites and symbols is not sufficient for interpreting them, because far from constituting a means for the organization of cultural and social discourse, they have the specific goal of disorganizing and destroying it, in the function of a nonhuman experience determined by its intention and its practices.

Mircea Eliade wrote that we must not imagine this opening of the human to the nonhuman as taking place through a bucolic conception of existence:

The myths of "primitive" people and the rituals that are connected with them do not present to us an ancient Arcadia. . . .

Paleo-cultivators, taking on the responsibility of making the plant world prosper, accepted torture, sexual orgies, cannibalism, and head hunting, for profitable harvests. This is a tragic conception of existence, the result of the religious validation of torture and violent death. . . . The paleo-cultivator accepted cruelty and murder as an integral part of his mode of being. Certainly, cruelty, torture, and murder are not specific and exclusive behaviors of "primitives." They are found all throughout history, sometimes with an unheard-of climax in archaic societies. The difference is above all in the fact that for primitive people, this violent behavior had religious value and was copied from *trans-human models*. . . . The myth is not in itself a guarantee of "goodness" or morals. Its function is to display models, and thus to provide meaning for the World and for human existence. Thus its role in the constitution of man is immense.[38]

Moreover, the redoubtable and often sinister aspect of the intervention of "spirits" or the nonhuman in the human experience constitutes one of the major, irreducible characteristics of the first manifestations of the sacred or numinous.

In his analysis of *Mysterium Tremendum,* Rudolf Otto points out that the Hebrew word *hiq'dich* ("hallow") corresponds to a special feeling of dread that is not to be confused with other forms of fear and that belongs strictly to the category of the sacred or numinous: "The Old Testament throughout is rich in parallel expressions for this feeling. Specially noticeable is the *emah* of Yahweh ('fear of God'), which Yahweh can pour forth, dispatching almost like daemon, and which seizes upon a man with paralyzing effect."[39]

Otto connects this with the idea of the "panicked fright" of the Greeks, *deima panikon,* and cites a passage from Exodus (23:27): "I will send my fear before thee, and will destroy all the people to whom thou shalt come." This terror, he writes, is

. . . fraught with an inward shuddering such as not even the most menacing and overpowering created thing can instill. It has something spectral in it. In the Greek language we have a corresponding term in *sebastos*. The early Christians could clearly feel that the title *sebastos* (*augustus*) was one that could not fittingly be given to any creature, not even to the emperor. They felt that to call a man *sebastos* was to give a human being a name proper only to the *numen,* to rank him by the category proper only to the *numen,* and that it therefore *amounted to a kind of idolatry.*[40]

The symbol therefore does not belong entirely to the signs of the human universe of discourse or solely to the categories of the concept or the imaginary. Symbolic function is inseparable from its sacral orientation or its hierophanic aim at the numinous or nonhuman powers to which myths and rites link the human being, reunifying *anthropos* and cosmos by the power of the logos that here is not *language,* but *verb* and *speech* resurrected (re-created) beyond the cultural and social sense of the words of the tribe. The circulation of symbols and their rules, the exchange of wives in matrimonial alliance, of objects and goods in economic relationships, whatever may be the anthropological interest presented by the study of their structures, can account only for the immanent expressions of this transcendent experience of primordial hierophanic communication. Their causes and conditions cannot be known in this way.

Certainly, the passage from nature to culture, as Lévi-Strauss so clearly showed, implies an aptitude for the use of the symbol without which no society can be formed. But although semiology can describe the symbolic dispositive as a function, it cannot explain it as a formation in its genetic and transhistorical reality. Instead, the study of this problem falls under general symbology—that is, the science of symbols—which cannot attain this goal alone or before many years, because neither its methods nor principles nor vocabulary is yet established. Thus, given its current state, we at first need at least agreement among all terms.

PSYCHOANALYTICAL SEMIOLOGY

If, in its spiritual, initiatory, and religious life, the symbol goes so far beyond the limits of the sociosphere that it is impossible to reduce it to an entirely decipherable cultural code that can be interpreted simply by the analysis of signs, then this difference separating semiology from symbolism is no less observable in the domain of psychological life.

C. G. Jung—whom, despite occasionally justified criticism from his Freudian adversaries, we must at least thank for having broadened our knowledge of the process of symbolization in the unconscious—insisted on the necessity of not confusing symbols with signs and not assigning to them any conceptualized content predetermined by ideological meaning. He writes:

> It is far wiser in practice not to regard the dream-symbols as signs or symptoms of a fixed character [i.e., not to view them semiotically]. We should rather take them as true symbols—that is to say, as expressions of something not yet consciously recognized or conceptually formulated. In addition to this, they must be considered in relation to the dreamer's immediate state of consciousness.[41]

Of course, C. G. Jung admits "*theoretically* there do exist relatively fixed symbols,"[42] a postulate without which "it would be impossible to determine the structure of the unconscious. There would be nothing in it which could be in any way laid hold of or described." But *in practice,* in the course of interpretation, he emphasizes that these fixed symbols "must on no account be referred to anything whose content is known, or to anything that can be formulated in concepts."[43]

Jung adds that attributing indefinite content to fixed symbols implies that

> . . . it is the indefinite content that marks the symbol as against the mere *sign* or *symptom*. It is well known that the Freudian school

operates with hard and fast sexual "symbols"; but these are just what I should call *signs,* for they are made to stand for sexuality, and this is supposed to be something definitive. As a matter of fact, Freud's concept of sexuality is thoroughly elastic, and so vague that it can be made to include almost anything. . . . Instead of taking a dogmatic stand that rests upon the illusion that we know something because we have a familiar word for it, I prefer to regard the symbol as the announcement of *something unknown, hard to recognize, and not to be fully determined.* Take, for instance, the so-called phallic symbols, which are supposed to stand for the *membrum virile* and nothing more. Psychologically speaking, the *membrum* is itself—as Kranefeldt has recently pointed out—a symbolic image whose wider content cannot easily be determined. As was customary throughout antiquity, primitive people today make a free use of phallic symbols, yet it never occurs to them to confuse the phallus, as a ritualistic symbol, with the penis.[44]

This criticism of Freudian hermeneutics by C. G. Jung appears to be justified more by the excessive dogmatic tendencies of certain disciples of Freudianism than by Freud's ideas. Here I would like to recall a crucial and too often forgotten statement made by Freud in *Totem and Taboo,* which shows with what moderation and what prudence—as befits his erudition and genius—the "father of psychoanalysis" expressly stated the limits of his discoveries and indicated their contribution to future, essentially interdisciplinary research:

The reader need not fear that psychoanalysis, which first revealed the regular over-determination of psychic acts and formations, will be tempted to derive anything so complicated as religion from a single source. If it necessarily seeks, as in duty bound, to gain recognition for one of the sources of this institution, it by no means claims exclusiveness for this source or even first rank among the concurring factors. Only a synthesis from various fields of research can decide what relative importance in the genesis of religion is to be assigned to the mechanism, which we are to discuss; but such a task exceeds the means as well as the intentions of the psychoanalyst.[45]

In the following chapters, dedicated to the study of problems in the interpretation of symbols, we will discover to what degree a fundamental methodological principle can be imposed in this vast, complex, and still-obscure realm: All hermeneutics must be considered as simultaneously necessary and insufficient. They therefore require from all their specialists a minimum of tolerance with regard to systems that do not agree with what they hold as most coherent, and they also require a sufficient capacity for self-criticism in order that specialists not turn away from the hypotheses and postulates, which, inevitably, interfere in all choices of a criterion of knowledge and an experiential order of reference.

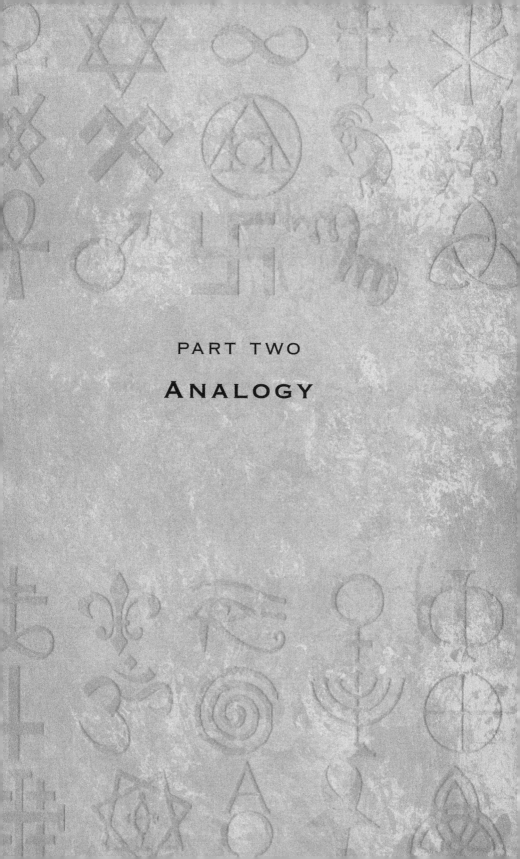

PART TWO

ANALOGY

3 THE EXPERIENTIAL ORIGINS OF THE ANALOGICAL PROCESS

THE CORPOREAL EXPERIENCE
OF INITIATION

Every rupture at the ontological level and every inner modification of the consciousness of existing in a certain state necessarily corresponds to a transformation from a prior language. A sick person does not speak in the same way as a healthy person; the words torn from him by the pain are easily comprehensible in appearance, but the meaning with which they are charged weighs them down with a new content, a focusing, and a capacity for evocation that they did not possess before. Every dramatic or exceptional existential experience takes place amid the necessity to reinvent its expression. How could the language of initiation, a process that requires ritual agony, death, and resurrection, escape this law?

It is too often imagined that this rupture at the ontological level is a metaphor, an allusion to purely interior transformations of being of the psychological order, or else that it corresponds only to the particular aspects of mystical life and religious sentiment. In the rites of a masculine brotherhood in the Mandan tribe of North America, initiation took the following form: Two men would force knives through the muscles of the chest and back of the neophyte, stick their fingers into the wounds, insert a fastener beneath the muscles, attach ropes to it, and lift his body into the air, having attached heavy stones and buffalo heads to hooks stuck into the muscles of the initiate's arms and legs. Ethnologist George Catlin, from whom we have the details, assures us that "[t]he way in which the young men endured this terrible torture . . . verges on the fabulous: not a feature of their faces moved while the torturers were butchering their flesh."[1] Once suspended in the air, the novice was rotated like a whirligig, faster and faster, until he lost consciousness, his body hanging as if broken.

After these trials, more terrible than natural death in most cases, how could a man feel any fear in battle? Who and what could he be afraid of, after knowing this pain beyond all pain? How could he not feel truly resurrected to the consciousness of existence, in a state that was absolutely different not only from his prior experience, but also from that of "profane" people who could never even imagine what he had known? The "wholly other" who reveals the direct experience of the sacred in the flesh, as well as in the spirit, is not a theoretical conception by historians of religion. It is a high and profound reality, an experiential surplus, a surreality in the most precise sense of this term.

For this reason, the language and name of the initiate also change after ritual resurrection. A secret language is taught to the new member of the brotherhood, on condition that he take an oath not to reveal it to anyone profane. These arrangements and traditional rules can be found in all epochs and in the most varied civilizations. Above all, we can find the same fundamental initiatory pattern comprising the same phases, as if there were a permanent and universal prototype. The classic works of Mircea Eliade relieve me from having to insist further on this point and offer more abundant proof. I will only repeat one of his conclusions: "The mystery of spiritual regeneration consists of an archetypal process which is realized on different planes in many ways; it is effected whenever the need is to surpass one mode of being and to enter upon another, higher mode, or, more precisely, whenever it is a question of *spiritual transmutation.*"[2]

This expression alludes to an initiatory "alchemy," and I wish to insist, in this regard, upon a point too often neglected: The Mandan rite described here was inspired not by some innate cruelty of the Amerindians, as Eliade rightly points out, but by the ritual significance of torture—"tearing into pieces"—by initiating demons. Is this sufficient? Eliade compares it to the famous temptation of St. Anthony, which is valid, because temptation is often associated with initiatory trials. Moreover, in both cases, the pain and suffering of existence must be endured, often in connection to demonic possession, but also to possession by spirits. In my view, in both the Mandan rite and St. Anthony's temptation, this is not the only aspect that should be taken into consideration. There is also an allusion to a material transmutation of the actual body of the initiate, assimilated into the earth, raised into the air, and cut by fire until the blood or the fire flows. The buffalo heads and the stones fixed to the legs and arms are fairly transparent symbols of these cosmological analogies, as is confirmed by the final rotation of the initiate's body, which can be likened to the movement of the starry celestial vault.

I have dwelled upon this particular aspect of the Mandan rite—which of course merits further, more specific commentaries—in order to show that the notion of interior or spiritual transmutation in traditional initiation on this archaic level is not the only notion we must consider in the perspective of symbolic interpretation.

The rupture at the ontological level has also taken place on the corporeal level in conditions of this kind, and we must admit that it is impossible for us to know scientifically what might be the consequences of such torture in terms of an initiate's perceptions and sensations. We may at least assume that these must have become more or less profoundly modified, even if only in their relationships to general cenesthesia. If we accept this hypothesis, it is possible that some experiment of unknown nature in our modern psychology might explain the impassivity of these neophytes and the incomprehensible absence of any contraction of a single muscle in their faces.

We should at least understand that the passage from one level of language to another—or, more precisely, from the tribal language of the profane to that of the initiates—involved not only learning the secret language of a brotherhood, but also learning about the close relationships that existed between this language and the existential experience of initiation, and, in a way, the incarnation of these myths, rites, and symbols. The body itself, in a certain manner, had to reinvent its image completely, just as the consciousness had to reinvent its language, by way of the trials of this new "birth."

In certain tribes, the initiates are alleged to have forgotten everything from their previous lives. Immediately after the ritual ceremonies, they were taken by the hand, fed like infants, and taught anew the elementary behaviors indispensable for life, including a new vocabulary, which imparted to them the secret names of living beings and things.

Among certain Bantu peoples, circumcision ceremonies required a preliminary rebirth. The father would sacrifice a ram, and three days later wrap the child in the animal's stomach membrane and skin. Before being thus enveloped, however, the child had to climb into bed, lie down by his mother, and cry like a newborn. He would remain in the ram's skin for three days, and on the fourth day, the father would sleep with his wife. It has been observed that in this Bantu tradition, the dead are also buried in a ram's skin and are placed in a fetal position.[3] In ancient Egypt and India and other ancient civilizations, ritual clothing in the skin of an animal was connected to the symbolism of mystical rebirth. Of course, tribal initiations must not be confused with those of secret societies and brotherhoods, but in many cases, the latter are marked by traditions derived from the former—not that these relationships are always easily determined.

We can note, furthermore, that the guardians and keepers of the traditions were always themselves initiates to these brotherhoods, which dated back to a long-ago time and often corresponded to intertribal associations. Therefore, it is at least probable that the authority of these secret societies imposed ritual and symbolic names upon various tribes, adapted to their various local customs and particular beliefs.

This is why, in most cases, it is very difficult to separate initiatory and magical symbols clearly from religious symbols, especially because they often appear in the form of veritable ritual stratifications, a precise historical analysis of which is almost impossible to undertake. I fail to understand how some prehistorians can claim that one such rite was the expression of a religious belief among early peoples whereas another was a magical practice, when these distinctions could have meaning only if we knew the actual thoughts of the early people concerning the subjects of magic and religion and the various values they assigned to them.

THE SYMBOLIC MEANING OF EARLY PEOPLES' MAGICAL AND RELIGIOUS RITES

It is likewise questionable whether we can argue for a comparison between the religions of archaic civilizations and those of Lower Paleolithic bear hunters, as was done by the Swiss prehistorian E. Baechler. Baechler is credited with one of the most important contemporary prehistorical discoveries: the sacrificial worship of bearheads in caves, dating to the Lower Paleolithic. A. Gahs, however, has voiced many objections in this regard.[4]

We hasten to reject, as quickly as possible, the interpretation of a magic related to hunting, in order to establish the notion of a primitive sacrificial cult or even a god of the world to whom the people of the Lower Paleolithic would have offered the objects "that had the greatest value for them,"[5] as E. Baechler arbitrarily assures us. Kurt Lindner, in turn, goes so far as to deduce from this "*spiritual bases* which led to the development of hunting magic and the hunter's art."[6]

Without denying the possibility of spirituality among early humans, for theoretically nothing negates this, we must admit that the indications do not permit us to claim it so peremptorily. On the other hand, it is certain that our distant ancestors attributed an eminent function to cave bears, as the discoveries show. We must remember at this point that early humans shared daily existence with bears, and that bear flesh was probably the main kind of meat in their diet. We may at least assume that they attached a whole complex of values—magical, religious, and utilitarian—to the heads of their victims. These values remain unknown to us. This archaeological testimony, which according to Kurt Lindner is the oldest mythical-religious representation by humans that has been found, therefore poses still more problems that are difficult to resolve.

Because of its importance, however, even though Baechler affirms arbitrarily that this worship had no symbolic meaning, I deem it necessary to briefly summarize the discoveries at Drachenloch and the facts:

Exploring these stations, about fifty centimeters [about twenty inches] from the cavern walls, there were little walls, some of which were as much as eighty centimeters [about thirty-one inches] high. These were built from loose stone without mortar, and their horizontal stratification confirmed that they had been built by human hands. Innumerable cave bear bones were piled up in the space between the little wall and the rock face; especially skulls, often arranged parallel, side by side, or in stacks, some intact, others damaged and full of holes. . . . The discoveries in the third cavern were still more curious. Here there were six stone chests, made of stone slabs and closed with a stone lid. They contained carefully arranged bear skulls, and also the bones of the extremities, as in the crypt in the vestibule. Continuing to search the third cavern, between the overturned blocks that must have existed in this form when the prehistoric hunters lived in the cave, there were well-preserved bear skulls inserted into stone niches. But the cultural character of all this bone debris was manifested above all in one bear skull, which was surrounded by flat stones the size of a hand, matching exactly with the shape of its skull.[7]

The first point that must be considered when we propose a symbolic interpretation is that it must always be associated with a liturgical or ritual dynamic. Consequently, these skulls had either merely banal alimentary significance, which seems unanimously excluded by specialists, or else symbolic and ritual significance. This significance is not necessarily worshipful—religious—because such an interpretation can be established only by comparative ethnology at a distance of at least ten thousand years from the conditions of archaic and Paleolithic civilizations, which is really too great a gap, both historically and psychologically.

On the other hand, we do know the alimentary habits of early peoples with complete certainty. Thus only one consistent hypothesis remains: the symbolic ritual value of a communally shared meal. Most remarkably, no spinal vertebrae were found, only bones from the extremities and skulls. We may then deduce that these body parts were chosen carefully by reason of the importance attributed to them.

Contemporary hunters have observed that the power of a bear's attack depends chiefly on its paws and head. An adult male bear of the species found in the caves would have been at least eight feet tall when standing upright. This ancient species has disappeared, but it is assumed that in size and appearance it resembled the American grizzly. Its bones were large and heavy; its head was particularly massive. Nothing is known of its personality, but the behavior of the modern grizzly when it is provoked or injured is extremely dangerous. Even in modern times animal handlers who deal with different species observe that unlike other creatures, a bear is an unpredictable menace because it gives no sign that enables us to predict its attack. Our distant ancestors therefore had every possible reason to fear bears, while at the same time respecting them, because they were the basis for the hunting economy of the Lower Paleolithic.

Eating the enemy together, in this case, would represent an assimilation of the bear's vital forces by the hunters, in particular the valuable contents of the head—which, in the feasts of cannibal tribes, were generally reserved for chiefs and high dignitaries celebrating victory over their adversaries.

Does not the positioning of the six chests itself indicate a distribution of the skulls either among individuals or among distinct groups? And the entirely isolated skull that was discovered, surrounded by stones corresponding exactly to its shape, constitutes a seventh element that must, in all probability, correspond to the place of the person who carried out this distribution among the hunters.

From these observations, we can at least draw a probable hypothesis: These caves were reserved for symbolic ritual operations of alimentary magic by the assimilation of the vital forces of the sacrificed animal, in the same way that the oldest mythical ritual testimony we know of is not, strictly speaking, religious, but rather magical—which does not exclude it from having sacred value.

In this prehistoric example, we also observe the major role of the body in ceremonies of this kind, which we have already noted previously in initiations. When we inquire into the origin of the consciousness of analogy on which the logic of symbols is based, we often forget that the law of similitude, or action of the similar upon the similar, may have experiential and existential origins: the assimilation of the living by the living—nutrition.

These paleopsychic depths must be plumbed beginning with the universality of nutrition, not merely with sexuality. To eat or be eaten: In an immediate and spontaneous fashion, this is the first law imposed upon all living beings. Consequently, for the most archaic level of living—assimilation—we must draw an essential consequence: All living beings, not only humans, apply in their behavior the logic of assimilation—analogy—which makes this logic not a specific language but the universal language of nature. This is shown to us by the phenomenon of mimicry.

THE PHENOMENON OF MIMICRY

In order to understand the phenomenon of mimicry better, we must first isolate a general principle: Organic movement covers the natural surroundings in the thematic state, subordinated in the organic form, before being differentiated in a distinct fashion as a territory. In this structure, markings made by organic liquids such as urine play the role of inductive signs intended for delineating the extraorganic form of the space occupied, and at the same time they function as inhibitors of the formation of a space altered by a concurrent presence capable of modifying the space for its own advantage. Moreover, these markings make the association of these signs into the primitive model of the association of our individual memories in time, because they allow an animal to recognize the territory as its own by means of the continuity of its traces, just as our memory, by means of our memories, bears witness to the continuous character of our individuality.

The power of assimilation of the extraorganic by the organic on the level of the living analogy of forms implies an essential homology, which is made evident enough by mollusk shells. Yet this condition can be exactly reversed, as in the case of the hermit crab. Here we see mimicry, which, in a way, transposes the thematics of the projection of the similarity of forms and rhythms by means of introversion and not extroversion. There are other examples: the dances of bees, in which these insects indicate to each other, through a truly abstract spatiotemporal reduction that is almost intraorganic, the configuration and conditions of the area of nutrition. And there is the web of the garden spider: If it loses a leg, the mutilation has repercussions upon the structure of its territory, and the angles of the web's radial lines are altered.

Mimicry, in fact, is not limited to its most apparent manifestations or to those best known to naturalists. It begins when the territory, instead of being simply recognized and occupied by inductive, inhibitory, and mnemonic markings, becomes somehow secreted and structured by the animal by means of a thematic transposition of its conditions, as an artificial and instrumental means for capture, nutrition, aggression, and defense. This external structuring of the territory arises from purely internal elements. For example, in the case of the spider *Zilla x-notata,* according to the famous experiments of P. N. Witt, neurotropic substances perturb the external organization of the web. Raymond Ruyer compares these facts with the intoxication of embryos at certain moments, which disturb the internal organization.[8] It is possible that the web of our bodies may be subject to aberrant inductions produced by false markings. We might at least assume a hypothesis—very little examined, to my knowledge—of a phenomenon of this kind in the growth of cancers.

If we have imparted to this notion of mimicry a rather unusual logical extension, it is also because it may be indispensable in understanding general movement on the basis of its most primitive conditions: those of the inversion of the process of thematic projection, most often required by the capture of prey upon which a lure must be imposed by the interposition of a formal similitude. This question is all the more important because it is directly linked to the existential experience of the efficacy of analogy, primarily in the function of archaic hunting practices.

An attentive observation of the behavior of animals has been the source of most mimetic trapping techniques invented and perfected by humans. I will give a few examples, generally not well known. Imitating the territory in which fish like to swim is an ingenious idea, ensuring that a bird has incontestable magical prestige if it is capable of achieving such mimicry. A certain New Guinea cassowary has probably given the Aborigines a natural example, which may in part explain the symbolic role of its attributes in their ritual ceremonies. Lying low in the water, the bird's long feathers wave just like aquatic plants, and it waits there, completely still. The fish, naturally curious and perhaps detecting an interesting smell, approach and gather around this new species of plant. Then the cassowary, compressing its wings, shoots abruptly out of the water and has a fine meal of all the small fry caught by the barbs of its feathers and scattered all around it.

La Fontaine showed us the heron, with its long beak, passively awaiting its prey. This was an error. Like any good fisherman, the heron uses bait: the whitish flakes of skin that fall from its oily breast feathers, which hold an irresistible attraction for fish. As soon as a ripple appears on the water's surface, the bird's long beak reaches down and snatches its prey.

And how does a polar bear capture a seal? By scratching the ice. Once in a while, the seal will come up to a hole in the ice for air, but it is too hard for the bear to know where its prey will emerge and then arrive at just the right moment. Undoubtedly—for there is no other explanation—the bear has observed that it is enough to scratch loudly at the edge of a hole; the seal, attracted to this noise, will come up from the water. The bear hides nearby, then pounces and grabs the seal in its paws, seizes the neck in its jaws, and drags off the fat prize to devour it, throwing away the skin. The Eskimos have learned from this lesson of nature; they attach a piece of wood to a walrus tusk, and generally fit the end of it with four or five bear claws held on by whale baleen. They precisely imitate the cadence of the polar bear's scratching, then stand back, harpoons at the ready.

Meanwhile, far away, the Bozo fishermen of Niger, also armed with harpoons, stalk catfish, which they attract with a decoy created according to the laws of efficacy of the action of the similar upon the similar: a catfish cranial bone fixed on a piece of board garnished with sorghum, to which are attached the feathers of the *anhinga* ("serpent bird") or cormorant.

The use of camouflage and mimetic screens or masks by hunters is immemorial. Bushmen hunting antelope use the same strategies as the Yaqui people of Sonora hunting deer and the Huichol people of Mexico, who wear wood on their heads like the famous prehistoric "sorcerer" of the Trois-Frères Cave. Stress was used by the Syrian poachers of Baniyas and likewise by the illiterate poachers of my childhood in Champagne, who taught me facts on this subject unknown to plenty of learned naturalists. The Syrian hunters would cover their fists with a material resembling panther hide, decorated with two ears and pierced with holes in which eyes were embedded. At daybreak they would creep up on partridges, surround them, and suddenly reveal their masks. The birds, immobilized by fear, could be captured by hand. Even quails can be caught with just two sticks, a black cloth, and a net. Because they have become rare, however, it is best not to explain this further.

These examples will suffice to show that the magic of hunting and the logic of analogy that can be deduced from it, far from being illusions of the primitive mentality known as prelogic, had rigorously experiential and concrete foundations based on the everyday experience of the efficacy of mimicry.

If psychologists and sociologists were educated in the school of nature rather than within the walls of the library, they would understand that their ideas of the animism, totemism, and infantilism and the naïveté of primitive peoples are the ideological abstractions of "civilized" thinkers. Intelligence certainly has its different ages, but the human species has no infancy. The extraordinary complexity exhibited by, for example, the initiatory and religious lives of the Australian Aborigines makes the analogical intuition of modern Western society appear impoverished by comparison, in terms of its archaic content.

If we cannot opt for what can no longer be chosen—history being what it is—then we should at least restore full meaning to those kinds of logic that are farthest removed from our own, rather than constantly devaluing them. The universal language of analogy and symbols is not only the language of the gods, but also the language of nature, of the suprahuman and the infrahuman, the language of the spirit, but also of the depths of the body.

NUTRITION AND THE MIMETIC ORIGINS OF ANALOGY

The phenomenon of nutrition presents two opposing characteristics, depending on whether we are considering vegetable or animal life: *autotrophy* or *heterotrophy*. A plant can build its organic elements autonomously, using elements from the mineral kingdom. An animal, on the other hand, must gain its energy from demolishing complex organic molecules that come from other living beings. This necessity to eat or be eaten therefore requires species and individuals to have mobility of action; this is indispensable for their survival, and requires aggression and attacking, as well as defense and evasion. At the same time, another new condition appears in contrast with vegetable life: the mobility of expression of forms and behavior.

Expressivity leads to the capacity to modify colors, odors, attitudes, aspects, and relationships between what is perceptible and what is perceived, between signs expressed and signs understood. Thus, besides the direct mechanisms of attack and defense, there are also indirect processes of diversion of these mechanisms through similarities to models or signs that are judged harmless by prey or dangerous by predators. Analogy can therefore play a part on all levels of the phenomenon of mimicry, and in a certain way, it is the primordial and universal logic of expressivity in the animal kingdom.

The similitude implied by every mimetic phenomenon is not merely a matter of a superficial apparent resemblance whereby one animal species, taking on an aspect uncharacteristic of its group, imitates another species in the same place or in two coexisting places. There is also, on the one hand, the dynamic relationship of the model and the mimic to their surroundings, and on the other hand, their relationship to a third term closely related to the origin and perpetuation of this mimicry: the animal that is tricked or lured by the resemblance between the first two terms. For example, a North American harrier, *Buteo albonatatus,* glides in the sky in the company of vultures, resembling them with its dark silhouette and long, straight wings. The relationship between the mimic species and the model species is explainable only as a function of the analogical interpretation of a third species, the dupe species: small rodents or other living prey that are not afraid of vultures, which the harrier can consequently approach without the risk of being spotted.[9]

The relations between mimetic behaviors and the environment also depend to a great extent on conditions of the visibility of shapes, ambient light or absence of light, and tricks of the light on the animal and its surroundings. On this subject, see Yveline Leroy's excellent article "Le mimétisme animal" [The animal mimic], in *La Recherche,* no. 45, May 1974.

Certain modalities of mimicry can also be nonvisual: for example, the ants that, in the following case, play the role of the dupes. The larvae of the beetle *Atemeles pubicollis* imitate the movements of ant larvae demanding food. They take advantage of not only a tactile analogy for extracting drops of regurgitated nourishment, but also an olfactory analogy, by means of glandular secretions whose smell resembles that of the pheromones emitted by ant larvae. Thus they are carried into the nest. If they are brushed with a coating that prevents the volatilization of the pheromones, the ants recognize the false larvae as strangers, and seize and expel them.

Mimetic homochromy refers to a certain harmony of coloration between an animal and its surroundings. It can be reinforced by *homotypy,* a similarity of form between the animal and some element in its surroundings, whether vegetable, such as a twig, leaf, or thorn; mineral, such as a rock; or animal, by the imitation of another species. In certain cases, the similitude between the mime and the model reaches the point of morphological and dynamic assimilation with a compact group, which then constitutes, according to Yveline Leroy's appropriate expression, "a veritable living microenvironment into which certain species incorporate themselves to gain advantage from it."[10] For example, some beetles, crickets, and spiders, called myrmecomorphs, look like ants and live around them, thus protecting themselves from many predators.

In mimetic homochromy, colorations are essentially variable, whereas they are fixed in what is known as *ostentatious homochromy,* as is evidenced by tent caterpillars, whose colorations continually protect them against predators. Thus a model species with bright colors that is dangerous, toxic, or venomous is imitated by a harmless mime species that has no active natural protection. In this case, we can see that expressiveness through imitation of forms and colors (the basis of all art) is prefigured as a condition of survival through the mimetic analogy, which thus perfects and completes a natural, imperfect process. *Isotypic mimicry,*[11] moreover, shows that species of more or less distant zoological groups naturally protect against predators by exhibiting similarly colored designs. One of

these designs, for example, is conspicuously worn by the black tent cater-
pillar, blotched with bright red. Other species, such as harmless *Simophis*
snakes, imitate coral snakes, whose bite is deadly, with red, black, and
white rings.

Mimicry does not have merely a defensive and protective function.
The analogical behavior whereby an animal simulates a model or a lure,
hiding it from its prey or attracting the prey, is used as an aggressive and
offensive function by predators. These homo-structuring hunting mechanisms are highly diverse. They use processes comparable to the mimicry
we have already examined in cases such as, for example, the insectivo-
rous mantis *Hymenopus coronatus,* which blends in so completely with
red orchid flowers that insects visiting for nectar trustingly land on the
mantis. In the case of anglerfish such as *Antennarius commersioni,* we
may observe a double mimicry, homochromic and homotypic, with the
use of a lure: a wormlike appendage attached to a filament, producing
an innate response of attraction in prey. In this case, the mime develops
a perfect resemblance to the model: *Antennarius* looks exactly like the
rocks among which it lurks, from its color and its rough or rippling
surface formed of false bryozoans to its apparent immobility. Moreover,
when the duped little fish rush to snap up the lure, they precipitate themselves into the mouth of their hidden predator. In fact, *Antennarius* has
taken the economy of fishing further than human fishermen, because
without expending the least amount of energy on movement, it uses its
victim's energy in its own direction, all the better to eat its prey.

Offensive and defensive mimicry may be partial or total, individual
or collective. In the latter case, the grouping of many animals achieves a
homotypy capable of evoking, for example, an inflorescence or a branch
bearing berries—a common form in which the individual's outline van-
ishes. Other phenomena often linked to symbiosis in a sense achieve
the paradox developed by Edgar Allan Poe in "The Purloined Letter":
hiding something in plain sight. For example, the very obvious designs
of the clownfish, with its transverse white stripes close in width to a
sea anemone's tentacles, allow the fish to blend in with the anemone's

colors and blur its outlines in a phenomenon of *somatolysis,* remaining unseen although directly exposed to the view of its predators.

All these facts are of crucial importance for the study of the experiential origins of the analogical process and the relationship of expressiveness to conditions of survival in an environment where the source of coveted energy or desirable nourishment—any living organism—must perform similitude if it is to escape the permanent threat of identification. In other words, it is not identity that saves, but analogy, with its possibilities of slipping through the holes in the net of logic in which all living beings are caught, at all levels of their adventures as predators or prey. The expressiveness of similitudes and the archaic manifestations of animal mimicry therefore constitute the archetypal corporeal and concrete experience of the vital efficacy of analogy, which is linked to the very foundation of all animal life: Eat or be eaten. The illusion implied by mimetic expressiveness can be extended to all language. But it is precisely due to to this illusion that the living dominates the devouring absurdity of the real and gives it an incontestable, immediate, and certain meaning: that of its own survival.

4 THE LOGIC OF ANALOGY

DEFINITION OF ANALOGY

Harald Höffding defined *analogy* in these terms: "A similitude of relations between two objects, a similitude that is not founded upon particular properties or on the parts of these objects, but upon the reciprocal relationship between these properties or these parts."[1]

Aristotle distinguished a quantitative analogy (*isotes logon*), which, in the strict sense of the word, is a proportionality, from a qualitative analogy, which can be observed, for example, between geometric figures or biological structures in different states. In fact, in his *Categories,* Aristotle specifically analyzed analogies, but only *paronyms (denominativa):*[2] *Grammarian* comes from *grammar, courageous* from *courage,* and so forth. Scholastics have developed the analogy of proportionality alongside the analogy of attribution (or proportion), which Aristotle made use of in his study of being, the object of metaphysics. "The analogous term is fitting to many according to a relationship in part identical, in part different."[3]

We must distinguish the analogy of attribution from the analogy of proportionality. The former is found most explicitly in Aristotle. In this analogy, unity stems from the relationship of various analogued to a single chosen: principal analogued. The analogous term of attribution is what applies to many as a result of ordering into a single one.[4]

In the analogy of proportionality, there is no principal analogued, but instead there are mutual proportions or relationships that create unity among the analogued. Thus we say "the eye sees" and "the intellect sees" because understanding is to the intellect what vision of the perceptible is to the eye: Vision/Eye = Understanding/Intellect. In this analogy, all terms can be represented, in a certain way, by one unique concept, even if it is imperfectly unified. We must therefore not interpret " = " with mathematical rigor. *The analogical term of proportionality is what applies to many due to a certain similitude of proportion (or of relationship).*[5]

We must also distinguish proper analogy from metaphorical analogy: Proper analogy is the case in which the reason signified by the term is found formally in each of the analogued, as we see in the example of vision by the eye and the intellect. Metaphorical (or improper) analogy is the case in which reason applies specifically to only one analogued and applies to others through an intellectual construction. Thus, to take a classic example, we would say that the walls have ears when really people are the ones who have ears.

In the first, mathematical sense of proportion, analogy designates the comparison of two relationships between four terms taken in pairs. Qualitatively, in biology this comparison may indicate functional similitudes and in linguistics, the assimilation of certain forms of expression. In all cases involving the unification of different objects or domains by linking them via a similitude of relationships, analogy takes part as an exploratory and unifying process capable of deriving perspectives of the whole and harmonic or of regulating relations that the logic of identity by itself does not allow us to perceive and explore.

Harald Höffding, supporting himself with the fact that analogy plays a fundamental role in every act of thought applied to concrete objects— whereas the identity of the object and relationship, of a logical and arithmetical type, is a pure abstraction—did not follow Aristotle or Kant[6] in not counting analogy among the categories (that is, the fundamental concepts of human thought). Höffding was also the first modern philosopher to introduce the concept of analogy into the formal categories, immediately after the concept of identity. Höffding showed that analogy is the basis for the reduction of serial relationships of quality, and for this reason, it takes part in the evolution of the concepts of number, degree, time, and place—hence the major importance of analogy in the principal operations of human knowledge.

We must first remember that there is not only an absolute identity of type—"A is A"—in the purely formal thought of logic and (for example) in axiomatics but also a relative identity or an identity of relationship in arithmetic. There is also an identity of difference, which is used in establishing a series of identically variable differences. Without this means, it would be impossible to conceive of the qualitatively identical series (in reality, assumed to be such) that are at the basis of all our so-called exact sciences: series of numbers, time, degree, and place.

Absolute identity is purely ideal and therefore experientially nonexistent in the empirical world as well as in everyday practice, and thus it has no concrete or existential meaning. The formal world of logical and mathematical abstractions therefore cannot oppose any kind of physical refutation or any ontological criticism because, being purely tautological, it is founded upon a single principle: "the same" (*tautos*), whose absolute equality is with the one it postulates ideally in all relationships considered rationally coherent. This logical perspective implies no postulate other than the meaning it assumes initially: the principle of identity, on which all further formalization depends.

Voluntary and conscious analogy begins with a reflection upon similarities and dissimilarities, and these may include numerous degrees between chaotic dissimilarity and absolute identity. Western thought always evolves around two poles: the indeterminate and the determinate, total inequality and perfect equality. To assimilate the one to the identical always equal to itself has in fact characterized the mark and, in a way, the model of Western philosophy since Plato, because this essential theme is found throughout all its melodic variations.

It is also not surprising to note that reasoning by analogy, which has played a fundamental role in the process of mythic thought and continues to play a basic role in civilizations different from our own, has been unceasingly reduced by Western thought either to a sort of "false thinking" or to an inferior form of consciousness, which, according to Aristotle and Kant, is unworthy of appearing among the categories of understanding. In short, it is reduced to a psychological process or even an aesthetic one.

Here, furthermore, is another constant postulate of Western philosophy: Only that which is thought to be true is true. It may well be, however, that the thinkable is as closely connected to the unthinkable as the audible to the inaudible and the visible to the invisible. What we perceive of the octaves of light is no more real than what we do not perceive at all; it is only more real relative to us and to our means of perceiving it. The inclination to attain an absolute identity as a form and supreme result of thought—the desire finally to find repose in a thought that is perfectly equal and united to its object, beyond all that is chaotic, multiple, and diverse—characterizes a permanent obsession of the West: a need for a unique order of truth in the universe, which alone would be capable of taking into account the infinite diversity of all real manifestations. From this perspective, interpretation can just as well be materialist as idealist, and its hidden basis does not vary. This is the logic of identity, as determining for the mentality of contemporary civilization as that of prelogic preparation for the primitive. Thus we have created a world of thoughts that have become mechanical without questioning attentively enough the foundations of our logic, our reasoning, and our interpretations of nature, humankind, and the universe.

The fundamental problem that analogy continues to pose, however, relates not to a schematism of a unity of order, purely ideal and abstract, which would permit us, starting with a first term identical and always equal to itself, to conceive metaphysically a proportional similitude of terms analogous to one another. The problem of analogy, still current, is one of a concrete experience of the multiplicity of the meanings of being among which the analogical process explores and presents similitudes of relationships, albeit without being able to prove logically that this is a matter of absolute identities. Humans, in fact, are not only capable of knowing at least part of what is real, rationally and scientifically. We must also concede that humans have the power to infer the rest and at least catch a glimpse of what our knowledge does not attain.

If we admit the reality of the glimmerings of intelligence that sometimes flicker in the eyes of dogs, then we would take humility too far in refusing to believe in our own glimmerings of spirit and the corresponding intuition indispensable for every animal or human search. This postulate does not require ambitious theories on the ultimate nature of the science of being as being or on the difference between the being common to the things in the universe and the first and unique being. The logical basis I propose can be stated in a few words: Every experience and every concept has meaning only as an experiential and conceptual increase, which is not exhausted by the logic of identity but remains open to the logic of analogy.

THE ANALOGICAL PROCESS

The analogical process offers the benefit of stimulating research, orienting its perspectives, and transferring an order discovered in one system to another system. For Galileo, for example, the discovery of Jupiter's moons offered an analogy that could show us the sun's relationship to the other planets, thus confirming Copernicus's conception. In modern times, the analogy between the solar system and the atom, although it has been recognized as arbitrary after a certain point, has nevertheless given us a better understanding of the atomic phenomena studied.

The great danger in reasoning by analogy, however, comes from the fact that it tends to cause the isolation of the particular object to disappear, placing it in relation to an ever greater number of other objects and, ultimately, to all of them. This process therefore terminates by making the specific characteristics of the initial object and its real singularity disappear within a global explanation and an artificial systematization, which, most often, effaces the dissimilarities and places emphasis only on the similarities. Analogy is not proof. This can never be repeated enough. Likewise, identity, even if it is sufficient for all demonstrations, proves nothing other than the truth of these demonstrations, and not truth in itself. These are the two vectors of orientation of the human spirit, both necessary and both insufficient if they are not the objects of a permanent critique of the interpretations they propose.

We must also not confuse analogy with homology. The former is based upon a concordance of functions, the latter on one of structures, for example in biology. Physiological analogies—but not homologies—can be discerned between the lungs of mammals and the gills of fish. On the other hand, the swim bladders of fish and the lungs of mammals, which are not analogous, can be considered as anatomically homologous. A whole given as such is not necessarily identical to that whole reconstructed using its elements. When we reduce the biological form to the physico-chemical elements that compose it, it is a matter of understanding how these elements constitute a whole that is the initial condition, or, if we prefer, all the preceding elements *plus* the unity of their combination; and ultimately, it is this unity that poses the principal problem. When we refer to *life,* we have simply substituted one term for another, with the difference that we designate as a totality something that, experientially, remains a unity. Kant noted in his *Critique of Judgment* that "the organization of nature has nothing analogical to any kind of causality that we know of."[7] Two eminent theoreticians of consciousness, Émile Meyerson and Léon Brunschvicg, are totally opposed on the subject of analogy.[8]

Furthermore, this is only one episode among many in the conflict between the logic of identity and the logic of analogy, which has continued throughout the history of philosophy from antiquity to the present. Without attempting to resolve it, we may at least wonder how to reconnect the various means and different areas of consciousness and experience without using the concept of analogy. But also, a similarity of relationship does not imply a necessary identity, just as our agreements of expectation on which all the objectivity of scientific thought depends cannot be limited to analogy for studying objects new to experience. Identity therefore remains the most effective methodological principle of our thought, which does not necessarily mean it is the most true.

Analogy acts through unification, but also through observation, stimulation, and anticipation. It reveals truths, particularly through the questions it raises, and it may lead to new knowledge, even if it turns out that its value is subsequently contested. This was the case, for example, for the analogical solar model proposed by Niels Bohr for interpreting atomic phenomena. Moreover, the history of the sciences shows us that often enough, a correct conclusion is drawn from false premises because, in many experiments, analogy plays a role in the hypothesis, poses a problem, and invites us to research the conditions of its resolution, leading to a critique of the initial conditions or premises. Those that are finally recognized as correct are generally discovered only at the end, but without false analogies, they would never have been found. Analogy, therefore, can deceive all the more often because it does not always deceive. In this case, its solution is found in the determination of a relationship definitively based on identity, that touchstone of the coherent in all domains of science—hence, the necessity of the logical and mathematical tool for the formalized solution of all rational problems.

UNCONSCIOUS AND INVOLUNTARY ANALOGIES

The aforementioned role of the analogy assumes the intervention of a conscious and voluntary analytical reduction of differences to an identical and unique object of understanding. But it also happens that involuntary psychic processes, such as sensory intuition, memory, and imagination, present to us not expressly different objects, but totalities. Analysis and reflection then tend to resolve them into combined parts, but these are able to determine only that the elements are identical at all points to those that constitute the initial involuntary or unconscious totalities.

In fact, the emergence of new elements can also intervene, immediately and involuntarily, and mix with content already given without us being able to distinguish them clearly. Moreover, analysis itself brings its own distortions into this process in that it grasps analogically only that which was already analogical. Thus it needs a "code of the code" in order to be interpreted.

On this subject, Höffding observed the extent to which the expression "unconscious conclusions" is incorrect. These are only processes, transitions that can be conceived only if they present analogies with true conclusions—for example, when we propose the concept of *synthesis* to express the nature of all conscious life. We must first decide theoretically whether or not the condition itself is constituted by differences that can be either large or small, but in any case irreducible. If these chaotic series existed, only approximations could be attempted, and the range of one single intense and penetrating reflection could only, at best, be limited to the true condition of one particular case.

The concept of analogy itself is used analogously, Harald Höffding observes, "when we say that primitive men interpreted every new experience in *analogy* with the traditions by which they lived."[9] We must always distinguish the logical basis of an interpretation and condition from the actual interpretation of the phenomenon using this basis. If images, names, or ceremonies are not parts present as such in the reflection of primitive man, but instead constitute a whole that is what it signifies, then this is only a prelogical basis or, better, an alogical basis in relation to our own. Yet the primitive interpretation, based on this initial condition, is rigorously rational. The image is not like the object but is the object itself; therefore primitives may fear falling into the power of someone who possesses their portrait, and dread, for example, failing as a hunter.

This reasoning is as rigorously coherent as our own, because in all times and at all degrees of culture, human reflection operates based on hypotheses determining a logical basis for the interpretation of phenomena—a basis that does not intervene immediately in this process as an object of reflection and critical analysis. When a contemporary mathematician checks the correctness of an equation, he does not question the principle of identity; nor does he consider whether, in reality, the second *A* in the formula *A* = *A* is or is not considered "in the same terms as the first," as Aristotle himself somewhat perversely expressed it. The primitive person would find the contestation of the identity of image and object or name and person no less absurd.

On the other hand, the constancy of rational process in all mentalities and the variations of the logical bases of interpretation pose the hardest anthropological problems to resolve. Each person, in fact, understands his fellow creatures only if they use the same logical basis for interpreting things and beings—although in most cases, he will be incapable of conceiving and critiquing this basis. Thus, for example, words in foreign languages can sometimes sound bizarrely inappropriate for the things they designate. A German visiting Paris once wrote in a letter to his family that he was surprised by the French word for bread, *pain,* adding: "We call it *Brot,* and this word describes it much better."

Involuntary and spontaneous analogies also depend on the practical conditions of action. An analogical representation of an isolated part or property in relation to a whole is also an indication that is sufficient for the instinct to bring about a movement. The sign acts as if the object were present. Moreover, in each recognition, similitude with prior experiences plays a role, and analogy may be considered as intervening as a stimulation of the analytical intuition as well as the synthetic intuition.

When we observe the behavior of children who are completely engaged in action by their games, we also observe their great aptitude for immediate and spontaneous analogical experiences. If a state or situation is linked to a pleasure or satisfaction, the child desires it to continue in an analogous relationship bearing a scheme similar to the previous one, even if the old forms have changed in appearance. For example, a child listens to stories and plays, sitting at his grandfather's knee, but it is time for him to go to bed. Shortly afterward, he runs back in with his teddy bear, which he immediately places in the spot where he was playing. The child does not want the situation to be interrupted. At least the bear will enjoy it, and what's more, later the bear will tell him everything Grandpa said. Likewise, if play is interrupted from outside, tears and anger are inevitable without an analogically substituted intermediary. The toy that continues to play while the child sleeps is capable of rendering appreciable services to parents.

ANALOGY AND THE INDIRECT CONSCIOUSNESS OF EXPERIENTIAL AND CONCEPTUAL EXPANSION

If we wish to understand the principal problem of symbolism and the expansion that it implies, let us pose a simple question: Assuming that fish are reasonable animals, how can we teach them what clouds are?

If we told them the pure truth—that clouds are vesicular vapors containing water suspended in air—we would completely mislead our little listeners. Have they not always known that in the environment of the sea, air is lighter than water? Have they ever seen water vapor in the sea or a cloud from which rain might fall? The wisest of fish could not conceive of this unthinkable thing, which nevertheless does exist in nature above them and is not unusual for other beings, who find it so banal that they often fail to notice it.

Because the fish are not able to understand an experiential and conceptual expansion directly in relation to a given living and thinking environment, we must therefore use an indirect means of communication—not the logic of identity, but the logic of analogy, not a clear and distinct idea, but an allegory or a symbol. The white masses of fish eggs that float on the surface of the water and from which a rain of tiny fish fall when they hatch offer us the material for a metaphor or parable. Thus we might say: "Just as here, in the ocean, countless living drops fall from these white masses you see, so elsewhere, the rain falls from the clouds in the realm of the sky . . ."

But a comparison is not sufficient for the fish themselves to verify what we say. We must give them another typical example, a model of experience, a dynamic scheme relating at the same time to their environment and to another environment where we can see that clouds exist.

Thus we are led to propose to them a typological symbol, a halfway point between air and water: the flying fish. Only through attempting to imitate its behavior can our listeners themselves have a chance of seeing or at least understanding what they cannot know. In this way, we can better understand that the analogy of similitudes finds its most perfect form closest to the truth in the imitation of a model, and in personal participation in its experience. On this level we can see that symbol, myth, and rite become inseparable. This is why, through a sufficiently obvious gradation, the entire analogical process of symbolism extends from the simplest synthematic convention to the most complex typological unification, passing through the multiple intermediaries of allegory.

From this perspective, we can better discern why analogical unification itself is always necessarily incomplete—because by definition, it never reaches total identification as such. Thus it remains forever open to the reciprocal interplay of the constitutive parts and changing relationships of experiential and conceptual expansion between the concrete totalities. This dynamic process of analogy finds its legitimate place within every dialectical process.

ANALOGY IN THE ECONOMY
OF SIGNS AND VALUES

How can we describe generally a communication of a signification by a similitude of relations between object A and object B, according to the definition of analogy proposed by Höffding? We know that this similitude is founded not upon the particular properties or parts of these objects, but on the reciprocal relationships between these properties or these parts. Consequently, we necessarily exclude their own use value and retain only their exchange value in the relationships in question.

It is important to observe immediately that we thus discover the same theoretical perspective in the domain of general symbology—that is, the economy of signs, as in that of the economy of merchandise. Both are related to the universal processes of exchange and of individual and collective interrelations.

In Marxian analysis, for example, value theory is the starting point for the entire system proposed.[10] Contrary to current beliefs, Marx's thought, summarized here, can be easily understood by all, and does not require specialized economic knowledge.

Suppose we have two commodities in a certain quantity, wheat and iron, for example, and assume the following equation.

$$A = \text{a peck of wheat} = \text{a kilogram of iron} = B$$

What can this equation mean if not that these two objects, A and B, have something in common and are of the same quantity?

The problem is finding this common element. Marx eliminated all the natural, geometric, physical, and chemical properties of merchandise. "Such properties," he wrote, "claim our attention only insofar as they affect the utility of these commodities, and make them use-values. *But the exchange of commodities is evidently an act characterized by a total abstraction from use-value.* Then one use-value is just as good as another, provided only it be present in sufficient quantity."[11] The only exchangeable value in which economic science is interested is the social function of the goods, not their individual function. This, then, is a matter of finding the social substance of goods; all their individual qualities must be eliminated.[12] When the use-value is set aside, all that remains is a quality common to all things that are exchanged: the quality of being "products of labor." Marx concludes that labor is the common principle of merchandise. It is its only common objective.

In Marx's analysis, there is one expression that has not been sufficiently examined by his countless commentators: the phrase "provided only it be present in sufficient quantity." Here, Marx clearly isolates a fundamental problem of economics: the *proportionality of value,* which had already been posed by the medieval theologians and canonists—for example, Albertus Magnus and St. Thomas Aquinas, on the subject of determining the fair price in exchanges. These two theologians drew their general economic theories from patristics, condemning riches and the love of gain for its own sake and espousing the prohibition of interest-lending and usury. But the inspiration of the economic ideas of Albertus Magnus (Thomas Aquinas's master) was Aristotle, and in this case, the model of the isotes logon of Aristotelianism: the analogy of proportionality. The scholastic theory of the fair price is based entirely on the proportional reciprocity (*contrapassum*) applied in Albertus Magnus's *Ethica*.[13] In trade, Albertus wrote, there must be a certain equality between the parties, but the special characteristic of this equality is proportional reciprocity, because each party must experience for itself what it makes adversary experience, *contrapati*. This is also the Thomist position: *Videtur quod justum sit simpliciter idem contrapassum, in commutativa justicia*.* The "justice" in question is that of the contracts known as *communicativi*—trade contracts—which shows that trade is thus assimilated to communication.

Moreover, Albertus Magnus synthesized this relationship into a "figure of proportionality" (*figura proportionalitatis*), the idea and terms of which are borrowed from Aristotle.[14] An architect offers a house and a cobbler offers shoes. How do we find the fair price ratio between them? We can draw the scheme on page 85.

The proportion, Albertus tells us, must be formed by the diameter, *per diametrum: $A/D = B/C$*. This is the isotes logon, the Aristotelian quantitative analogy. What is the nature of this relationship, and on what basis is it founded? Should the size of the objects exchanged serve as a criterion? No, that would be absurd. According to Albertus Magnus, the exchange must be made according to each party's *indigentia*. Langenstein, who taught in Vienna a century later, defined *indigentia* as the lack of useful or somehow necessary things—that is, the greater or lesser degree of utility that the thing possesses in relation to the person who buys it, his need for the object of economic exchange. Thus the quantity of shoes (D) given in exchange for the house (C) must be in the same ratio as the utility of a shoe for the architect relative to the utility of a house for the cobbler.

---

*Thomas Aquinas, *Summa Theologica*, vol. 2, part II-II (*Secunda Secundae*), quaestio LXI, art. 4.

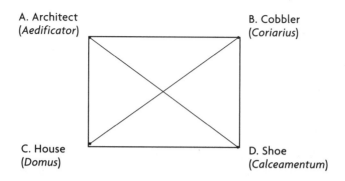

St. Thomas Aquinas was more precise than Langenstein and followed the ideas of Albertus Magnus on this point: "The architect must accept the work of the cobbler, and the cobbler that of the architect, according to a fair equivalent in expenditure and work (*in labore et expensis*); otherwise, society is compromised."[15] This passage seems to show that the notion of the value of merchandise in work is not a modern invention.

Human indigence, moreover, was considered by Albertus Magnus as the true and natural measure of commutable things (*Indigentia humana est vera et naturalis mensura commutabilium*).[16] The idea of work as value is even more clearly present in Thomas Aquinas's rule according to which the architect must receive a quantity of shoes such that the work and expenditure contained in the shoes equals the work and expenditure contained in the house: *Oportet igitur ad hoc quod sit justa commutatio ut tanta calceamenta dentur pro uno domo . . . quantum oedificator . . . excedit coriarium in labore et in expensis.*[17]

We may note that on this point, Thomas Aquinas appears to be more precise than Albertus Magnus: He calculates equivalency according to the work and costs of production. These two examples at least show clearly that medieval scholastic thought in this era—and the thought that would evolve after it in a perceptibly different manner, especially in the fifteenth century—was seeking objective economic justice exterior to the particularity of things. Its concepts were built upon Aristotelian quantitative analogy—which is to say, in that era, they were scientifically and mathematically constructed. This doctrine is founded upon an already formalized and synthemized logic. Consequently, the idea of *æqualitas* was developed by the canonists concurrently with that of the *justum contrapassum*. We must at least remember from this that the relationship between lending and counterlending, which constitutes the form of justice in the lending contract, was not conceived by medieval scholastic thought as being of a psychological nature or by any equivalence of desires between buyer and seller. This relationship had to be the same for all sales, fixed and independent from the particular circumstances of each exchange.

This, therefore, is the fair price, the value of work; and at least on this point, Marxian analysis, according to which the basis of the value of merchandise is the quantity of work that it contains and the measure of value is the unit of work, can be considered as being very close to scholastic analysis. In other words, according to Marx's own expression, the value is a crystallization, a "freezing" of human work (*Arbeitsgallerie*). Hence, the incomprehensible side of work in itself, because when all values are measured, work has no criterion other than being its own value in itself. Marx recognized this: "In the expression 'value of labor,' the idea of value is not only completely obliterated, but actually reversed. It is an expression as imaginary as the value of the earth."[18]

Thus substantified, that which is sold from the work will then be dynamized, according to Marx, thanks to the concept of labor-power, no less obscure than the preceding concept. How can we measure "the expenditure of simple labor-power, *i.e.*, of the labor-power, which, on an average, apart from any special development, exists in the organism of every ordinary individual,"[19] according to the definition of work proposed by Marx? The notions of complex labor, psychological value, equivalency of desires in exchange, and even the finality of work escape both Marxian analysis and medieval scholastics for the same profound reason: They eliminate the nonmeasurable—the irrational—from all economic relations.

Moreover, these two systems of thought, although so different on other levels, neglect an essential fact: The value of exchange is not an initial condition of the economy of merchandise or of the economy of signs. Society is not an initial given. The initial cause is the individual use-value, the subjective determination of the value of exchange from the point of view of the subject's *indigentia*. If we do not want to buy a good, whatever it may be, we will determine its abundance and even its overabundance, and consequently the decline of its exchange value and market prices. There is no fair price when the buyers no longer desire a given good. The bids will prove it: If a suspicion or rumor of a lack of authenticity circulates in an auction room, then even without any objective proof, the object will have no buyer or will be sold below its initially fixed value. Its price, therefore, is not independent from the oscillations of desire or, ultimately, from irrational causes.

Likewise, a relationship between a signal and a signification depends on the desire for communication between the two parties, in terms of the sign in question. All dead religions prove it. The symbols of a forgotten god have no more meaning for people who no longer wish to communicate with each other concerning this god. The symbols have not lost their initial meaning, but the process of their exchange no longer takes place; it no longer corresponds to a real production of information or to the determination of values. Axiological order does not exist in itself; it is built only through the realization of a desire by the psychological and spiritual lives of individuals.

Likewise, work has no meaning entirely independent from its personal goal, from the inner vocation to which it corresponds. This is why there is no fair salary that can be determined quantitatively. A worker who struggles more than another worker to accomplish the same task should, in strict fairness, be paid more than the worker whose effort is less. One individual's hour of work is not worth the same as another's. The different quality of the results obtained from the same task is sufficient to prove this, as is the variable quantity of these results. Thus, in addition to quantitative analogy in the realm of economics—formalized logic—we must add a pure abstraction of exchange, a qualitative analogy, which is necessarily symbolic. In fact, it restores concrete and universal reality to individual desires and to the life of desire, alienated and dissociated by the abusive generalization of the rational concepts of the exchange of merchandise and the communication of signs.

Clearly determining and distinguishing the various operations of the analogical process of symbolism can thus allow us to develop a coherent classification of the various signs of similitude—that is, all symbols. There are three of these operations: (1) assembling a signification arbitrarily with a signal that has an appointed sign, giving it an unequivocal and constant predetermined meaning; (2) reconnecting a signification with a signal without first explicitly determining the meaning of the signification between the parties who communicate concerning it; and (3) joining a signal and a signification to a typical significator in two possible relationships: either active, in which the type acts as a model, or passive, in which the type functions as an imprint.

The first operation corresponds to what I call synthematic symbolism; the second to metaphorical or allegorical symbolism; and the third to anaphoric or typological symbolism. These three terms will be explained later. We must merely remember here that in both metaphors and anaphoras, the similitude is neither conventional nor arbitrary, which it always is in the syntheme. This is why, although we could speak of synthematic symbolism in general, the signs it uses are based not on real or somehow natural or internal analogies, but on external and artificial analogies. In this sense, the signs of formalized logic and so-called symbolic calculation, for example, are not true symbols and must be called synthemes, like all other conventional signs of the logical-scientific type.

As a function of this preliminary separation, it seems clear that the dynamic character of analogy and symbolism is verified only on the level of the continued metaphor that is allegory and on the level of the intervention of the significator type in the relationship between signal and signification.

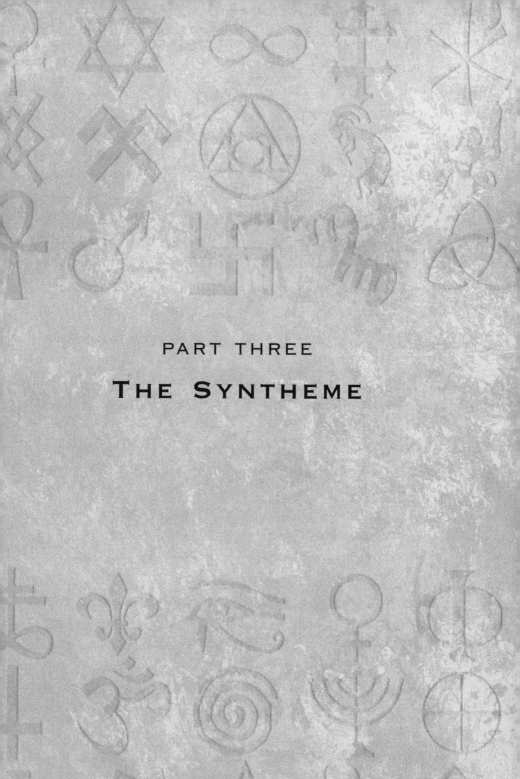

PART THREE

THE SYNTHEME

5 THE SYNTHEMATIC FUNCTION OF SYMBOLISM

LOGICAL AND MATHEMATICAL SYNTHEMES

It is regrettable that logicians and mathematicians do not use the word *syntheme* rather than *symbol*—not only because the former term more correctly designates the conventional character of the arbitrarily chosen sign, and thus distinguishes it from signs that are purely abstract in the Saussurean sense of the unmotivated linguistic type; but also because *syntheme* does not imply any particular conceptual or intuitive residual in the ideographic use of signs and their textual assembly in the mathematical—theoretical—sense of the term.

In fact, a mathematical text or theory is composed of assemblies of synthemes classifiable into logical and literal signs specific to the theory considered. The rules of synthemization of these assemblies constitute formal mathematics. They may be enunciated in various ways, which are not all equivalent. Summarily describing logical synthemization, according to Bourbaki,[1] we must remember that this system constitutes not symbolization but rather a device structured by *ideogrammatic assemblies*.

Almost all mathematical signs have been borrowed from various writing systems derived generally from Greek and Latin alphabets and consciously diverted from their initial usage as characters in Phoenician writing. These letters have been used in italic, gothic, or inverted typographical designs to signify various values. With the addition of the ancient and cursive forms of these letters borrowed from the Greek and Latin alphabets; Arabic numerals; punctuation, emphasis, and linking signs; certain characters of Hebrew and Japanese origin; specific signs such as =, +, C; and glyphs and brackets such as ( ), [ ], and 占占, we end up with a total of about five hundred synthemes of the logical and mathematical type.

Their assemblies take place through a linear device that has often been codified by usage. If a text is long (and may contain many thousands of signs), we substitute these assemblies with abbreviating synthemes or words and phrases of the usual language. The logical synthemes used are *or, not,* and τ ("the object which")—for example τ B, in the sense of "the object such as B."

The assemblies of a text or a theory T appear in phrases or formative constructions. These are obtained by certain juxtapositions of assemblies called *terms* or *objects* if they are reduced to one letter or if they begin with the syntheme τ ("the object which"), or with a sign that is substantific of T. In the opposite case, they are called *relations* or *assertions*. The phrases are formed of assemblies A, having one of the following properties:

- A is a letter.
- In T there is a relationship B preceding A such that A is the assembly τ x (B). τ x (B) designates the assembly obtained by replacing the letter *x* in B with □ and writing the sign τ in front of this assembly, τ being linked to the signs □ by a "gallows."
- In T there is a relationship B preceding A such that A is the assembly that is *not* B.
- In T there are the relations B and C preceding A such that A is the assembly B *or* C.
- A is obtained by following a sign specific to T with assemblies preceding A, according to certain rules specific to the sign in question.

Once these general processes of construction are conventionally admitted, we may deduce their terms and relations from the text or theory T. We now use *abbreviating synthemes*. For example, if A and B are relations of T, the assembly (*not* A) *or* B is represented by A $\Rightarrow$ B, and the assembly *not* (*not* A) or (*not* B) by A *and* B.

The term or relation corresponding to an assembly of T is obtained in an assembly A of T by substituting a term *t* of T with a given letter *x*. This result is notated (t | x) A.

Thus, substituting the letter *x* in the relationship A with the assembly τ *x* (A), we obtain an assembly designated by ($\exists x$) A, which reads: "There exists an *x* such as A." The assembly *not* ($\exists x$) *not* A) is designated by the assembly ($\forall x$) A and reads: "For each *x*, A."

The synthemization of a mathematical theory T is operated by first writing out the relationships in which the specific synthemes or signs of T (the axioms of T) appear, then the rules or patterns of axioms of T that determine the relationships of T. Here, we should distinguish axiomatic theoretical or textual synthemes from axiomatic schematic synthemes.

Thus we can more clearly distinguish the operations that allow us to obtain a proof of the theory T:

1. Transcription of the theoretic synthemes—that is, the formative constructions of assemblies of T.
2. Transcription of the axiomatic and schematic synthemes of the relations of T applied to these assemblies.
3. Transcription of the synthemes of form A $\Rightarrow$ B known as relational, designated by R, such that A and B are assemblies of T preceding R.

Because all these relationships thus written constitute the true relationships in T, they can be considered as theorems of T, signifiable in their turn by synthemes of the theorematic type, strictly speaking. Thus we can prove that: A synthemization syn T' being compared to a synthemization syn T, in order for theorem T' to be "stronger" than theorem

T, it is necessary and sufficient to combine the following conditions:

- syn T = syn T' (the signs of T are the signs of T')
- The axiomatic theoretical synthemes of T are the theorematic synthemes of T', namely [syn Xi T = syn T']
- The axiomatic schematic synthemes of T are schemes of T' [syn schem T = schem T']

The scope of this book does not allow me to explain the proofs of a general synthematic theory of mathematics or the topical analysis of the usual methods of axiomatic formalization. I have simply recalled that the idea of synthematics is not only more appropriate than that of symbolics in systems of the logical and mathematical type, but also that synthematics allows them to be separated by a specific abstraction from certain linguistic confusions that are perpetuated by specialists in the humanities rather than by logicians and mathematicians themselves—especially in the realm of the homology of structures.

It is important not to forget that mathematical reasoning is always tautological in its processes of formalization and construction of theoretical assemblies. It is therefore dangerous[2] to use it ontologically and empirically when describing concrete psychological or sociological phenomena. Strictly speaking, mathematical theories are purely logical and are most often obtained by introducing new axiomatics or schematic synthemes, for example, in algebra, topology, category theory, functional analysis, and algebraic geometry. This language has its own grammar and syntax, and like all other languages, it is capable of evolving and transforming. Because it is distinguished from both linguistics and symbology itself, synthematics—the general science of synthemes—may offer a useful contribution to future logical-mathematic formalization.

My position on this point, therefore, is different from that of Ernst Cassirer, who treats the signs of mathematical language as if they could be assimilated to those of axiological language, as formers and operators of a meaning that does not come to them entirely from the abstraction of empirical conditions and which is comparable to the meaning relating to a preliminary domain of essences or values. Cassirer draws a philosophical conclusion from this: Symbolism is the universal in action, using its communicability to surmount isolation and the particularity of individual consciousness.

It may be that Cassirer confused two distinct operations: the operations of symbolic communicability itself and the logical operations that make it possible. Between these two, some signs are based on the abstraction of empirical conditions, such as those of mathematical language, while others are based on the similitude of concrete relationships, such as those of the analogical process. Serious misunderstandings result from confusing the logic of identity, essential to every logical or mathematical language, with the logic of analogy, characteristic of every axiological language.

Nor do I share the opinion of Alfred North Whitehead, who considers the symbolic function to be exercised beyond the signals that lead to the actual object, well delimited in space and time, inside or outside this object, thus achieving the operation by which eternal entities are invested with concrete forms. This philosopher thus assimilates all analogical intuition into mathematical, aesthetic, and religious thought, all three of which have their own capacity for logical appropriation to the symbolic function in question. Moreover, transcendence of meaning is nonsensical on the level of alleged mathematical symbolism, which is purely synthematic and ideogrammatic.

It would also be erroneous, inversely, to reduce the whole philosophy of symbols to a single system of designative and practical synthematic references. Informational-deductive languages and their logical-mathematical or logical-scientific expressions structure acts of thought into well-regulated, rigorously assembled, and controlled operations by a process of consolidation or ordering of experiential or empirical realities previously formalized. This does not mean, however, that they can absolutely ensure the ideal truth of their theses—truth that is denominating in itself. In other words, there is no absolute of the signification in the consistency of theoretical languages, which remains constructive, effective, and operative, but also purely formal. Mathematical discourse does not relate to essences and its rules are not norms in the axiological or transcendent sense of the term; they present a universal ontological meaning in themselves. We can grant informational-deductive languages the power of abstractly ensuring the coherence of formalized experiential processes, their communicability, and their generalization, without having to add to these privileges—already exceptional in comparison to the other languages we know of—an empire that is no less exorbitant than it is illusory.

Moreover, synthemization that is logical-mathematical or logical-scientific presents the considerable interest of not being entirely reducible to its domains of determination of currently schematized empirical or experiential facts. Synthemization intervenes again because it is more general than what it determines. It has a capacity for questioning the empirical and experiential limits attained. This anticipating function of synthemization is all the more remarkable in that it is not only potential, but also rigorously coherent, so that in many cases, it somehow gives the experience a firm and straight path for the exploration and interpretation of its conditions.

On the level of mathematics, the idea of the synthematic should be preferred over that of the symbolic for numerous reasons, as I have tried to show in these few insights. (To develop them would require a separate work devoted to them alone.) The foremost among these reasons, however, may be the fact that the object of mathematics is a product that extends farther the more we complicate it and the more rigorously we control its specific processes of production. This process of self-constitution of a purely tautological nature is limitless in its extent, like so many radii going out from the center of a single circle, where the center is the principle of identity. A simple geometric comparison, however, allows us to understand why mathematical power is attained by the very essence of the real.

This is because, limitless though they are, radii going out from the center of a circle in a sphere with infinite radii are not infinitely diverse, a property belonging only to radii going out from the center of the sphere, each of which corresponds precisely to the plane of a single circle. Given that the human mind uses the principle of identity, it is clear that mathematics on a single plane constitutes the mind's most effective and most extensive tool, but also that all the other planes of reality are somehow projected onto our own in such a way that we can grasp them only indirectly in their mutual relations, due to the concept of analogy and its specific logical process.

Clearly distinguishing these two epistemological orientations, refusing to confuse their operations and their interpretations, is a matter not of opposing them to each other but, on the contrary, of understanding their necessary complementary nature in order to place in perspective the conditions of human consciousness.

The fact that the problem of essences remains unresolved (identity does not solve it any better than analogy does—the former fails by excess and the latter fails by insufficiency) is not the most important thing for consciousness, because it may also be a false problem on our scale and level. On the other hand, for our correct and true understanding, it is important that we use both eyes rather than just one. The mathematical view of the universe is that of a Cyclops, unless the analogical view compensates for its relative aberration and vice versa. Reconciling our views of the world, nature, humans, and society within ourselves requires us to make this difficult alternation of a logic of "sometimes this, sometimes that." It has obvious merits over the alternative "yes or no," because it integrates rather than excludes and because it distinguishes the languages from each other instead of merging them or attempting to reduce them to a single language.

The synthematic function of symbolism therefore constitutes only one of its fundamental operations. The more we separate it from its allegorical and typological functions, the better we can unite the symphony of consciousness and its interpretations with the integral scope and profundity of their real and possible developments.

LOGICAL-SCIENTIFIC SYNTHEMES

The history of scientific nomenclatures requires a lengthy discussion, but we can analyze its important and significant aspects in the history of chemical and mineralogical nomenclatures, as well as the characters or synthemes that conventionally represent various substances and natural bodies.

The first synthemization in this area was that of the ancient alchemists, but strictly speaking, it was neither purely conventional nor arbitrary in that it was inspired not only by allegorical themes, but also by an esoteric and initiatory symbolic typology. This is why it is too complex to be studied within the space of this book. On the other hand, we may consider the tables of characters devised by the famous Swedish chemist Torbern Olof Bergmann (1734–84) as documents characteristic of a first systematic synthemization of artificial and natural physicochemical substances.

As general characters, Bergmann used a triangle, a circle, a ring, and a cross. The triangular syntheme, modified in various ways, was the sign of the four elements, for example, fire △, water ▽, air ⏃, and earth ⏀ and inflammable substances ⏁ such as sulfur and mercury. The ring designated metallic substances. A circle ○ indicated salts, and a dotted circle ⊕ indicated alkalis. A cross represented acids and acidified substances.

Using these conventional signs, Bergmann represented various types of earth—"siliceous," "heavy," or "argillaceous." For metals, he also used crosses, circles, and semicircles, which appears to mean, in keeping with his general synthematic system, that he allowed for an analogy among acids, salts, and metallic compounds. No less strangely, he represented lime with the same sign as metal oxides, which, according to his nomenclature, were considered "metallic limes."

Thus, in Bergmann's primitive chemical synthemization, we may observe vestiges of alchemical theories more or less exactly preserved. Yet all late-eighteenth-century chemists believed in the necessity of inventing a new nomenclature. Bergmann himself was so convinced of this that he wrote to Guyton de Morveau: "Do not favor any improper naming; those who already know will understand forever; those who do not yet know soon will."

Around the middle of the year 1786, Morveau, Berthollet, Fourcroy, and Lavoisier met to examine a nomenclature project that had been proposed by Morveau around 1782. Several geometers from the Royal Academy of Science in Paris attended these conferences almost daily, and after eight months of discussion and study, Lavoisier, at a public session of the academy on April 18, 1787, presented the foundations for the "reform and perfection of the nomenclature of chemistry," which he further developed in a presentation on May 2, 1787.

Compounds were divided into acids, bases, and salts. This was therefore a general classification in chemistry. The rule of nomenclature had established that "every naming of a compound must indicate the names of the elements in that compound." Thus the old oil of vitriol became sulfuric acid, spirit of salt became muriatic acid (our hydrochloric acid), and so forth. For the most part, the nomenclature of 1787 remains the basis of what is used currently.

We may consider it as the spoken language of chemistry, while the synthematic notion is the written language of that science. Both are modified with ever-increasing precision as a function of the development of this discipline in order to establish uniformity in the naming of analogous compounds as well as the most characteristic properties of a substance.

By the late nineteenth century, it was well established that matter is made up of atoms that are identical to one another within a given chemical type. Physicists believed that this identity and uniformity corresponded to the inner composition of matter. After the discovery of natural radioactivity by Henri Becquerel in 1896, there were theories of a new world within the atom and of far more powerful electromagnetic and gravitational interactions than those known at the time. The first synthematic representation of the theoretical model of the atom, the planetary model, did not appear until 1920, and was the result of Rutherford's work. It pictured a cloud of electrons orbiting a nucleus. It had been proved that only electrons play a role in chemical bonds between atoms, while the nuclei remain passive and isolated from one another.

Decisive progress in the understanding of the nucleus's composition was achieved in 1933 with the discovery of a new particle, the neutron, by James Chadwick, subsequent to the work of Frédéric and Irène Joliot-Curie. The neutron is thus named because it is electrically neutral. Its mass is equal to that of the proton, which is the nucleus of the hydrogen atom and has an electrical charge, designated synthematically by $+e$. The nucleus is therefore composed of Z protons corresponding to $Z + e$ and N neutrons. If one or the other of the constituents of the nucleus, Z or N, is designated by the term *nucleon,* a nucleus contains a total of $Z + N = A$ nucleons.

For a given chemical type, all the nuclei contain the same number of protons, but they may differ in their number of neutrons. They are then considered various *isotopes* of the chemical element in question.

The syntheme of the atomic nucleus is:

$$\underset{Z \quad N}{\overset{A}{\times}}$$

In this system, X corresponds to the chemical syntheme of the element—such as Au or P6—to which it belongs. Z designates the number of protons or the atomic number; N, the number of neutrons; and A, the total number $Z + N$ of nucleons or the *mass number* of the nucleus. Thus, the synthemes of the isotopes of oxygen are represented by the notations:

$$\underset{8 \quad 7}{\overset{15}{O}}, \ \underset{8 \quad 8}{\overset{16}{O}}, \ \underset{8 \quad 9}{\overset{17}{O}}, \ \underset{8 \quad 10}{\overset{18}{O}}.$$

An abbreviating synthemization is also used:

$$X: \ \underset{\ }{\overset{15}{O}}, \ \underset{\ }{\overset{16}{O}}, \ \underset{\ }{\overset{17}{O}}, \ \underset{\ }{\overset{18}{O}}.$$

Between the synthemes devised by Bergmann and those of nuclear physics, we can see that the conventional logical-scientific representations, although arbitrary, are not *unmotivated,* in Saussure's purely linguistic sense of this term. They correspond to various phases of the development of scientific thought, and depend on them analogically to a certain extent. But this similitude is too general and too vague for us to be in a position to speak of a true process of symbolization regarding them. Neither chemical and physicochemical notations nor logical-scientific notations in general are symbols. Thus, just as in the case of the language of formal mathematics, we must call them *synthemes.*

THE VARIOUS APPLICATIONS
OF SYNTHEMATICS

Synthematics, in its principal concern, must not be confused with linguistic semiology in the sense that it describes forms using an analogical operation of a determined type on the subject of which no psychological research seems necessary, because synthematics is relatively simple in its principles. Admitting and observing the existence of artificial and external analogy imposed conventionally upon every syntheme as such, this discipline proposes to study and research only the forms that are most appropriate for this operation and most useful for various physical and social sciences, technologies, pedagogies, and economic exchanges.

Here we will be limited to discovering briefly its principal possible applications, which depend, in most cases, on the means of communication and information. We can distinguish spatial and static synthemes from temporal and dynamic ones. The former use extended and fixed intermediaries, at least in their recording of information, such as paper, punch cards, photographs, or magnetic media. The latter use rhythmic modifications of the physical environment, such as sound and electrical or electromagnetic waves. The former allow for a reversibility of operations of deciphering or reading of recorded synthemes. The latter are initially irreversible and become reversible only if their information is recorded.

Topological synthemes, for example, are conventional signs that serve to convey information relative to a place and to depict a terrestrial or celestial expanse. Topography is only one of the applications of topological synthemes of the static or spatial type, through the intermediary of drawing and writing. We can, however, conceive of topological synthemes transmitted through modifications of the physical environment by waves—that is, synthemes of the temporal and dynamic type. Instruments exploring an unknown environment can be connected to receptors and to a computer producing an automatic reading of the planimetry and elevation of the terrain recognized and analyzed automatically.

Likewise, chronological synthemes—those that allow us to know a determined duration for the proportional movement of a mobile indicator in relation to them—can either be marked on a dial or indicated by a signal transmitted by waves. In the first case, they are spatial and static; in the second, rhythmic and dynamic.

Mnemonic synthemes are conventional signs that use indicators to represent an action performed that must be remembered, recalling an action that we must accomplish or representing facts or conditions that the memory must retain. Some are recorded in a material, extended, fixed medium: a knot in a handkerchief or notches on a wooden rod. Others are dynamic and temporal, such as the sound of an alarm clock, the notes of a trumpet, and other such processes. The same category can include schematic or abbreviating synthemes that are used pedagogically, such as chronological tables of the events of an epoch. The transposition from synthemes of the first type to those of the second forms one of the important aspects of contemporary audiovisual teaching.

Metabolic synthemes—from the Greek *metabolikos,* literally "changeable," which the grammarian Heraclides used to mean "relating to exchanges of merchandise and negotiation"—are conventional signs used in economic exchanges and necessarily linked by a guarantee to a value determined by consensus. Any object, provided it is more easily exchangeable than the merchandise or value for which it is the sign, may become a metabolic syntheme. Exchanges in nature and the use of shells were replaced by exchanges first of livestock, then of metals—in piles of raw and unshaped nuggets, as they are found in mines; in purses or little bags containing powder or flakes of metal; in bricks or tiles, bars, or plates obtained by melting or forging; or in rings of various size. Weight was linked primitively to the act of counting,[3] as is confirmed by the double meaning of *shekel* in areas of Palestinian and Phoenician civilization. The emergence of money around the seventh century BC came from the invention of a metabolic syntheme applied initially to metal ingots using a punch or stamp, which guaranteed their weight and value to the public as a function of confidence placed in the authority and honesty of governmental powers.

Metabolic synthematics constitutes a discipline that is accessory both to numismatics on the historical level and to the logical-scientific synthematics of the economic sciences on the theoretical level. In "traditional" civilizations, its study is more complex, because it is linked by some of its aspects to civil allegory and to mythical and religious typology.

The preceding applications of synthematics do not constitute a definitive list, but they do at least allow us to observe that the use of the word *symbol* in all realms is improper and should be avoided, especially in relation to the logical-scientific realm. This is not a matter for the signs corresponding to the operations of the logic of analogy, which I call synthematics, from the Greek *sun-desmeo,* literally "to link together," hence *sun desmos* (plural *ta sundesmo,* "links") and *suntema,* "synthemes." In fact, in their case, the relationship of analogy is of an external order in relation to the signal and the signification that it "links together" in an arbitrary and conventional manner. It is clear that we must not confuse a conscious, voluntary, artificial, and imposed analogy between two terms (depending only on a free choice between the parts that communicate among themselves regarding it) with a real, intuitive analogy dealing with a relationship of convenience of the internal order between the signal and the signification.

This is expressed, for its part, in two distinct ways: either by allegory, whose principal process is the metaphor, or by typology, whose primary expression is the anaphora, terms that we will examine later.

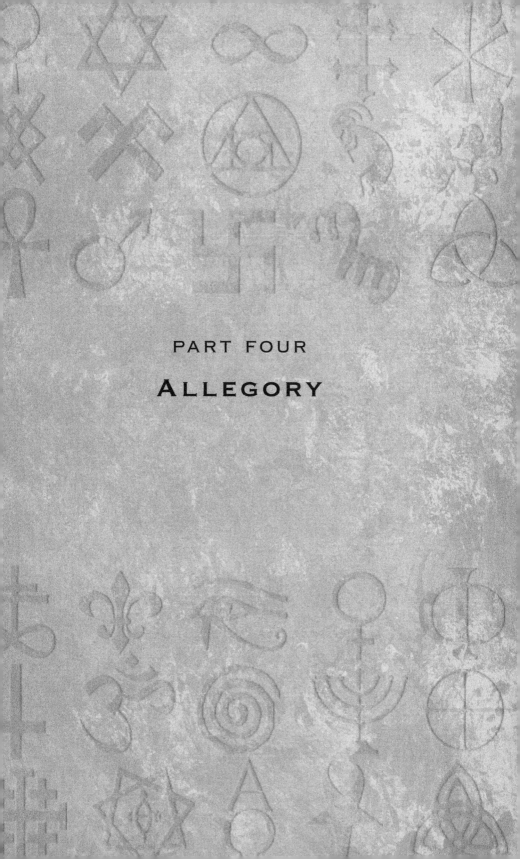

PART FOUR

ALLEGORY

6 THE ALLEGORICAL FUNCTION OF SYMBOLISM

METAPHOR AND ANAPHORA

Under the influence of German Romanticism and depth psychology, as Jean Pépin correctly relates, "people today have acquired the habit of distinguishing clearly between *allegory* and *symbol,* as between didactic artifice and the spontaneity of life. In order that this distinction, which is well justified, may be taken into consideration in view of Dante, it seems it must be placed within the mores of its epoch. This is in no way obvious. The ancient and medieval definition of *allegory* is so broad that it fits with almost all varieties of figurative expression and with every case of symbolic expression.[1]

With Philo, as with Clement of Alexandria, the ideas of symbol and allegory are not as clearly separated as many modern authors seem to believe. But they should not be confused with one another. Allegory is both a rhetorical process and a hermeneutic attitude relating to discourse and interpretation—that is to say, to expression and thought—whereas the symbol escorts the signal and the signification back to the significator itself. This is why allegory is founded upon metaphor and not upon anaphora.

Thus allegory is not associated with the sacred myth or rite, whereas the symbol is the basis of every initiatory and religious dynamic. Yet just as we cannot separate the flesh from the soul or the spirit, so traditional sacred texts do not separate the three levels of understanding, instead presenting a direct association among the levels of this inner realization already clearly distinguished by Origen: "The most simple is instructed by what one could call the flesh of Scripture, the current reading. He who has progressed a little is instructed, one might say, by the soul of Scripture. The perfect student . . . is instructed by the spiritual law, which is the shadow of the good to come."[2] Origen had good reason to repeat the word *instructed* three times. He explains his ideas in a fragment of commentary on Leviticus: "The Scripture is constituted, in a way, by a visible body, a soul which can be known by way of the body, and a spirit which is the example and shadow of celestial good."[3]

These three degrees of the hermeneutic process are interdependent, and each is known through the others. This is why allegory, although distinct from symbol, is as profoundly linked to it as literal meaning is linked to allegorical meaning—something that is often forgotten. The logic of analogy, in fact, is founded upon a concrete reality, and in order for this reality to be the true sign of *another* reality, this initial condition itself must not be fictitious. The use of metaphor that is allegory is enough to prove it. There have been hollow and sterile allegories—for example, in the fifteenth century, as a result of literary abuse by rhetoricians—as well as other allegories that teach important hidden truths. We can admit that the cultural and didactic role of allegory is no less important than that of the symbol, because the allegorical process is implied in all forms of artistic expression and is linked, via iconography, to the vast world of images and memory.

It has been noted, without doubt, that Origen spoke of the *shadow* and associated this word both to spiritual law and to the spirit of the scripture, which was at once the example and the shadow[4] of celestial good. This is because death is not yet destroyed and eternity is not yet restored. The truth cannot be expressed without the veil of signs and models. Only through anaphora, through an ascending movement of the visible toward the invisible, from the apparent to the hidden, from the sensible to the intelligible, and from the intellectual to the supraintelligible, can we rise to the level of spiritual interpretation no longer allegorical but anagogical[5]—and the principal means of this interpretation is the symbol. Of course the resurrection of the significator takes place in the shadows, but as Clement of Alexandria said, "The shadow of the light is not darkness, but illumination."[6]

A passage of the *Contra Celsum* concerning certain details of the resurrection of Jesus criticized by Celsus (the angels, the white clothing, etc.) suffices to show how much Origen's teaching directly links this spiritual interpretation, this tropology,[7] to an operation of resurrection of the significator itself: "For each one of these events, it must be shown that it is possible, that it took place, and that it signifies some tropology, which can be operated, based on appearances, by those who are ready to contemplate the resurrection of the Word."[8]

These various levels of interpretation relate only to texts recognized as sacred by an initiatory or religious tradition, particularly by the Judeo-Christian tradition. Of course, we must study these problems differently in the framework of other religions of the Book. We may observe, for example, in the case of Islam and the Qur'an, that Sunni orthodoxy is violently opposed to the allegorical exegesis favored by mystics. These latter have been accused of substituting the usual conceptions and interpretations with a hermeneutics founded upon personal modes of intuition and symbolization that is incompatible with the customs and rules of Qur'anic exegesis.

The founder of Sunni Islam, al-Tabari (839–923), declared around the end of the ninth century: "Whoever uses his judgment alone for dealing with the Qur'an, *even if he attains the truth by this manner,* is still in error from having used his judgment alone. His progress, in fact, is not that of a man certain of being in the right. It is only that of a man who conjectures and supposes; whoever deals with religion using conjecture is uttering insults to Allah the nature of which he does not know."[9]

This inflexible, dogmatic position can be explained historically. It was a matter of preserving unity in a community menaced from within by theological schools or philosophical sects that had dared to ask questions concerning the subject of free will. The school of the Mu'tazilites, for example, gained great importance in ninth-century Iraq under the influence of Hellenistic ideas introduced by the translation of Greek philosophers. It combined with the preoccupations of thinkers who, like Avicenna and Averroës, attempted to reconcile pure reason with Islamic dogma. The Mu'tazilites' skills allowed them to ward off the danger of merciless repression. They used the tradition of the schools of readers and the plurality of allowed readings to infer and propose some variations on the vocalism of the text—variations that gave them the means to preserve a personal interpretation without clashing with dogmatic positions.

Exegesis, as we know, is always dominated by the principle of authority. The critics of the Shiite sects, for example, attained theological and political authority. They implicated not only the Qur'anic texts of Caliphs Bakr and 'Umar but also the probity of the Umayyads, accused of having removed, for dynastic purposes, all the passages in the Qur'an attesting to the caliphic legitimacy of Ali, Muhammad's son-in-law. The general position of Qur'anic exegesis was no less based upon the authority of the consensus of all concerning the interpretations and readings proposed. This *consensus omnium* is expressed in the ancestral and consecrated custom, the *sunna*.

Writes Régis Blachère:

From the life of Muhammad himself a plethora of anecdotes, collected later in the *Life of the Prophet* and the collections of traditions, or *hadîth,* shows us the believers coming to consult the master regarding an obscure word or passage of the revelation, the scope of a prohibition, or a Qur'anic authorization regarding worship. . . . Here we see the Prophet explaining the term or giving the line's meaning: in a word, doing the work of the exegete. After the death of the founder of Islam, its principal members found themselves in an identical situation. The principle of a perpetual commentary of Qur'anic revelation is, as we can see, inherent in the authority that is attached to it; this perpetuates the role of edification that has played in the life of the Muslim world since its origins.[10]

The precariousness of Arabic writing, defective in its appearance, also leads to obscurities in the material form of the text. This, attracting the sagacity of grammarians, became a source of perpetual investigation by its "readers" in the domain of the writing system. Yet at the origin of Qur'anic exegesis lies the fact that the world of Islam, not being dominated by any single ecclesiastical, conciliar, or pontifical authority, could not limit excesses of interpretation, which risked harming the development of the Law, because it lacked the principle of an agreement founded upon unity in the Islamic community and lacked a consensus preserved by ancestral custom. Such is the meaning of the word *idjmâ'*, which denotes an "agreement formed by uncontested canonists."[11]

But the history of Qur'anic exegesis shows the coexistence of two general tendencies, two attitudes toward the sacred Book, and two distinct approaches toward the revelation: "literal commentary," or *tafsîr,* and "interpretive explication," or *ta'wîl.* Among the various forms of ta'wîl, that of the Ismaili philosophers has become better known thanks to the profound research of Henry Corbin.[12] This is a spiritual exegesis that contrasts, in its esotericism and its initiatory scope, with the exoteric interpretations of the literal commentators, which are necessarily subject to the principle of authority that constitutes the consensus of all. The Ismaili *ta'wîl* is "a forever incomplete operation, recommencing each time with each person; this is why it is linked to the 'spiritual birth' (*wilâdat-e-kûhâni*) of each person until the end of the 'cycle of cycles.'"[13]

The free initiative and free research to which this Ismaili ta'wîl, in relation to literal tafsîr, bears witness are notions to which Henry Corbin frequently returns in his works. He must be recognized as having correctly insisted on the error committed by so many amateurs in traditional studies who have claimed to maintain a dogmatic position in an area where, on the contrary, we must become conscious of the limits and insufficiencies of this position on a level of inner experience besides that of the relationship between a community and its legitimate principle of authority and unity. Henry Corbin writes:

> The *free initiative* also shows us how fictitious and nontraditional is a certain notion of tradition, which has been fashionable for a few decades in the West; the dogmatic manner of dealing with symbols is one of the strangest symptoms of the spirit that nourishes it. Without doubt, people are not even conscious of distorting the notions of which they pretend to take advantage when we assume a more despotic authority than that of any other repudiated dogmatics! On the other hand, it would be difficult to reproach an Ismaili on matters of esotericism; neither Nâsir-e-khosraw, vehemently denouncing the dogmatic furor of the *haswîyân,* nor Master Abû'l-Haitham nor his disciple telling of his years of feverish searching allow us to suppose that their esoteric tradition might have implied a renunciation of the spirit of free research, and this is the most precious legacy that those who created the origins of Ismailism can pass on to the Ismailism of the future.[14]

This, in fact, is an essential point that seems to be of capital importance, not only for Ismailism but for all true esoteric and initiatory traditions as well. It was not said in vain that the truth could set us free: "The Lord is the Spirit, and where the Spirit of the Lord is, there is freedom."[15] Knowledge has no goal other than deliverance. If it were a matter only of forging and wearing more chains, esoteric and initiatory experience would have no meaning and no justification.

On the other hand, if "the veil is removed," according to St. Paul's expression—the veil of the "written code that kills"—it can be removed only by a new covenant with the "spirit of the living God," with the resurrected freedom that gives life. This is no longer a community; this is a unity, the unity of each one of us, and not only the unity of all, which bears witness to the life of the unique. Freedom is not only the goal of all human history; it is also the very essence of the spiritual principle that glows among the ashes of our personal history, without which it could not manifest. Exegesis in this sense—which is, strictly speaking, only one explanation—must therefore not be separated from an implication of the significator in the sense that it reveals, not dogmatically but freely and in particular, as it pleases, when it pleases, and to whom it pleases. The freedom of the principle assumes the freedom of the gift. It is therefore not possible to establish dogmatically limits for spiritual interpretation in its relations to the personal life of the believer. Simple good sense is enough to persuade us that if this is a matter of the life of a community subject to historical and legal necessities, the consensus omnium is no less necessary for the preservation of its axiological cohesiveness and social existence. This is why, for both religious communities and secular societies, the main problem remains one of reconciling among themselves and agreeing on the free life of the unique in everyone and the organized life of unity in all.

On this point as well as on many others, we must at least be aware of the value of a logic of alternation in relation to a logic of alternative. The meaning of the sacred texts is not either literal or allegorical, either allegorical or historical, either moral or anagogical. These meanings coexist in the scriptures, as theologians unanimously agree. And they are not the only ones, for if the words conceal things other than what they mean literally, these things are also figures of other things, especially in relation to the spiritual meaning of anagogy.

Under these conditions, we can see that all hermeneutics imply the interpretation of distinct levels of sacred texts, some of which arise in relation to others in the ascending movement of the strictly symbolic anaphora that was emphasized earlier in this book. In other words, the metaphorical process as a whole can be represented by a horizontal expression of analogy and the anaphorical process by a vertical orientation toward the significator itself. Coming from the word, speech returns to it. This return of the river to the source corresponds to an ascension revealing new horizons, ever vaster and more profound, to the spirit that contemplates them and recognizes itself in them, unveiling each of its mirrors.

THE ALLEGORICAL EXEGESIS
OF PHILO OF ALEXANDRIA

One of the best-known examples of this traditional method is that of Philo of Alexandria, although it is common to all pagan and Christian philosophers who followed Platonic or Stoic teachings in this area. The Philonian hermeneutics of the holy scriptures comprises three levels: cosmological, anthropological, and mystical. The cosmological interpretation of mythology is not a modern invention. It is found in Plutarch: "These are such as pretend, like the Greeks, that Saturn symbolizes Time, Juno the Air, the birth of Vulcan, the change of Air into Fire; and similarly amongst the Egyptians, that Osiris is the Nile, copulating with Isis the Earth."[16] And a little further: "This however is of the same kind with the theological theories of the Stoics, for they too say that the generative and nutritive spirit is Bacchus; the impulsive and separative, Hercules; the receptive, Ammon; Ceres and Proserpine, that which pervades the earth and her fruits; and Neptune that pervading the sea."[17]

Plutarch mentions that Isis's clothes are of many colors because her power extends over matter, which receives all forms. This allegorical interpretation was known to the Alexandrian Jews before Philo. According to Flavius Josephus, the multicolored robe of the great priest of Israel is an allegory of the four elements of the cosmos,[18] and the candelabra with seven branches represents the seven planets.[19] According to Philo, in "Explanation of the Law": "We ought to look upon the universal world as the highest and truest temple of God, having for its most holy place that most sacred part of the essence of all existing things, namely, the heaven; and for ornaments, the stars; and for priests, the subordinate ministers of his power, namely, the angels, incorporeal souls."[20]

Philo takes this cosmological allegorical exegesis quite far. He explains, for example, that the two sides of the arch correspond to the two equinoxes and the four animals to the four seasons. If the sacred candelabra glows only in one place, this, he says, is because "the planets do not revolve in all the parts of the celestial sphere, but only in the southern hemisphere."[21] The cherubim represent the two hemispheres, and the veil that separates the rest of the temple from the Holy of Holies is the firmament that separates the terrestrial world from the heaven of the stars.

Philo clearly distinguishes anthropological or moral (*moralis*) exegesis from cosmological or natural (*naturalis*) interpretation. The latter, in addition, is more frequent than the former and often borrows from animal allegories characteristic of the iconology of medieval bestiaries, which was studied considerably in the sixteenth century. Philo writes:

> In every one of us there are three things: flesh, the outward sense, and reason; therefore the calf exhibits a familiarity with the corporeal substance, since our flesh is subdued by, and kept in subservience to, and in connection with the ministrations of life. . . . But the similitude of the she-goat is connected with the communion of the outward senses, either because all the objects of those outward senses are each borne towards their appropriate sensation, or because each impulse and motion of the soul takes place in consequence of an imagination formed of the objects received through the medium of the external senses. . . . But the ram is akin to the word, or to reason. In the first place, because it is a male animal; secondly, because it is a working animal. . . . And there are two species of reason; the one derived from that nature by which the affairs of the world subjected to the outward senses are finished; the other from that of those things, which are called incorporeal species, by which the affairs of that world, which is the object of the intellect are brought

to their accomplishment. . . . The pigeon, forsooth, resembles speculation in natural philosophy; for it is a more familiar bird . . . the
turtle dove imitates that species, which is the subject of intellect and
incorporeal; for as that animal is fond of solitude, so it is superior to
the violent species which come under the outward sense, associating
itself as it does with the invisible species by its essence.[22]

From this same psychological perspective, according to Philo, Adam
represents the spirit and Eve the sensation:

"The Lord God," says Moses, "cast a deep trance upon Adam, and
sent him to sleep." He speaks here with great correctness, for a trance
and perversion of the mind is its sleep. And the mind is rendered
beside itself when it ceases to be occupied about the things perceptible only by the intellect which present themselves to it. . . . "He
took one of his ribs." He took one of the many powers of the mind,
namely, that power which dwells in the outward senses. . . . "He built
it up into a woman": showing by this expression that woman is the
most natural and felicitously given name for the external sense.[23]

Regarding the animals led before Adam so that he could give them
names, Philo wrote: "But the passions he compares to beasts and birds,
because they injure the mind, being untamed and wild, and because,
after the manner of birds, they descend upon the intellect; for their
onset is swift and difficult to withstand."[24] These moral allegories are
ancient. In Plato's *Republic,* the spirit holds sovereignty over the passions like a king over a herd of chained animals—serpents, lions, and
apes.

Mystical exegesis presents problems far more complex than both
anthropological and cosmological exegesis, which, in a way, constitute
the traditional allegorical interpretation of the neo-Alexandrian philosophers, and are intended to be fairly easily understood by educated
readers and by the humanities. In many respects, we can connect these

two successive levels—cosmological and natural, anthropological and moral—of the initiatory teaching of the ancient small mysteries. Later, we will examine the third level, concerning the typological function of symbolism and analogy, for its basis is no longer the metaphor, as in the allegorical process—a comparison between the sensible signification and the intelligible signal—but is instead the anaphora, a process that leads the signal and signification back to the significator itself.

Only at this third, typological level do we see the beginning of the initiation into the great mysteries of the symbol, which are neither cosmological nor anthropological nor theological, but are rather *theogonic*. Indeed, they originate neither from the language of nature nor from that of culture nor even from the science of religion and its various branches and doctrines. Instead, these mysteries are rooted in the depths of the mysterious itself.

Here is what Philo writes on this subject. This passage, regarding a verse from Genesis (28:11) concerning Jacob's dream, is sufficient to distinguish mystical exegesis from all the other types: "And he lighted upon a certain place, and tarried there all night, because the sun was set."[25] Philo writes:

Some persons—supposing that what is meant here by the figurative expression of the sun is the external sense and the mind, which are looked upon as the things which have the power of judging; and that what is meant by place is the divine word—understand the allegory in this manner: the practicer of virtue met with the divine word, after the mortal and human light had set; for as long as the mind thinks that it attains to a firm comprehension of the objects of intellect, and the outward sense conceives that it has a similar understanding of its appropriate objects, and that it dwells amid sublime objects, the divine word stands aloof at a distance; but when each of these comes to confess its own weakness, and sets in a manner while availing itself of concealment, then immediately the right reason of a soul well-practiced in virtue comes in a welcome manner to their assistance, when they have begun to despair of their own strength, and await the aid which is invisibly coming to them from without.[26]

At this point, Rashi notes that the Torah does not give the name of the place, but the place is named elsewhere: the land of Mori'ah (Genesis 22:4): "Abraham lifted up his eyes and saw the place afar off." Regarding the words "he lighted," Rashi adds: "Our masters explain this word in the sense of prayer. We thus learn that it was Jacob who introduced evening prayer."[27] Regarding the sun, Rashi believes it better to say: "'The sun set and he spent the night in the place,' because 'the sun was set' suggests that the sun set suddenly before its time in order that Jacob might be obliged to spend the night there."[28]

Here, in Rashi's apparently simple commentaries, there are in fact a number of complex allusions that partially explain the mystical interpretation proposed by Philo. Both Philo and Rashi knew what profound mysteries were at hand here, and they conveyed them by different processes, the less subtle of which was Philo's. In short, after the second or third reading, Rashi goes much further in his mystical exegesis, veiled by a laconic and literal commentary that interprets the Law.

We should remember that in Rashi's era (the eleventh and twelfth centuries AD), in relation to the time of the sacred texts of the Israelite tradition and also to the time of those texts in the Christian and Islamic traditions, people were still practicing very cautious exegesis, which was consequently much more allusive than in later times. This caution required the readers of these interpretations to have a much more highly developed symbolic ear, or musical sense in a manner of speaking, than we have today. The dangers that threatened overly audacious interpreters were not imaginary. Under these conditions we may observe, for example, that the older alchemical treatises from the twelfth to early fifteenth centuries are much harder to decipher than those of the sixteenth and seventeenth centuries. This is not a question merely of language and style, but also of the evolution of the process by which works were composed.

THE CRYPTIC STRUCTURE
OF SACRED TEXTS

The historical method, despite its obvious advantages, is incapable of resolving by itself the extraordinarily complex problems posed by sacred texts. E. C. Hoskyns, for example, showed this regarding the Gospel of St. John:

> Say that the Fourth Gospel is Hellenic, or that it emerges from the background of some mixture of Greek thought and Oriental mythology, and we are confounded by the Hebraic quality of the language in which it is written, by the author's rigid adherence to the Old Testament for his literary allusions, and by the frequent occurrence of Palestinian topographical details. Say that there is both historical reminiscence and spiritual interpretation in the book, and no doubt we are right; but go on and demand that the critic, or the spiritually minded interpreter, shall separate the history from the interpretation, and we force him to give up the attempt in despair, for the author of the book has set a barricade across that road, a barricade through which no one has yet passed or is likely to pass, since the Spiritual meaning of the life and death of Jesus belongs to the history and, indeed, made it what is was, for the Spirit gave reality to His observable words and to His observable actions—*it is the Spirit that quickeneth, the flesh profiteth nothing.*"[29]

Facing a sacred text, what is the most correct attitude if not one that admits the existence of a superposition of perspectives and views, assembled as if on the same sensory plate that has been used several times over to photograph the same object? After immersing it in the developing bath, we sometimes see landscapes, sometimes details about people, sometimes a coherent succession of connections between actions, sometimes a historically reparable structure, sometimes a series of figures and models alien to all historical reality. If we observe attentively these phenomena of the superposition of readings, we will note an undeniable fact: Each one of us reads and sees nothing other than what he is able to read and see—that is, what he is capable of learning and knowing. In other words, the levels of reading of sacred texts are in constant and direct connection to their readers' various degrees of initiation or, if we prefer, their intellectual, moral, and spiritual evolution. This is something that goes far beyond an ordinary author's capacity for composition and elaboration, however great his talent may be.

This can be judged by the fact that the minute study of the vocabulary of the Apocalypse and the Gospel of St. John shows the existence of a symbolic numerological structure that is both global and partial. In global terms, words are used a specific number of times, and this number itself has symbolic significance that can in each case be connected to the meanings of the numbers according to mystical Pythagorean doctrine. For example, the word *psuke*—"breath of life," "life"—is mentioned ten times in the Gospel of St. John, which corresponds to the total or global symbology of the denary or the Pythagorean *tetraktys*: $10 = 1 + 2 + 3 + 4$. Moreover, the word is used in the text once in the discourse on the vine and branches (John 15:13), twice in Peter's denial (13:37–38), three times in the glorification of the Son of Man (12:25–27), and four times in the discourse on the good shepherd (10:11, 15, 17, 24), corresponding to the partial numerological symbology of the tetraktys: $1 + 2 + 3 + 4$.

François Quiévreux's remarkable research has shown that "an analogous structure appears for a certain number of words, and that the series of numbers that can thus be made evident in each case possesses symbolic significance."[30] The work as a whole becomes comparable "to the mechanism of an extraordinarily complex and precise clock in which everything is connected and concatenated, so that it is impossible to change a single word without betrayal."[31] M. E. Laubscher, of Basel, arrived at conclusions analogous to those of Quiévreux with regard to the Apocalypse in his work *Neues aus der Offenbarung Johannes,* containing a study of several hundred vocabulary words.

Of course, Quiévreux posed the question of whether the numeric arrangements might be the effect of chance. "The calculation of probabilities," he writes,

> . . . allows this hypothesis to be refuted with certainty, showing that the probability of encountering such a number of coincidences is absolutely infinitesimal. . . . How did the holy author manage to compose a book in this manner? The difficulty appears astounding at first sight, but a musical comparison clarifies it for us. Imagine that in the year 3000, every notion of what music is has been lost, and one day a musical score is discovered. Scholars study it; they notice signs distributed along five lines. This is a musical range, but they have never heard of such a thing. After much research, they finally find mathematical ratios in the order of repetition of these signs. Little by little, they discover musical notation, but it appears to them only as a series of numbers. They marvel at it, and wonder how it can have been possible to achieve a work of such amazing complexity through the calculation of numbers. Of course, we know how this is achieved: a musical composer listens to his inspiration, and doesn't bother with numbers—yet numbers in fact measure the harmonies he writes down. In the same manner, the evangelist, inspired by the Holy Spirit, certainly had no need to make any calculations in order to achieve such a perfect work. If objections come to mind, it is because we do not conceive of the possibility of another way of thinking besides logical thinking; this is merely an infirmity of the modern mind.[32]

Our historicism never reveals itself to be more insufficient than in matters of sacred texts—no matter what their verifiable historical nature may be. The symbolic ear mentioned earlier existed not only in St. John's first readers, but also in the Evangelist himself. Directly hearing the living music of the Word, he noted it without changing anything; indeed he could not modify it, at the risk of disrupting it.

Likewise, the transcendence of the mission revealed to the Prophet is formulated in the Qur'an, Sura 81:

> *Verily I swear by the stars, which are retrograde,*
> *Which move swiftly, which hide themselves;*
> *And by the night, when it cometh on;*
> *And by the morning, when it appeareth;*
> *That these are the words of an honorable messenger,*
> *Endued with strength, of established dignity in the*
> *   sight of the possessor of the throne,*
> *Obeyed and faithful:*
> *And your companion is not distracted.*
> *He had already seen him in the clear horizon:*
> *And he suspected not the secrets.*
> *Neither are these the words of an accursed devil.*
> *Whither, therefore, are you going?*
> *This is no other than an admonition unto all creatures;*
> *Unto him among you who shall be willing to walk*
> *   uprightly.*[33]

7 Apologue, Fable, and Parable

APOLOGUE AND FABLE

A *fable,* in the proper (albeit seldom used) sense of this word, is "something that is said, something that is told," according to Littré, who mentions six other meanings: "subject of clever tales," "imaginary tale, i.e., from the imagination," "mythological tales relating to polytheism," "term of epic or dramatic poetry," "short tale concealing a moral under the veil of fiction, in which animals are characters," and "a lie, something made up."[1] Littré also distinguishes the fable from the apologue and the parable, in the following terms:

> The fable is the most general term; it is anything we say, anything we tell; in the fables of Phaedrus and La Fontaine there are ingenious stories that are not apologues at all. The apologue is always based on an allegory that has been applied to man. The parable is an apologue contained in holy scripture; we speak of the parable, and not the apologue, of the prodigal son, although at heart they are the same thing.[2]

Littré appears to have taken into account La Fontaine's preface to his *Fables,* in which *apologue* itself, not *fable,* is considered the more general term. La Fontaine, in fact, divides the apologue into two parts, one of which could be called the body, the other the soul. The body is the fable and the soul is the moral. Moreover, he declares expressly that "the Apologue is a gift that comes from the Immortals,"[3] which he does not say of the fable itself.

La Fontaine's expression is all the more correct given that the Greek preposition *apo* itself implies this general meaning, as Campos Leyza notes in *Analyse étymologique des racines de la langue grecque:* "This preposition has numerous meanings, which can be equated to 'coming from,' 'based on,' 'starting with,' hence 'outside of,' 'far from.'"[4]

Apologue, in Greek *apologos,* does not indicate simply a tale or a story. It is the exposing of a moral truth in allegorical form, wherein the teaching is imparted by an analogical likening of humans to the beings who speak and act in the fable. Giving life and words to all the actors in the theater of nature, the apologue also teaches the universality of physical and psychical similarities and homologies of relation between interior passions and exterior forms. This method is not limited to moral and social pedagogy. In India, for example, the subject of metempsychosis and reincarnation—a metaphysical teaching—is also evoked or suggested by the apologues and fables of the Brahmanic tradition.

In the fourth century AD, a Brahman named Pilpay, or Bidpaï, composed the earliest collection of this type, the *Hitopaseda* (Friendly Instruction), translated by C. Wilkins and W. Jones. A second collection, transcribed in Pahlavi in the sixth century, was so successful that it was translated into Arabic, Turkish, and, finally, more than twenty other languages. The work did not remain in its original state; the parts were published separately. For example, *Kalila and Dimna*[5] was translated from Sanskrit into Persian and from Persian into Greek.

The Western fable writers had certainly not heard Eastern tales before composing their works; all civilizations have had artists gifted with the particular type of genius that is the innate sense of the apologue. Madame de la Sablière called La Fontaine her fabler and said that he bore fables as naturally as a plum tree bore plums. "To speak of the apologue," La Harpe said, "is to speak of La Fontaine; the genre and the author are as one. Aesop, Phaedrus, Bidpaï, Avenius, these are the fables of La Fontaine."

In the winter of the French mind's history, La Fontaine seemed to gather and distill the fruits and perfumes of the springtime orchard. No color was missing from his palette, nor any essence from his alembic. And there are many things to be divined in those animal devices that are fables, for they are "a comedy with a hundred different acts, whose scene is the universe." Not without reason did Madame de Sévigné write: "La Fontaine's fables are divine." Fénelon was not exaggerating in comparing La Fontaine to the greatest ancient poets: "Anacreon knew not how to jest with more charm; Horace could not adorn philosophy and morals with more seductive ornaments. Terence painted the mores of men no more naturally and truly; Virgil was not more touching, nor more harmonious." Lessing's Germanic attack—daring to claim that La Fontaine "had distorted" the apologue "to the point of making it merely a poetic pompom"—was merely the exasperated reaction of a learned but tedious rival. As for Florian, all honey and sugar compared to La Fontaine, he was merely—in the clever words of Beaumarchais—"the poet of the meringues."

Unlike Littré and other critics, La Fontaine connected fable to apologue. His authority on the matter absolves us from having to discuss this. He also added that the truth was spoken to us through parables, and that parables were nothing other than apologues—that is, allegorical examples capable of penetrating more easily the more common and familiar they are.

A few nuances, however, might be added to this statement. The parable relates to religious teaching, not to the social morals that are the principal goal of the apologue. In the Hebrew scriptures, priests and prophets express themselves in parables in order to warn people and kings of the dangers and promises of the Eternal. When Nathan reproaches David for his adultery with Bathsheba, it is in the form of a

parable of a rich man who took a poor man's sheep. When God orders
Ezekiel to predict the ruin of Jericho, he tells him to offer an enigma
and a parable: *Fili, propone enigma et narra parabolam ad domum Israël.*
In the Christian scriptures, the parable's role is essential; as St. Mark
says of Jesus' teachings: *Sine parabola non loquebatur illis.* Thus a great
deal of attention must be paid to the nature of the parable and its specific function, distinct from that of the apologue.

THE PARABLE AND THE TEACHINGS
OF THE GOSPEL

Clearly, every parable is a comparison in the Greek sense: *para-ballein.*
This word means literally "to throw or cast aside," hence *paraballein
tophtalmo,* for Plato, "to cast one's eyes aside." This means precisely "to
look around oneself" in the original sense of this expression, which, by
extension, can mean "to place by the side of" or "to connect"—hence
the notion of "comparing." When we *connect* two things via an analogy
founded upon their mutual relationship, we do not *unite* them or *assemble* them; we merely place them in parallel by reason of their similitude.
Hence the difference between *parable* and *symbol.* The former connects,
while the latter assembles in the sense of *sum-ballein,* explained earlier. A
parable, in a way, is a figure having the property of reflecting, in parallel
meanings, the signification of a luminous truth or a distinct metaphysical principle situated at its center. By contrast, the symbol tends to make
the meanings converge in the direction of this truth, orienting them and
focusing them by this principle. The symbol, so to speak, focuses and
concentrates the meanings in itself, whereas the parable diffuses, extends,
and propagates them in parallel.

Jesus did not speak symbolically, but in parallel, just as light reflected
in a "parabolic" mirror is perceived in the form of parallel rays only after
first being concentrated at a luminous center. Consequently, the parables in the gospels have meaning only because they are like radiations
from the center of revelation. They can, in a manner of speaking, be no

"newer" than La Fontaine's apologues; they bear no less of the mark of the creative spirit who illuminates them with a different light. This is why, although most evangelical parables, including those in the Hebrew scriptures, belong to the common treasure of the great religions—just as the apologues come from the allegorical tradition of universal morals—both parables and apologues have been reformulated, re-created in such a way that we can no longer totally understand them on the basis of what has come before. The parables of the prophets of Israel are no more sufficient to explain all the meanings of the parables in the Christian scriptures than Aesop's fables can explain those of La Fontaine. For example, the fig-tree parable is used by Jesus in a very complex sense, despite appearances. This is from Mark 13:28–31:

> Now learn a parable of the fig tree; When her branch is yet tender, and putteth forth leaves, ye know that summer is near: So ye in like manner, when ye shall see these things come to pass, know that it is nigh, even at the doors. Verily I say unto you, that this generation shall not pass, till all these things be done. Heaven and earth shall pass away: but my words shall not pass away.

The fig tree was venerated in antiquity as being anthropogonic, the archetypal generator and nourisher. The famous *Ficus ruminalis* of Rome protected the wolf nursing Romulus and Remus; and Tacitus, in his *Annals* (XIII, 58), wrote of the sacred fig tree concerning which Pliny gave curious details, explaining to us that *rumen* is equivalent to "mamalla" (XV, 18). Moreover, the god Mars was "the father of the twins" and of the "sons of the wolf." The fig was the first cultivated fruit to be eaten by humans, and Adam, of course, hid behind a fig tree after having eaten the forbidden fruit. In the mystic container of the Dionysian rites, there were, among other objects, fig branches (*kradai*). The archetypal Indian sacred tree is the *açvattha* or *pippala*—either *Ficus religiosa* or *Ficus indica,* for which one Sanskrit name is *bahupâdah,* "many-footed." In the Vedic language, both are called *çikhandin. Ficus indica,* also known as *vata* or *nyagrodha,* "is reborn from its own branches," or "from its trunk," hence the terms *skandhaga,* "born of the trunk," *avakohi,* "downward-pushing," and *skandharuha,* "pushing on its own trunk."

The Kathaka Upanishad tells us: "The eternal açvattha has its roots above, its branches below . . . it is called the seed. Brahman, ambrosia; all the worlds rest upon him; above him, nothing exists." The açvattha is used to rub the *çami* to produce fire, a symbol of generation. The sacrificial vessel destined to receive the *soma,* the divine drink, must be made of açvattha wood.

It is also the sacred tree of Buddhism, the Bodhipâdapa, described in texts as "sacrificial," "wise," "deserving worship," the *pippala* or *pipal,* the *açoka* or the "tree without suffering," which should not be confused with another plant bearing the same name, one of the most beautiful plants of India, with blood-red flowers: *Jonesia asoka.* The confusion comes from the fact that the tree beneath which the Buddha achieved "the end of suffering," thanks to enlightenment, has been compared allegorically to the plant that women cause to bloom by touching it with their feet, thus bringing about the birth of love in the "heart of the king."

These connections may be enough to establish that the fig tree corresponds to the archetypal tree of generation—the tree of successive lives—from the Indian perspective, as well as in the teaching of the ancient mysteries, by all appearances. When Jesus uses the fig-tree parable in the passage from St. Mark, we should not forget that earlier, regarding the parable of the sower, he said: "Know ye not this parable? and how then will ye know all parables? The sower soweth the word" (Mark 4:13–14). Further, earlier (Mark 4:10–12) Jesus tells the apostles privately, when "they that were about him with the twelve asked of him the parable": "Unto you it is given to know the mystery of the kingdom of God: but unto them that are without, all these things are done in parables: That seeing they may see, and not perceive; and hearing they may hear, and not understand; lest at any time they should be converted, and their sins should be forgiven them."

These words show quite obviously that those "that are without" are the profane—"those who are in front of the temple"—in the literal sense of this word, *pro* and *fanum,* or "outside," in opposition to those to whom the mysteries have been given (that is, the initiated, those to whom Jesus was speaking privately of the kingdom of God).[6] Under these conditions, claiming that the gospels have no esoteric or initiatory meaning as distinct from their exoteric meaning, in that the symbol is different from the parable, is to refuse to listen to the teachings of Jesus. The Gospel of St. Mark returns many times to this separation between the two teachings, one public and open and the other private and closed: "With many such parables spake he the word unto them, as they were able to hear it. But without a parable spake he not unto them: and when they were alone, he expounded all things to his disciples" (Mark 4:33–34).

In the fig-tree parable, we read that "this generation shall not pass, till all these things be done" (Mark 13:30)—thus the first Christians concluded that "the time of the Son of Man" was near, and doubt began to reign among them, as they observed that the generations passed by without Jesus' words being fulfilled. Thus it was forgotten that this was a parable, and that it was first necessary to try to listen in a different manner from those who "hearing, may hear, and not understand" (Mark 4:12). The objective of Jesus' teachings was generation in the continuous, Adamic sense—that is, the "fig tree" of successive generations. The text, moreover, is situated in the perspective of an answer Jesus gives to a question posed privately by only four apostles—Peter, James, John, and Andrew—"as he sat upon the mount of Olives over against the temple" (see Mark 13:3–4). They are at first surprised by Jesus' answer to one of his disciples—"Seest thou these great buildings? there shall not be left one stone upon another, that shall not be thrown down" (Mark 13:2). The disciples demand of their master: "Tell us, when shall these things be? and what shall be the sign when all these things shall be fulfilled?" (Mark 13:4).

This was therefore a prophecy of the end of time. Why does the fig tree appear in this parable? In Hesiod's fragments, when the seer Mopsus, nephew of Tiresias, tells Calchas how many figs are on a nearby fig tree, Calchas then dies. Whoever eats a fig from the fig tree acquires new life, thus becoming like the immortals. But the fig tree itself is condemned to perish, and Calchas's life ends as soon as the seer measures the days of his life by the number of figs on the tree.

The Adamic fig tree has thus continued growing "from its own branches" ever since the origin. It was placed on earth in autumn; it went through the winter; Easter brought its springtime; its summer passed by. The four seasons correspond to the "cross of time." The summer, the "dog days" of Egyptian esotericism, corresponds to the birth of Typhon, the principle of evil. We may observe that Jesus' prophecy is typically Typhonian, both in the catastrophes he predicts and in his warnings against false Christs and false prophets (Mark 13:22). The cosmological side of this would require lengthy commentary, but here we limit ourselves to examining the complexity of the evangelical parables despite their apparent simplicity of expression. Each word must be examined, weighed, and interpreted not only in its connections to Christian teaching, but also in the sense that this teaching reveals that which has been much more deeply hidden than the mysteries of the ancient religions.

We can see by this example that the parable is the most complex form of allegory, beneath common and familiar appearances. It misleads the profane much more readily than other, complicated allegorical processes, because we immediately believe we have heard and understood everything. The alleged simplicity of the style of the gospels is illusory. The *Tao Te Ching* also often appears merely to repeat the obvious sayings of Chinese peasant wisdom. Nonetheless, it remains one of the most mysterious sacred books in the world, to the point that no Sinologist would boast of being able to translate it exactly.

The limits of the study here do not allow us to examine the question of the keys to the interpretation of the sacred texts of the great Eastern and Western religions. This problem also leads to the question of the relationship between the authority of the interpreters known as mystic and that of historically established religious orthodoxies. Here I mention only Goldhizer's work, published in 1920, on the Islamic interpretation of the Qur'an; Henry Corbin's work on Shiite and Ismaili gnosis, one of the most important works of our time on questions of esoteric and initiatory hermeneutics; and Gershom Scholem's equally remarkable book *On the Kabbalah and Its Symbolism.* Many works by Orientalists should also be mentioned, for example those of Sinologists such as Maspero and Kaltenmark in the field of Taoism.

It is quite paradoxical, on the other hand, to note the absence of works of comparable value and scope in the domain that is most directly important to us: Christian hermeneutics and its esotericism. What should we believe: error or truth? The most obvious consequence of this vast lacuna in Western Christian religious teaching is the tendency of an entire intellectual and spiritual elite to search, legitimately, in Eastern and Far Eastern spirituality for more-profound truths than those found in the insipid contemporary evangelical preaching.

Gershom Scholem notes, admirably:

> [T]he word of God must be infinite, or, to put it in a different way, the absolute word is as such meaningless, but it is *pregnant* with meaning. Under human eyes it enters into significant finite embodiments, which mark innumerable layers of meaning. Thus mystical exegesis, this *new* revelation imparted to the mystic, has the character of a key. The key itself may be lost, but an immense desire to look for it remains alive. In a day when such mystical impulses seem to have dwindled to the vanishing point they still retain an enormous force in the books of Franz Kafka.[7]

In his *Selecta in Psalmos* (Psalm I),[8] Origen relates that a "Hebrew" scholar told him that the holy scriptures were like a great house with many rooms. For each one of these there is a key, but it is not the right one. The keys to all the rooms have been switched around, so that the right keys must be found to open each room—a huge and difficult task. As we can see, in this epoch—probably the time of the Caesarean Rabbinic Academy, as Scholem assumes, citing this example—the revelation had been received but the key to it was already lost. Now, thanks to the extraordinary expansion of our historical perspectives and the continuously increasing precision of our methods of examining texts, we can do something today that the "separated" research of the old days was not able to do: approach things collectively—that is, through the vast resources of future interdisciplinary synthesis and on an ecumenical basis. This is the only path open to us in the reconquest of the keys—and meanings—of our own sacred traditions.

FABLES AND MYTHS

Greek polytheism presents a singular contrast to the aversion evinced by the Hellenic mind for all things excessive and monstrous—in short, for all the various forms of immoderation. A son, Chronos, brutally mutilates his father, Uranus, and he swallows his own children, then vomits them up again, still living; Apollo, the most beautiful of the gods, the incarnation of serenity, nails Marsyas to a tree and flays him alive; Demeter, sister of Zeus, eats one of the shoulders of Pelops, who has been killed and roasted by his own father. We could cite many other divine atrocities of this kind, worthy of the most barbaric people. A civilized Greek who taught his children the stories of the heroes and gods would have been unable to escape having to tell them these tales of absurd horror and carnage.

Certainly, though the origin of these fables was shrouded in mystery and they were considered with fear and respect, certain Greek philosophers dared to express doubt and scorn on the subject. Xenophanes accused Hesiod and Homer of having attributed to the gods everything that is dishonorable among men: thievery, adultery, and perfidy. Xenophanes states that "God is one, the greatest among gods and men, resembling men neither in form nor in thought."[9] This philosopher called the battles of the Titans, centaurs, and giants "inventions of the ancestors" (*Isocrates* II, 38), and demanded that divinity be praised in sacred tales and pure songs.

According to Diogenes Laertius (IX, 1), Heraclitus declared that Homer and Archilochus deserved to be expelled from public assemblies and beaten. The same author tells a story in which Pythagoras saw, in hell, the soul of Homer hanging from a tree and surrounded by snakes as a punishment for his lies about the gods.

Yet political power allowed nothing to affect sacred mythology. Anaxagoras, who tried to give a moral interpretation to the Homeric legends, and who is said to have explained the names of the gods allegorically, went so far as to declare that Fate was a name devoid of meaning. He was thrown in prison in Athens and was released due only to the powerful protection of his disciple and friend Pericles. Protagoras, another friend of Pericles, was banished from Athens and his books were burned in the public square because he had said that he could never know whether the gods existed or did not exist.[10]

All these facts—to which we might add the condemnation of Socrates, although he never attacked sacred traditions or even popular fables—prove that allegorical interpretation was not without its serious risks for the philosopher who dared to propose it. But after the death of Socrates, the Athenians appear to have admitted a certain freedom of thought. Plato, while declaring that myths could be interpreted, still banned the Homeric poems from his *Republic.* Diogenes Laertius (X, 123) attributed these words to Epicurus: "The gods exist, assuredly, but they are not what the common people believe they are. He who denies the gods of the masses is not impious, but he who attributes to the gods sentiments in common with mortals is impious." As we also know, Euripides' poetry oscillates between two extremes: Either he ascribes the same violent crimes and injustices to the gods that the fables ascribe to them or he denies the truth of the ancient myths because they attribute to the gods what is incompatible with their nature.

These situations may be enough to show that the fables of Greek mythology were founded upon sacred traditions whose meanings had become uncertain, either because they had been forgotten or because they were piously guarded by hierophants of the Mysteries. This latter hypothesis seems quite probable by reason of the familial character and inherited privileges of the ancient priesthood. The primordial deposit of the arts and sciences was never revealed openly or taught in any great ancient civilization in the East or the West. Aristotle seems to allude to this sacred deposit:

> Traditions, however, have been handed down from our predecessors, and the very ancient philosophers, and left to their posterity in the form of a Myth, to the effect that these many heavens—supposing them to exist—both are gods, and that the Divinity encompasses the entire of Nature. And the remainder of these traditions, in the present day, has been brought forward, clothed in a fabulous garb, for the purpose of winning the assent of the multitude, and enforcing the utility that is urged in favor of the laws, and of general expediency. For they speak of these as subsisting in the form of the human species, and as being like in appearance to certain of the rest of the animal kingdom. And other statements consequential upon these, and similar to those that have been declared, do they put forward.
>
> Now, if as regards these traditions any one having separated this from amongst the others may receive merely the first assertion—namely, that they supposed the First Substances to be gods—he would consider that this statement had been made after a divine manner; and in accordance with what is to be expected in the discovery—as frequently as is consistent with possibility—as well of every art as of every system of philosophy, and in the loss of these, again, he must conclude that likewise these opinions of those very ancient philosophers, as relics, have been preserved up to the time of the present day.[11]

From Socrates to the present, there have been innumerable attempts at the interpretation of Greek mythology. Because this subject alone would require a separate work or, better, an encyclopedia, we cannot approach it here, for this book is limited to the examination of the elementary conditions of general symbology. It does seem necessary, however, to recommend to the reader one documentary source, unfortunately no longer in print: Friedrich Creuzer's monumental work, *Symbolik und Mythologie der alten Völker* (1819–21), translated into French by Guigniaut under the title *Les religions de l'antiquité considérées principalement sous leurs formes symboliques.*[12] Although Creuzer's system, greatly admired by Hegel, does not correspond to contemporary conceptions of the history of religions, Creuzer's considerations still present a great deal of interest and do not deserve the unjust oblivion into which they have fallen.

Concerning the difference between myth and fable, we should first remember that the Greek language uses the same word for them: *mutos.* Plato, however, mentions their hidden meaning in another word besides *allegoria: uponoia,* "implied thought." What we might call a hyponoetic figure does not necessarily present another meaning, an entirely different signification from what it presents visibly—such as, in principle, a proper allegory should. Legends and fables are allegories in the general sense. But myths, strictly speaking, at least in their archaic forms, are like those rough, uncarved stones that are not the attributes of the deity, but rather the deity itself in its immediate and sensible opacity.

Under these conditions, we may admit the impossibility of explaining a myth allegorically, because the only way of understanding it is to live and experience for ourselves what it implies through its opacity, its shadows, its strangeness, its drama. There is no privileged viewpoint from which we can judge a myth by a value system different from those systems that the myth forcefully imposes if we allow it to penetrate. This is why every myth can truly be approached only through initiatory rites derived from its own nature and from its norms alone. A myth is nothing other than the mutation that it brings about in us when we let ourselves dissolve into it.

To live a myth is not within the range of ethnological observation or philosophical reflection or historical critique or sociological analysis. The fact that in our era we confuse what is mythical with what is fictitious or illusory is enough, for lack of other proofs, to measure our society's state of inner degradation and spiritual poverty. All great civilizations not only represented their mythologies in their monuments; they also perceived them existentially and lived them concretely in their everyday experiences.

Because people of these civilizations came no longer to have the vital force necessary for the mystical penetration of their ancestral myths, they began to question the myths instead of questioning themselves. When we speak of the Greece of Socrates and Plato, we tend to forget that the civilization was born three thousand years earlier, between the Tigris and Euphrates. A Platonic dialogue, *Critias,* relates the words of an Egyptian priest who considered the Athenians and Greeks to be "children," newborns in the ancient world. The myths are immemorial. In the current state of research, we can connect some of them to prehistory—that is, to time scales unrelated to those of written traditions. The myth began with man, like magic. It was perfected with the ages of fables and science.

8 DEVICE AND EMBLEM

DEFINITION OF *DEVICE*

In heraldic language, the word *device* is derived from the verb "to devise," which used to indicate the action of "placing by dividing," forming a plan or a *devis,* in the ancient sense of "description."[1] As a heraldic term, a device is a "division" of an honorable piece of the escutcheon. For example, a "fasces in device" is a fasces one third its usual size.

This definition is different from the one designating "an emblematic figure with some concise sentence explaining it," such as, for example, a dried-up, dead tree around which are written the words *Fin che sol ritorni* ("until the sun returns"). In this case, the figure is called the body and the sentence is the soul of the device. In coats of arms, devices are written on ribbons surrounding the shield or on the crest, sometimes at the bottom or on the sides. The devices of orders are written on their collars.

A device can also be a short sentence, sometimes reduced to a single word to signify some quality attributed to people or things—for example: "Diversity, that's my motto." The specific character of the device, in fact, is that it is an abbreviated similitude, as concise as possible. Cicero noted that a metaphor is both a comparison and an abbreviation in a single word: *Similitudinis est ad verbum contracta brevitas.*[2]

A metaphor can represent one idea with another idea or one object with another object presenting an analogical relationship with the former. The first process is intended for the eyes of the spirit, so to speak; it is immaterial and abstract. The second, sensible and concrete, speaks to the sense of sight: a visible speech, although it is silent, a mute language.

It is not easy, in all cases, to distinguish a device from an emblem, because the emblem may also contain an image and a legend, a body and a soul. For example, Aeschylus describes the figures engraved on the shields of the Seven Chiefs against Thebes: Polynices, he tells us, bears the goddess of Justice on his shield, with the legend "I will reestablish thee"; Eteocles' shield bears a soldier climbing up a tower, with the legend "Mars himself could not push me back"; and Capaneus displays a man brandishing a flaming torch with the words "I will burn Thebes." Are these emblems or devices?

It should be noted that in each case, the words correspond precisely to the figures, forming a literal and direct translation of each other. Their conformity clearly and immediately reveals both the thoughts of their authors and their meanings. The body allows the soul to be seen entirely, without veils. By their very nudity, these are *emblems* and not *devices,* because the latter always impose upon us a subtle detour, a singular and indirect allusion, a voluntary divergence between that which is shown and that which is signified. In other words, it is not enough to see the device in order to understand it immediately; we must also divine its resonances and its inner music, sometimes hardly perceptible upon first examination.

Further, the emblem is used for the expression of general ideas, maxims of public interest, collective moral truths, universal philosophical ideas, and social lessons, whereas the device is inspired by traits specific to a family, restricted group, or person. The device always expresses an irreducible and permanent characteristic of those who bear it in order to distinguish themselves from other members of society.

THE ART OF DEVICES

Of all the works of the mind, the device is the one that says the most in the fewest words. Apologue, parable, enigma, and even oracle all need a certain development of discourse in order to be expressed. A couple of lines, a few syllables, are enough for a device, which is a quintessence of meaning, a highly elaborate product of art and allegory. If it is not hieroglyphic or symbolic in itself, it is sometimes based on an esotericism that is specific to it and which relates to what Scipione Ammirato called *una filosofia del cavaliere,* a chivalric philosophy, also known as the language of gentlemen or noble wisdom.

This is a heritage and tradition whose origins go a long way back; by all appearances, they can be traced to the ancient Indo-European distribution of religious, military, and economic powers among castes and families possessing "sacred deposits" and passing on initiations specifically founded upon worship rendered to different gods from those of the priesthood. Georges Dumézil has already written and demonstrated a great deal on this subject.[3] Three primitive functions—those of the priests, warriors, and shepherd clans—corresponded to three groups of gods: the celestial and cosmic sovereigns, or Aditya; the fighters of the tempest, or Rudra; and the givers of goods, or Vasu. Roman horsemen and warriors were linked to the second group, to which the Roman cults of the god Mars would later correspond.

Medieval chivalric esotericism is still not well known, despite research by numerous specialists who have tried to show its specificity in relation to priestly esotericism. To tell the truth, we are even less well informed about the economic traditions of the third group (the Vasu) than about those of the second (Rudra), even though they have certainly played a substantial role in the history of our societies. Heraldry gives few directly usable indications in the realm of chivalric esotericism. Even its greatest specialists reject indignantly any hypothesis of this type.[4]

It would be going too far, however, to deny the existence of a soul in devices of nobility. Heraldry cannot be reduced to a game played by a computer' capable of making it into a positive and rational science. There is a singular naïveté in this, which is not without connection to certain excesses of erudition. Analyzing the most minute details of each tree, many heraldic specialists seem not to notice the forest.

Might we suggest to them at least the existence of devices, and ask them whether there is really no esoteric and initiatory meaning in the device of the Order of the Star (founded by Robert, son of Hugh Capet, and abolished by Louis XI)—*Monstrant regibus astra viam*—with, as its body, a star leading the three Magi? Or how about the device of the golden fleece, with a collar made of double fusils interlaced in the form of a letter *B* with firestones emitting rays and flames, and with the inscription *Ante ferit quam flamma micet*? Or its decoration: a golden sheepskin with the device *Pretium non vile laborum*?

Certainly, we must distinguish these devices from those that followed the French expedition into Italy under Charles VIII. The art of devices was fashionable by then. They were used in gallant jousting and in tournaments. They added charm to dances and court diversions; they were displayed on triumphal arches at the births of kings, at their coronations, at their entries into the cities of the kingdom. Engravers put them on tokens, medals, and furniture; they appeared on sculptures in palaces and on the dedications of public monuments; they were embroidered everywhere, reproduced on banners, harnesses in the field, cloaks at court. The Medicis and Concinis made their popularity and use still greater. In the seventeenth century, the French were the uncontested masters of the art of devices. By then, it was a literary genre that sometimes even managed to sum up an entire political program with one four-letter word.

A device of Richelieu, for example, showed a globe marked with three fleurs-de-lis supported by three chevrons and the single word *Stat* (without delay). Because the cardinal's arms bore three red chevrons, it was easy to conclude that while Richelieu was minister, the stability of the entire kingdom would not be weakened by anything. The political device of Louis XII is well known: a porcupine with the words *Cominus et eminus,* "from near and far." A little sagacity is enough to understand that the words *se tuetur* are implied. The porcupine "protects itself from near and far." Interior and exterior enemies are thus clearly warned by the king. The verb *tueri* itself is rich in implications. It means both "to protect oneself" and "to defend oneself"; also, its French phonetic equivalent, *tuer* ("to kill"), suggests that one prick from a spine of the French porcupine is enough to kill its adversary. Moreover, the same device can be read esoterically, transposing it by playing with the connection between *Cominus* and *Caminus,* as well as that between *eminus* and *animus.* In this sense, it evokes "the path, the hearth, the fire," and "the breath, the spirit, the heart." The porcupine thus changes meaning; it becomes the image of the radiant sun. It is with good reason that this device appears in a place of honor at the hotel L'allemand in Bourges.

The rebus, the *à-peu-près,* the double entendre resulting from phonetic assonance were all used by the Greeks and Romans well before medieval "speaking arms." The coins of Rhodes bore a rose with five leaves, because in Greek, the rose is called *rodon.* The cock, which Aristophanes called the *mede* or Persian bird, was given as an emblem to the Persians because of the similarity between the word for the "red fire" of its crest (*pursos* in Greek, derived from *puros*) and the word *perses,* "inhabitant of Persia." Assyrian ensigns bore doves, whose name was close to that of Queen Semiramis. The elephant, an emblem of caesar, came from the Phoenician name for this animal, *coesar.* Fabius's insignia was a fava bean; Lentulus, a lentil; Torquatus, a torch—just as today, the Mailly family have mallets, the La Saulsaye have willow trees (*saules* in French), the La Tour d'Auvergne have a crenellated tower (*tour* in French), the Colonas have columns, the Orsinis have a bear (*orso* in Italian), and the Cardonas have thistles (*cardo* in Italian). These are but a few examples.

In certain cases, we must search much further for the equivalence or the wordplay. For a long time, ensigns had preserved this ancient type of convenience for the illiterate. It was not necessary to know how to read in order to understand the ensign of an inn showing a gold lion: the French equivalent, *au lion d'or,* sounded like *au lit, on dort* ("in bed, one sleeps"), thus indicating to travelers that they could find rooms or beds there. Rabelais's work is a monument to the glory of this unsuspected language, which Fulcanelli quite rightly called the "phonetic Kabbalah," and which is the archetypal "language of chivalry"[6]—which, in Jonathan Swift's work, was the language of the horse.

Some devices evoke a great deal of drama in very few words. That of Francis II showed two spheres with the words *Unus non sufficit orbis:* "One world is not enough." Mary Stuart, before her death, chose as her device a licorice plant with its root in the ground and the words *Dulce meum terra tegit,* "The earth hides my sweetness" ("The earth hides my sweet friend").

Sometimes, a change of a famous device was used to punish someone powerful. For example, Holy Roman Emperor Charles V had chosen the Pillars of Hercules as the body of his device and for its soul, *Plus ultra:* "More beyond," "Farther beyond." When he lifted the siege of Metz, his retreat was mocked, and his device was depicted with the columns replaced by a crab and the words *Plus citra* ("Farther backward").

The inner, personal character of devices is one of their most engaging aspects. Shameless ambition is avowed, for example, in the rocket of the count of Illiers d'Entragues with the words *Poco duri, purchi m'innalzi* ("May I not last long, provided that it causes me to rise up"). The temperament of a princess who inflamed all hearts but remained frigid is described in three words accompanied by an image of the sun: *Uro nec uror*—"I burn but am not burned." And there is the haughty device of Erasmus—the god Terminus, with the inscription *Cedo nulli*—and the charming spiritual device of Madame de Salers: a pin, with the words *Je pique mais j'attache* ("I prick, but I attach").

Nothing is more difficult than the art of devices. Malherbe said that a good device was a life's work for one man. He was doubtless exaggerating, for he also said that after writing an elegy of a hundred verses, an individual might rest for ten years. Paul Jove, however, one of the greatest geniuses of his time in this area, stated that he had never been able to compose a single device with which he was entirely satisfied. Ruscelli said that to succeed in this genre, a person required clear judgment, an enlightened and educated mind rich in noble images, a lively style, and a delicate taste for discerning what was fine and exquisite in each thing. These are qualities that have depreciated for many ages; we must not hold our breath waiting for the subtle art of devices to flourish once again in this society that can no longer understand their implications and allusions, for we hardly even hear the jackhammers on the pavements of everyday hype.

EMBLEMS AND COLORS

The ancients originally gave the name "emblems" to stone or enamel mosaics; marquetry and damascene work; filigreed inlays; festoons; garlands; gold or silver bas-reliefs; and all the embellishments and decorations appearing on vases, furniture, and clothes. Homer, Hesiod, and the Greek mythographers relate how the doors of temples and sacred cups and vessels were decorated with emblems. Cicero, reproaching Verres for stealing vases and statues from Sicily, called these ornaments *emblemata*. In the sixteenth century, Montaigne wrote, in the Roman style: "My book is always the same, saving that upon every new edition . . . I take the liberty to add (as 'tis but an ill jointed marqueterie) some supernumerary emblem"[7]—that is to say, what is known as a "related piece."

The word *emblem* has also described engravings and seals. In 1261, Baldwin II, emperor of Constantinople, used the expression "Signed with our imperial emblems." In general, the emblem can be reduced to a soulless body—a figure by itself or accompanied by a sentence or legend that makes it alive. In this usage, as we discovered earlier, it expresses general truths—philosophical or religious, moral or political—of a collective, social, or universal type, making abstractions or ideas understandable. Known sentences materialized by a figure or a scene—as well as scenes idealized by a sentence—constitute the two principal processes of the composition of emblems.

Emblematics play an important role in ensigns. In ancient times, Roman brothels bore a phallic emblem with the words *Hic habitat felicitas.** We will return later to the question of marks and ensigns. Here, it is important to note only that emblems are connected to the plastic arts, unlike apologues and fables, which are connected to literary expression. The emblem has one trait in common with the symbol: its depictability. This is an important characteristic, because unlike a device, an emblem is essentially figurative; it speaks to the view rather than to the mind. It fascinates and fixes the view, and this is why we may consider the history of painting as being directly connected to that of emblematics.

The material character of primitive emblems in fact imposed a long, fastidious, and patient artisanal apprenticeship upon ancient and medieval painting. The great decorative displays of the past were the work not of a single artist, but of a collective animated by the mind and teachings of a master. A great deal of sweat and labor was required before anyone could be judged worthy of painting, as Cennino Cennini relates:

> Know that you cannot learn to paint in less time than thus. In the first place, you must study drawing for at least one year, on tablets; then you must remain with a master at the workshop; you must begin with grinding colors, and learn to boil down glues, to acquire the practice of laying grounds on panels, to work in relief upon them; and to rub them smooth and to gild; to engrave well; and this for six years; afterwards to practice coloring, to adorn with mordants, to make cloths of gold, and to be accustomed to paint on walls, for six more years—always drawing without intermission either on holidays or workdays. And so, through long habit, good practice becomes a second nature. Adopting other habits, do not hope to ever attain great perfection. There are many who say they have learned the art without having been with a master. Do not believe them . . .[8]

The masters guarded from all disclosure their knowledge, as well as the privileges acquired through their technical ability. They communicated

---

*Here dwells happiness.

their knowledge to pupils only little by little, by degrees, at the price of such obedience that Vasari, along with other authors, called the disciples the *creato* ("creatures") of the old masters, a term that passed from Spanish to Italian as a synonym of *servant*. Thus Taddeo Gaddi served Giotto for twenty-four years, just as Giotto had been Agnolo's disciple for twelve years. The art of painting corresponded to a gradual initiation and touched upon many areas besides that of painting itself.

Cennini wrote, for example: "There is a red color called cinnabar, and this color is made by a chemical process performed in an alembic, which I will leave alone, as it would take too much time to put in my explanation each method and recipe. If you wish to fatigue yourself with it, you will find plenty of recipes, especially collecting them among the monks."[9] The painters of old used considerable quantities of gold; they were therefore better informed than we might suppose concerning this precious metal in general. Alchemical influences on painting have not yet been sufficiently studied, neither from the viewpoint of the history of science and technique nor in relation to the history of emblems and works of art. Exploring the relationship between emblems and colors would require a thorough study of the correspondences between the teachings of hermetic philosophy and those of traditional Western painting. Here, we limit ourselves to the sense that this is a matter of artisanal and artistic magic rather than religious symbology. This is why it is necessary to remember what role the painter played in traditional societies. In Tibet, for example, painters and sculptors

... are regarded as humble craftsmen, and not as individual creators. Apart from a few monks, remembered for reasons unconnected with their art, only a few obscure names have been preserved for us, on fifteenth-century frescoes. The Tibetans tell us nothing, throughout their history, of any eminent painter, any remarkable or famous work of art, nor are their paintings and sculptures ever signed.[10]

These facts—reported by Rolf Stein, one of the greatest modern Tibetologists—did not prevent painters from being called "makers of deities" (*lha-bzo-ba*). Nor did it prevent their works from being artistic creations, for the Tibetans were as aware as we are of the more or less perfect execution of a work of art and of its quality. In Tibet, just as in medieval Europe, the painter was an artisan—but as such, he was responsible for the magical efficacy of his image on the level of its fabrication. This meant that he could not work at just any given time or with any color or material. His technique, like that of the painter of icons, was regulated by minute instructions. Upon leaving his hands, however, the work would be neither symbolic nor sacred in itself, but still emblematic. It would become a truly religious work only once traditional rites had transformed its initial nature, perfectly adapting it to the use for which it was intended—something that could be achieved only by following traditional magical-technical rules.

These rules are preserved materially in the construction of the geometric projection of the world that is found in the famous Indo-Tibetan psycho-cosmogram known as the *mandala*. On this subject, Giuseppe Tucci has written a crucial book[11] to which we should refer to complete the brief description of these operations.

The mandala is drawn in the sand on a surface consecrated by appropriate rites. The masters begin by determining the quality of the string that is to be used for tracing the various parts: the quality of the material that composes the string and the number of strands that must be twisted together (five, each of a different color). Rice powder of various colors is generally used to trace the lines and designs of the figures, and the choice of powder is determined by the section in which the figures will be drawn. The string is covered with this powder; it is placed flat on the surface to be decorated and is held at its ends. By lifting the string with one finger and "snapping" it so that it suddenly falls, the powder is released and lands in the chosen place. In general, the mandala is made up of an exterior enclosure and one or more concentric circles, each containing a square divided by diagonals. In this way, four triangles are created, and at their center (which is also the center of the whole figure), there is a circle containing emblems or depictions of deities.

The mandala is then surrounded on the outside by a circle in which are drawn a series of spirals representing the "mountain of fire," a barrier of flames closing off its entrance. Immediately afterward, a "diamond belt" is drawn, completing this cosmogram.

There are many additional details, making its construction very complex, but the most important ones to note are the division into five elements in the subtle and gross states, five colors, five objects of the senses, and five "faces" from which five directions derive, corresponding to the five "families" of the Buddhist schools. White corresponds to the west, yellow to the north, black to the south, red to the east, and green to the center.

Every civilization has given various and multiple meanings to colors. In all cases, we may observe certain correspondences that are more general than others. For example, red is more likely than white to be connected to the symbolism of the active powers of nature and to the sun, blood, fire, and supreme power. On feast days, the Romans painted red the statue of Jupiter Capitoline and the faces of triumphant warriors. Social dignity was proclaimed by this color. In the Eastern Empire, high honor was paid only to *porphyrogenes*—to those "who were born in the purple."

White, the color of innocence and purity, was used for sacred activities. Because of the purification required for all initiations, white is the archetypal color of those who have had a new birth through rites. It is also, analogically, the color of the spirits of the dead and the Manes.*

"To die," wrote Plutarch, "is to be initiated to the great mysteries." The color of mourning was white before it became black. White also corresponded to the blessed and the redeemed, and it was considered a luxurious color. In pompous festivals, the Romans wore white robes as a sign of joy. Joyous days were marked with a white stone. An honest and loyal man was said to be "white," *homo albus*. The white tunic was the garment of aspirants to chivalry, hence their name *candidates*.

---

*[Manes are the souls of deceased loved ones. —*Ed.*]

Kings and queens of Great Britain wear white coronation veils and white robes, and one name for the color is related to an ancient name for England: Albion.

Blue, the color of the sky and the sea that reflects it, is the archetypal cosmic color and, by extension, the color of universal wisdom and perfect serenity. It is a votive color and is appropriate for sovereign majesty: The royal cloak of the eldest branch of the Bourbons was blue.

Green naturally represents both the renewal of life and the putrefaction of death. This color can therefore suggest or evoke both spiritual rebirth and material decomposition. In olden days, for example, the fraudulently bankrupt were required to wear green wigs. This sanction has been forgotten, but it has a certain descriptive interest.

This subject cannot be covered in full within the limits of this book. Colors have served for many ages to distinguish political parties and rival sects. The *aurigae* and *quadrigae* (chariot racers) of the Roman circus were divided into four major factions: Whites, Reds, Blues, and Greens. Their rivalries and battles incited riots in the capital and, taking on a political character, became a serious form of sedition. Under Justinian, these rivalries shook the whole Byzantine Empire: Forty thousand partisans were massacred, and this bloody repression had far-reaching historical consequences.

In the era of the Crusades, the French wore a red cross on their robes; the Italians, a blue cross; the Germans, a black or orange cross; the English, a yellow cross; and the Saxons, a green cross. Florence was destroyed by the irreconcilable factions of the Whites and Blacks, Bianchi e Neri. In the fifteenth century, the members of the Burgundian faction were recognized by their red sashes and the red cross of St. Andrew. White was the color of the Armagnacs.

The three colors of the French flag are explainable not only historically. They also have an emblematic meaning: The body—blue, white, and red—corresponds to the French soul: liberty, equality, and fraternity. I will leave readers to decipher the deeper meaning behind this relating to distant ancestral traditions.

9 ALLEGORY AND ICONOLOGY

The ancient and medieval conception of the allegory, as I noted earlier, was applicable to all varieties of expression represented, although the anagogical and mystical spiritual interpretation might be distinguished from it, insofar as the anaphoric interpretation of this nature corresponds to an orientation toward the significator rather than to a metaphorical relationship between the signal and the signification. Only with this assumption can we speak of a symbolic typology as distinct from allegorical typology, because the difference relates to the dynamics of the prefiguration of the eternal model in the temporal fact, an *allegoria in facto* in the Augustinian sense, and not merely an *allegoria in verbis*. In other words, it is the historical fact itself that is allegorical from this perspective, because it can be understood in a different manner, no longer evidential but instead, so to speak, adventual.

John Chrysostom taught that "[c]ontrary to usage, [Paul] calls a type an allegory [*ton tupon allegorian ekalesen*]; his meaning is as follows; this history not only declares that which appears on the face of it, but announces somewhat farther, whence it is called an *allegory*."[1] For example, in the anagogical sense, the true historical fact of the exodus from Egypt indicates, according to the words of the Psalmist (Ps. 114), that the "house of Jacob" became free, and also that Judah became "a

146

sanctuary of the Eternal" and "Israel his dominion." But this historical event can be filled with typological significance of a spiritual order:
The soul departing from sin becomes holy and worthy of the gifts of
the Eternal.

It should be observed that the exegetes of the High Middle Ages,
such as the Venerable Bede and John the Scot, took up the Augustinian
conception of the allegoria in facto. St. Thomas Aquinas also referred
to the allegorical or typical meaning: According to him, "[T]hings that
occurred" (*ea quae contigerunt*) in the Hebrew scriptures—events—
are thus understood and revealed in their relationship to Jesus and the
church (*exponentur de Christo et Ecclesia*).[2] Moreover, Thomas Aquinas
sustained a thesis on this point with great consequences for allegorical
exegesis: namely, that the power to fill events themselves with a meaning of this kind is the privilege of God and the scripture of which he is
the author. No human science can lay claim to it, and thus sacred and
divinely inspired texts alone are bearers of anagogical meaning that can
receive a spiritual interpretation of this kind. Thus we can see how the
allegory of the theologians is not that of the poets. Plenty of nuances
remain to be determined on this point. As Jean Pépin shows in *Dante
et la tradition de l'allégorie,* these nuances are revealed with the greatest
precision on the subject of Dante and the tradition of allegory. This
work is indispensable for all seekers who desire to be precisely informed
of the current state of these questions. Latin grammarians have confirmed this restriction of the meaning of allegory, presenting it as a figure of rhetoric, a continued metaphor, according to Quintilian. Cicero
observed (*De Oratore,* chapter 27) that this denotation is a transition
from the proper meaning to the meaning depicted. Yet although the
grammarians of the Middle Ages observed the gap between what is said
and what is meant by this process of literary exposition—*Allegoria est
cum aliud dicitur et aliud significatur*—the theologians did not limit it
to this simple relationship or to its role as an ornament of rhetoric.

Allegory must not be confused with the allegorical process of
exegesis or with *allegorism*—the search for profound cosmological,

anthropological, metaphysical, and mystical relationships among the various levels of the analogical interpretation of things and beings, between the sensible and the intelligible, or between the image and the idea. Allegorical interpretation is a consequence of a symbolic vision of the world, nature, man, and their correspondences with a mysterious and suprahuman order that transcends them.

Allegorism expresses the symbolism from which it emanates and proceeds. Far from being opposed to the symbol, traditional allegory embodies it in its imaginary figures, magically makes it present, so to speak, rather than merely representing it philosophically as a system of ideas. Thus allegorical configurations oscillated during the Middle Ages between the vibration of Roman art and the precision of Gothic art through which was manifested an encyclopedic illustration of universal sapience: theological, ethical, and scientific. We can note, however, at the end of the medieval epoch, an overflowing of realism and a widening gap between discourse and image. Gothic allegorism, in a logical fashion and in an essentially coherent order, integrated the extraordinary wealth but also the obscurity of the original themes of Roman art, whose allegories correspond more to what Isidore of Seville, in his treatise on the allegories of the Holy Scripture, called "the prefigurations of the mystery."[3] These themes of the general ornamental line and particular ornaments enliven stone, metal, and parchment in order to evoke and magically signify the ordering powers that transcend the real, rather than representing their actual order. In Roman allegory, what is essential is the *theme;* in Gothic allegory, it is the *figure*. Little by little, around the middle of the thirteenth century, there took shape a new desire for the objective description of the world, a tendency toward naturalist allegorism, which also corresponded to the intellectualist directions that were triumphing during this era. According to this intellectualism, Nature herself appeared divinely ordered and organized. This evolution, accelerating in the fourteenth century and even more in the fifteenth century, profoundly transformed the allegorical process itself; by the end of the medieval epoch, the philosophical allegorism of the Renaissance had emerged.

THE DECLINE OF SYMBOLISM
IN THE FIFTEENTH CENTURY

People began to question symbology in an epoch when symbolism was no longer commonly listened to or understood. The first signs of this decline appeared in the fifteenth century, a time of transition between two worlds, marking the frontier between the bygone Middle Ages and the future Renaissance.

Johan Huizinga, in his fundamental work *The Waning of the Middle Ages,* shows that one of the main causes of this change was the decline of symbolism itself, which, by the fifteenth century, had degenerated into superficial and sterile games provoked by the abuse of allegories. Huizinga writes:

> Having attributed a real existence to an idea, the mind wants to see this idea alive, and can only effect this by personifying it. In this way allegory is born. It is not the same thing as symbolism. Symbolism expresses a mysterious connection between two ideas; allegory gives a visible form to the conception of such a connection. Symbolism is a very profound function of the mind; allegory is a superficial one. It aids symbolic thought to express itself, but endangers it at the same time by substituting a figure for a living idea. The force of the symbol is easily lost in the allegory.[4]

The symbolic interpretation of the world by medieval thought included nature, history, the human condition, and divinity. The unity it assumed was that of an architectonic order and a harmonic hierarchy of the functions shared between the powers of heaven and earth, which allowed for the conception of infinite analogical correspondences between beings and things.

From the perspective of scholastic realism—the "reality of ideas," according to a theology formed in the school of Neoplatonism—and despite the countercurrent of nominalism and the doctrine of the *universalia post rem,* which had neither the importance nor the influence of Neoplatonism, each thing acquired its essence and preexistence from ideas or from the *universalia ante rem.* According to this view, symbolic assimilation, founded upon the common properties shared by things and ideas, allowed for the discovery of the essence hidden behind appearances, a real reason for being between two terms—an analogical signification revealing the glory of the divine Word.

Each thing, by its various characteristics, could thus designate many ideas, just as a single one of its characteristics was itself rich in multiple symbolic meanings. Everything announced a transcending presence manifested in the most humble of earthly productions: A nut bore witness to the mystery of Christ; the edible kernel, to the divinity of the Word; its fleshy green shell, to Christ's humanity; the bark of the tree, to the cross. Every precious stone shone in the world of ideas as well as with its own splendor in the mineral and terrestrial world. Around each symbol, other symbols were grouped like filings attracted by a magnet; at the least movement of the mind, they could arrange themselves into ever-changing symmetrical figures, as in a kaleidoscope. At the limit of analogical assimilation, the universal symbolic process arrived at the mystery of the identity of the Eucharist itself. The host was really and truly Christ, and the priest absorbing it became the sepulchre of the Lord. Each symbol thus took part in the universal life of mystic unity.

One of the main consequences of this medieval vision of the world was the transfiguration of earthly occupations and, in particular, of all the trades. St. Bonaventure called the artisan's work the eternal incarnation of the Word and the covenant between God and the soul.[5] Individual suffering and profane love assumed symbolic significance: As shadows of God's suffering and love, they broke away from the dark sphere of the individual and rose up to the light of the universal. In fact, all medieval symbolism had meaning only via the relationship between the human and the divine, and this fundamental relationship could also become a principle of contradiction and decline, starting at the moment when anthropocentrism transferred symbolic thought to the moral and social realm in the degraded form of profane allegories stripped of spiritual meaning.

The usury of symbolism is evident enough in the political allegories of Chastellain and Molinet: The three states represent the qualities of the Virgin; the seven electors of the Empire signify the virtues; the five cities of Artois and Hainaut, which remained faithful to the house of Burgundy in 1477, are the five wise virgins.[6] It is also evident later on, in works such as Olivier de la Marche's *Parement et triumphe des Dames,* in which each piece of feminine clothing represents a virtue—an allegory also developed by Coquillart:[7] Shoes represent care and diligence, stockings perseverance, garters resolution, and so forth.

In order better to understand this degradation of symbolism in the fifteenth century, we should remember that the symbolic relationship is one not of cause and effect, but of a connection of meanings and mutual exchanges from the moment that the terms of the relationship have a common essential quality that we can connect to a general principle of classification. Medieval thought often conceived of relationships of origin as kinships of a genealogical type. The tree of the origin of justice and the laws, for example, symbolically classified all justice in the form of a tree with many branches.

The most obvious danger of such a method was its arbitrary schematism, which tended to replace experimentation—neglected in those days, along with deductive methods—with analogical relationships of procreation and ramification, principally inductive and intuitive. Knowing the models of beings and things was sufficient for medieval thought to determine their real nature—that is, the hierarchical place and degree of their functions and properties in the unity of the divine plan. All that we consider worthy of attention and interest in the symbolism of the Middle Ages—the transfiguration of the real that it performed to the point of producing an extraordinary spiritual surreality—should not conceal from us the fact that such a movement depended on a capacity for poetic and religious exaltation, rather than on a rational and systematic investigation, the necessity of which became apparent later under new economic and social conditions.

The medieval person, moreover, was characterized by a much freer religious individualism and search for personal salvation than is generally believed. The diversity of medieval civilization was one of the most singular—and in appearance most paradoxical—characteristics of an epoch marked by the unity of its symbolic thought. In fact, there is nothing contradictory in this. If the world is classified according to an analogical system of correspondences between the properties and qualities of beings and things and the ideas that are their real roots, we can always isolate some quality from this complex, and with it we can then establish a new symbolic relationship. When Foulques de Toulouse was faulted for giving alms to an Albigensian, he replied: "I gave not to the heretic, but to the pauper." And Margaret of Scotland, queen of France, after having kissed the lips of the poet Alain Chartier when she found him sleeping, justified her conduct thus: "I kissed not the man, but the priceless mouth from which so many great words and virtuous speeches have come forth."

It is commonly believed that the Middle Ages were marked by a rigorous moralism, especially in the domain of eroticism and sexuality. This is an error, as historians have pointed out with the support of numerous examples and documents. As Johan Huizinga writes, "[I]t is improbable that the restraint thus displayed in fifteenth-century art, in respect of erotic expression, was due to a sense of modesty, for in general an extreme license was tolerated."[8] In the most atrocious massacres and pillages, the victims were left with their shirts on, and feminine nudes were rarely depicted in art. On the other hand, when nobles entered cities, there were exhibitions of goddesses or nymphs without the least veil, and *tableaux vivants* on platforms, or sometimes in the water, for example, the "quite naked and disheveled" sirens "near the bridge over which Duke Philip had to pass, on his entry into Ghent in 1457."[9] The judgment of Paris was a favorite subject for these displays. This spectacle was offered to Louis XI when he entered Paris: "And there were also three very handsome girls, representing quite naked sirens, and one saw their beautiful turgid, separate, round and hard breasts, which was a very pleasant sight, and they recited little motets and bergerettes; and near them several deep-toned instruments were playing fine melodies."[10] These tableaux vivants also took place in the sixteenth century, upon the entrance of Charles V into Antwerp in 1521 and the entrance of William of Orange into Brussels in 1578. Moralism in this area came only after the Counter-Reformation of the seventeenth century.

Many aspects of fifteenth-century life thus suggest an evolution from allegory toward a bizarre mythological iconology, a strange mixture of pagan personifications, macabre themes, singular superstitions, and naive naturalism. There are many indications that the great plague epidemics, which at one point wiped out one third of Europe's population, left profound traces in the mentality of the epoch. Jean Gerson, the illustrious chancellor of the University of Paris and also one of the greatest mystics of his time, perceived the pathopsychological nature of this abundance of hollow allegories, superstitious images, and excessive and suspect ascetic practices mixed with sexual perversion. They arose, he said, from the malady of imagination and melancholy caused by diabolical inspirations: *hominum phantasione et melancholica imaginatione*.[11] Like barnacles attaching themselves to the keel of a ship, a coating of obscure and obstinate beliefs seemed to latch on to the sacred vessel of the church, weighing it down and degrading it. The Eucharist itself became a prophylactic tool; it was believed, for example, that a daily Mass could protect people from apoplexy and blindness until the next day, or even that people did not age while attending this holy service.[12]

At the end of medieval civilization, religious thought also seemed to be printed on minds in material forms contained in allegorical "plates," which from then on were easily reproducible and had no direct relation to their symbolic source. As we can observe in the phenomenon of saline saturation of a liquid medium, the essentially dynamic and fluid life of the High Middle Ages—so diverse and volatile in so many ways that all historians have been struck by its profound "nomadism"—seems to have become sedentary and to have suffered the effects of continually

increasing urban concentration. Perhaps Huizinga does not clearly iden-
tify the prebourgeois aspect of the fifteenth century, which, with its
social conflicts and the rise of its financiers and great European merchants, heralded what Ernst Bloch rightly called "the bourgeois philosophy of the Renaissance"[13]—that is to say, the birth of the modern era.

THE CULTURAL REVOLUTION
OF THE FIFTEENTH CENTURY

The true beginning of the return to antiquity was not in the sixteenth century, as is generally believed. Its origin was the capture of Constantinople
by the Turks in 1453 and the influence of Byzantine philosophers and
savants who, having fled their homeland, found refuge in Florence with
the Medicis. Completely safe under their lofty Italian protection, they
were able to introduce into the West not only the Greek language, but
also Neoplatonist doctrines and their mystical and magical practices. A
prime example is Marsilio Ficino (1433–99), the first Latin translator of
the Greek texts of Plato and Plotinus, whose works had previously been
translated only into Arabic; or Pico della Mirandola (1463–94), who
taught at the Platonic Academy in Florence, founded by the Medicis nine
centuries after the closing of the previous one by Emperor Justinian in
529. But too little has been said about two people who played a crucial
role in this cultural revolution: Georgius Gemistus, also known as Pletho,
and Cardinal Bessarion.

Gemistus, probably born around 1350 in Constantinople, appeared
in 1426 as among the closest advisers of Michael Paleologus. Bessarion
ensured that Pope Eugene IV was victorious over the fathers of the
schismatic Council of Constance[14] and thus contributed to the triumph of the Roman pontificate. Cardinal Bessarion became one of the
most powerful people in the church, twice coming close to occupying
the pontifical seat himself, and he protected Pletho just as Cosimo de
Medici had ensured Marsilio Ficino's safety.

Pletho was one of the representatives of the Greek church at the

Council of Florence in 1438. A fervent Platonist, he openly attacked George of Trebizond, the chief of the Aristotelian partisans, and went so far as to suspect him of wanting to replace Christianity with a Platonic religion. These rumors were not unfounded, judging by a singular letter written by Cardinal Bessarion to Pletho's son after the death of his father in which this high dignitary of the Roman church eulogized the deceased as having joined the gods of Olympus to celebrate with them "the mystical choir of Iacchos"—the song of the initiates to the Eleusinian mysteries, the day of Manifestation. Moreover, Georgius Gemistus Pletho was Marsilio Ficino's master. Because he himself was initiated at Adrianople by an eminent Jewish kabbalist who was accused of magic and condemned to the stake, Pletho was forced to flee that city and take refuge in Mizithra, the former Sparta.

All these personalities gravitated around the Medicis, who founded not only the Platonic Academy in Florence, but also the first bank in Europe. Under veils of secrecy, a considerable interest in trade with the East pitted against each other the great financier dynasties of Italy and Germany. Thus, the Reformation cannot be understood properly without taking into account the importance of conflicts between the Fuggers and the Medicis.

The cultural revolution of the Renaissance therefore truly began in the fifteenth century. The medieval economy responded to the heavy tread of corporations and to the easily predictable, seasonal, and limited needs of local markets. At the end of the Middle Ages, space-time changed as a result of new geographical, intellectual, and historical discoveries. The "here below" of the fifteenth century became a new world, no longer a "here below" with no meaning except as a function of the "hereafter."

Religious thought then crystallized into images of an end of time, a *memento mori,* also corresponding to the appearance of a new form of artistic representation: woodcuts that associated the image with the predication, which now, for the first time, pervaded all classes of society just as television does in modern times. In a simple, direct, and easily accessible form, realism presented only the death of the most complete and gross aspects, imposing fear rather than offering consolation and hope. If we examine this dance of Macabre—the proper noun from which the adjective comes—we will notice that it has very little connection to the Christian faith. This fantastical, hallucinatory death is a theatrical character; the *danse macabre* was performed as well as painted and depicted, for example for the duke of Burgundy at his mansion in Bruges in 1449. From 1424 on, this spectacle covered the walls of the gallery of the Cemetery of the Innocents in Paris. Thousands of people went there, as if to a cinema, to look at the images and read the stanzas, each one of which ended with a proverb.

Did this simian, snickering death have some function of exorcism toward real death, whose presence was never more evident than in times of epidemics and massacres? Or did it express a veiled form of political and social satire with the sinister egalitarianism that it suggested? Or was it the expression of a new anthropocentrism, contemplating images of the death of humans rather than the Passion of God? We may hesitate between these various hypotheses, but it is at least certain that at the end of the Middle Ages, the image was marked with a naturalism and realism very different from the traditional principles of Gothic and especially Roman iconology.

Theater and scenic representation doubtless played an important role in this evolution. The new pedagogical methods of wood engraving and printing, beginning in the Renaissance and continuing into modern times, gave the art of images an importance that is the direct origin of our present-day, image-based civilization, with all the profound anthropocentric and narcissistic consequences that it implies. This function of the allegorical mirror was clearly defined in Calderón's *Autos sacramentales:*

> *The allegory is only*
> *A mirror, a mirror that translates*
> *That which is into that which is not,*

And all its elegance
Lies in the faithfulness
Of the image to the original,
In the observer of the former
Believing he is contemplating both at once.[15]

The great dramaturge, at the opening of his play *The Labyrinth of the World,* declared that this mirror must be shown to everyone through the use of allegory, "desiring that the people should know that there is no fable without mystery, if it is viewed allegorically in the light of that mystery."[16]

This pedagogical capacity for allegory is essentially collective and social. It therefore differs from the initiatory or religious symbol, which acquires meaning at the level only of each person's spiritual interpretation or of the closed community that constitutes the assembly of believers and the faithful. The way in which the iconological or theatrical process of allegory is open to the profane and incredulous, in fact, implies no relationship other than that of spectator and spectacle. From this, the possibility also arises of applying the processes of personification used by allegory to the objects as well as the subjects. The fetishism of merchandise and its contemporary heterosacramental theater of advertising are a testimony to this. To translate that which is simple economic exchange into that which is not—the complex communication of a new personal power or a magical and mythical prestige through the acquisition of the object sold—constitutes the entire drive behind modern advertising. Thus, the contemporary pseudo-Eucharist is a transubstantiation rigorously inverse from the old one, and hence is essentially parodic. Those who lack the means for buying bread and wine immediately take refuge in the communion of the faithful clients, and their only salvation lies in earning enough money to be worthy of participating anew in the unanimous life of the church of consumers. How can we not see that the concept of cash as money with legal value and the strange ceremonies of banker's rites signify a sacralization of our economy? Thus, allegory has entirely changed its orientation, but not its processes. In this sense, our image civilization is founded no longer on symbolic anaphora, but on a continuous metaphor through which bourgeois philosophy accomplishes the feat of embodying in everyday life the permanent passage from the proper meaning to the represented meaning.

ALLEGORY AND ARCHAEOLOGY

One of the most important eighteenth-century works in the history of symbology is *Versuch einer Allegorie,*[17] by the German archaeologist Johann Joachim Winckelmann (1717–68). Winckelmann was the first to attempt a scientific interpretation of the monuments of antiquity. As librarian to the count of Bunau, near Dresden, then curator of Cardinal Albani's collection of antiquities, he studied the recently discovered ruins at Naples and Pompei in 1758 before being made prefect of Roman antiquities and, somewhat later, librarian of the Vatican. Upon his return from a voyage to Germany, he was assassinated in Trieste by a certain Archangeli, whose cupidity had been aroused by the sight of the gold medals his victim possessed.

Winckelmann published various erudite works, principally *Sendschreiben von den Herculanischen Entdeckungen* (1762), *Geschichte der Kunst des Alterthums* (1764), and *Monumenti antichi inediti* (1767). His interpretations had an influence on the Kantian conceptions of symbolism and, by this intermediary, on an important sector of nineteenth-century German philosophy.

Winckelmann likened allegory not only to iconology, but also to ideography: "The allegory that the Greeks said was invented by the Egyptians was more in favor among these people than in other nations; it was their sacred language, in which intelligible signs, that is to say sensible images of things, appeared to have been most ancient."[18] For this reason, Winckelmann connected the Chinese language to the Egyptian, considering it allegorical because he identified allegories with all images, whether abstract or concrete.

Winckelmann also referred to the works of the authors who had previously explored the principles and applications of the allegorical process, in particular the treatise *Emblematum libellus,* by the Milanese jurist Andrea Alciato; *Les Hiéroglyphes,* by the writer and philologist Valeriano Bolzani, a.k.a. Valerianus Pierus or Pierius, according to certain authors; and *Researches and Figures,* by Cesare Ripa, revived by Jean-Baptiste Boudard and published as *Iconology or the Science of Images.* The first two of these treatises appeared in the sixteenth century and went through several editions in various languages until the seventeenth century. They are monuments of erudition characteristic of the lights and shadows of Renaissance philosophy, and they—especially the second one—do not deserve Winckelmann's unjust severity in judging them: "What is indicated by these authors," he writes, "is for the most part founded only upon feeble conjecture, and in the case of Valerianus, the good contained in his work is drowned in a jumble of useless reasonings, which serve only to make it voluminous."[19] The Lyon edition of *Les Hiéroglyphes* by Ian-Pierre Valerian, commonly named Pierius, newly given to the French by I. de Montlyard and published by Paul Frellon in 1615, was subtitled "Further Commentaries on the Sacred Letters and Figures of the Egyptians and Other Nations, a Work Reduced to Fifty-eight Books to Which Are Added Two Others by Caelius Curio, Concerning What Is Signified by Various Effigies and Portraits of the Gods and Men." This heavy in-folio volume totaled 807 pages, plus the index and many engravings. It has been plundered by numerous authors, ancient and modern—though most of these authors do not cite their sources; Cesare Ripa, who borrowed the remainder of his 1644 work from Alciato's *Emblematum,* added only a few of his own interpretations.

Jean-Baptiste Boudard's *Iconology* came long after the aforementioned works. It consisted of three volumes published in 1759 in French and Italian. Boudard was a sculptor employed in artistic service to the duke of Parma. Most of his images come from Ripa's *Iconology,* which was also reproduced in numerous editions "for the use of artists" without the author's name, bearing titles such as, for example, *Petit Trésor des Artistes et des Amateurs des Arts* (Little Treasure of Artists and Some Amateurs of Art). In publications of this kind, the engravings were slightly altered, and the captions were often different from those in the original. A separate study ought to be devoted to these sixteenth- and seventeenth-century allegorical distortions, for they played a definite role in the history of art and symbolism.

Here we cite only one example: Boudard represents the image of "fever" with the allegorical figure of a woman reclining upon a lion with vapors coming from its mouth. In his interpretation, Boudard explains the meaning of this relationship between fever and lion: It is "by reason of the melancholic nature of the lion." Winckelmann legitimately criticizes Boudard on this point, and proposes a pseudo-explanation probably drawn from Pierius's *Hiéroglyphes:* According to Winckelmann, Boudard should have known and noted that ancient naturalists believed lions to be susceptible to fever, especially quartan fever; this was why the lion was used in the representation of this illness.[20]

In fact, this allegory comes from meteorology and astronomy. In the month of August, the sun traverses the zodiacal sign of Leo. During the dog days, the atmosphere becomes heavy and stifling; vapors rise from the ground. The earth appears to have a fever, hence this representation of a reclining woman during the hottest part of the year, marked by the rising and setting of the sun in the ancient constellation of the Great Dog. These dog days were believed to have a disastrous influence. Hippocrates himself advised against taking medicine at this time of the year: *Sub Cane et ante Canem, difficiles sunt purgationes.* Those who are born at its rising, according to Firmicus Maternus, are predisposed to fevers and madness that can drive them to all kinds of excesses. It is significant to note that the simplest and most obvious cosmological interpretation appears not to have been understood by Boudard or by Winckelmann in the eighteenth century.

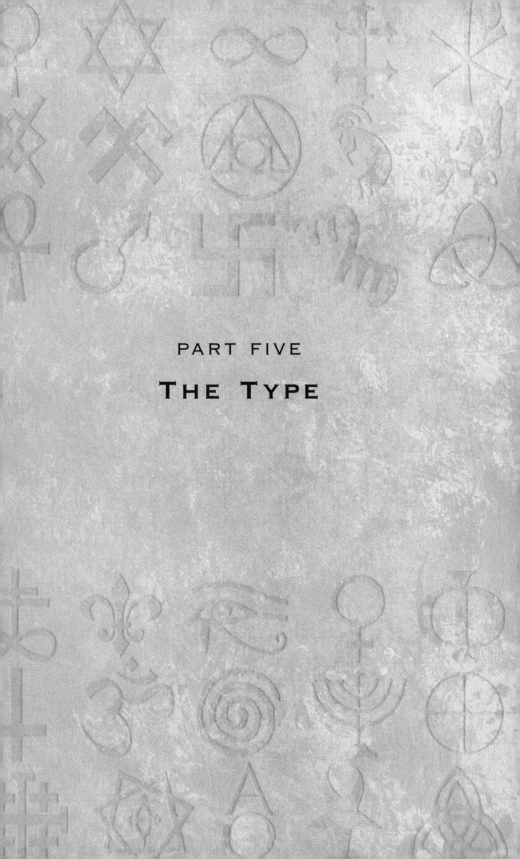

PART FIVE

The Type

10 The Typological Function of Symbolism

Earlier, connecting the archaic foundations of the logic of analogy to prehistoric experiences of hunting, trapping, animal mimicry, and nutrition, we endeavored to discover the concrete character of an essentially dynamic process based, on all infrahuman and human levels, on the principle of the assimilation of the living by the living and the action of similar upon similar.

This is a matter of a general thematicism of perception and action in their relationship to analogy—and it is not a specifically human prerogative: Raymond Ruyer tells us:

> The striking thematicism of mental and conscious perception and action characterizes every life and every individual. It characterizes primary organic consciousness as well as secondary mental consciousness. Organisms are not masses of molecules, but organic wholes that have a function, a theme of constitution and action, and mental consciousness simply applies to the perceived world the thematics inherent in the organism. . . . This is why, seen from outside and at a distance, humanity, with its works, appears to continue the order of organic productions. Human activity takes place

in works that have typical forms, just as biological activity takes place in organic forms. Works of art, monuments, machines, their codes, religions, and languages, although they are also something entirely different, are, from a certain point of view, as Cournot has shown, natural organic productions. . . . This is because man is not the only conscious being who makes efforts according to themes "sensed," although he is the only one that has found the means for "signifying" the meaning.[1]

Animals, moreover, are capable of intelligent actions. Norway rats, in certain experiments, learned their way around a labyrinth more quickly than human students. Many animals are architects and use tools. In *Animal Architecture,* Karl von Frisch[2] shows that real technology is applied by certain species to create works of art. Australian turkeys (*megapodes*), who lay enormous eggs up to a quarter of their own weight and as many as thirty-five in one season, build artificial incubators for them. These consist of sand used as a thermal insulator and a hole about ten feet in diameter and about five feet in depth in which there is a compost of leaves and plants. Here myriad bacteria produce considerable heat, regulated to a constant temperature of 33°C due to the installation of ventilation holes and, in summer, layers of sand whose thickness the bird controls depending on exterior conditions. Frank Lloyd Wright, one of America's greatest architects, often stated that humans could profit from studying the forms and constructions built by animals, whose main tools are their own bodies.

All these facts observed in the infrahuman and human realms not only present the problem of passage from unconscious thematicism to conscious symbolism and of transition between themes associated with motor schemes or stimuli signals and much more complex mythical and symbolic models; they also incite us to question the very origin of these models and themes.

SIGNALIZATION AND SIGNIFICATION

Raymond Ruyer proposed a theory of symbolic function and its origin that is worth repeating here, because it appears more correct than that of Ernst Cassirer,[3] according to whom, from a quasi-Kantian perspective, symbolizing categories constitute the world of culture—while in Kant's system, the categories of sensibility and understanding constitute the world of phenomena.

Remembering Cassirer's principle according to which the specific unity of human works and various sectors of culture is to be found in the symbolic function and in the handling of signs and symbols that are very different from the animal's stimuli signals, Ruyer explains that this passage is crossed when the sign "is understood no longer as announcing or indicating a nearby or imminent object or situation, but as something that can be used in itself, to conceive the object, even in the absence of this object."[4]

The same word, for example *water,* can serve two different uses and can be situated on distinct levels. It designates the presence of the object that it indicates—"Here is water"—or else it establishes the concept or the idea, as an instrument of thought but not of immediate action, in the absence of the object and without a realizing intention regarding it. Ruyer notes:

Therefore, it is not language in the most general sense of the word, but rather language as a symbolic system, which, permitting noncurrent conceptions and thoughts, is at once the instrument and indicator of the human level. . . . Animals, with or without words, are able to express themselves by gestures, mimicry, vocalization, by speaking to someone. Humanity began when, through an apparently insignificant functional change, through a mental mutation that implied not the least organic mutation or any new miraculous animation, a prehistoric human used a signal as a sign, spoke to someone or even to himself about someone or something, using symbolic utterances or gestures.[5]

Ruyer observes that the intent to communicate is not enough to explain symbolic behavior. In fact, communication is established spontaneously by sign-signals, whose immediate utilitarian side hinders rather than helps the change from function into signal and symbol: "A ceasing of immediate action and communication," he emphasizes, "is, on the contrary, the indispensable condition of mental experience and symbolic behavior. An animal communicates current needs spontaneously. The first conceptions of the animal-human must have been produced outside of, or even in opposition to, the pantomimes of communication."[6]

This is an important observation. Edward Sapir noted that the first vocalizations of infants have a definite "autistic" character. Attempts to learn language by chimpanzees, wild children, and people born deaf, mute, and blind have always failed when their educators insisted on sticking to the level of utilitarian communication. But they appear to have succeeded when the subjects, often by chance, found themselves in a state of detachment and conceived, in an aesthetic or magical sense, the expressive value specific to certain objects.

In her case study of the deaf and blind Helen Keller, Susanne Langer shows that when Keller, after three weeks of practice, had learned to interpret tactile signs traced on the palm of her hand and thus knew twenty-one words, these were at first only signals for her, because she did not yet have the notion of everything having a name. For example, she confused the word-signal *mug* with the word-signal *water,* both associated with the action of drinking—just as a conditioned dog might confuse the sound of the bell with Pavlov's white coat. The mystery of language was revealed to Helen Keller when her instructor, taking her hand and placing it beneath a stream of fresh water, indicated on her other hand, with tactile signs, the word *water:* "I knew then that 'w-a-t-e-r' meant the wonderful cool something that was flowing over my hand." Thus, this word was no longer simply a signal by which water was expected, requested, or obtained. It was also "the name of this substance, with which one can mention it, evoke it, conceive it, celebrate it."[7]

The discovery of the poetic and symbolic meaning of the word is an

experience absolutely distinct from the utilitarian and pragmatic interpretation of its signalization. A chimpanzee can learn to pronounce the
word *papa* when it sees its adoptive father, as in Kellogg's experiments
with Gua, or the word *banana,* as Yerkes accomplished with Chun.
But this is only specific training, an application of the word-signal to
a behavior. The animal understands no better than Helen Keller did
before her sudden enlightenment that everything has a name and that
every name can evoke an absent object, its repetition making the images
of memories and their analogical relationships newly present in the
inner experience. Moreover, animals, although aware of the expressiveness of visual forms, are not as clearly aware as infants of the expressiveness of vocal forms. Lacking spontaneous vocalizations, they are not
able to develop easily repeatable vocalizations, some of which could be
striking in their expressiveness or could facilitate a mental connection
corresponding to the visual forms of an object or a situation. There is
more than one difference in the degree of evolution between signalization and signification. Between animal and human, an interval remains
that is not yet explained and perhaps inexplicable, an abyss that is called
consciousness. This—consciousness—is the cause and the condition of
the symbolic function of language. The mutual relations, however, are
cybernetic in nature and involve retroactive effects, like those of the
hand and the brain.

INTERVAL, CONSCIOUSNESS, AND TIME

The capacity to delay action, the possibility of distancing the sign-sym-
bol from the sign-signal, and the perception of multiple levels of signification of things and beings are specifically human characteristics. From
this perspective, Heidegger saw our condition profoundly, conceiving of
humans as "inhabitants of Time." Essentially, with the interval indispensable to every distinction between the present and nonpresent, the
perceived and the conceived, there appear simultaneously the consciousness, the subjective-objective discontinuum, and time. That which char-

acterizes humans as human is therefore also what separates us from a total integration of action into the eternal present, from an immediate and spontaneous existential experience that is also that of the animal and the very young infant. This interval can be perceived as a fall into time and, from this point of view, as a sin that is truly "original" because its consequence is that we are able to conceive of our own death as a predictable and certain event. To live in time or to know that we must die sooner or later is an original condition of our state of being.

Here, another experience intervenes that is also inaccessible to the animal: the signification of an absent object, the experience of the word-symbol in contrast to the signalization of the present object. Thus we can see what prodigious architecture human language constructs and sets in opposition to time and death, even though its foundations are rooted in these things. The logosphere, for humans, has become a new living means that transcends duration and nature and their ephemeral limits. By naming beings and things, humans are born into another life, that of their meaning, their symbolic function. For this reason, the symbolizing animal that we humans are is nourished by the products of this new, living medium, the logosphere, just as the animal is nourished by the products of the biosphere. A society without symbols therefore cannot avoid falling to the level of infrahuman societies, when only signals and stimuli-signals affect and regulate it.

Conversely, if the process of assimilation of the living by the living rises by successive levels from the lowest degrees of nutrition to the highest, we may conceive that these levels are not limited to human realities, and that the symbolic function is also a means of relation between the human and the suprahuman.

Under these conditions, how can suprahuman states of being not be linked to human states by symbols, when we observe that humans are obviously linked to the whole infrahuman part of our condition by other signs and by stimuli-signals? This, at least, is what all initiatory and religious traditions claim regarding the suprahuman and divine institution of their symbols, myths, and rites. There is certainly good reason to doubt it, but unanimity on this crucial point cannot be contested.

Moreover, what can such a hypothesis mean if not that spiritual realities exist in forms as diverse as material, psychical, and intellectual realities? Constituting an enigma in itself is the fact that a single act of charity can take place even once in a physical universe and a nature that seem to ignore it totally. Where does it come from? What is its true origin? Charity is neither material nor natural, because if it were either, we would notice its existence in observed phenomena. If it is of social origin, it is not manifested in animal societies, coming into being only on the level of human societies. From this perspective, we arrive at the paradoxical claim that humans, by their own genius, have invented something that exists nowhere outside of them in all the immensity of the cosmos. So where did we find the model for it? If the model is not outside us, it is within us, in our own heart. But we must now admit that this heart is different from all the others in the cosmos, or that if it has not always been different, it has become different. We therefore find ourselves facing two unavoidable conclusions: Either nature evolves toward the supernatural or the supernatural exists in nature—or else the universe contains a charity of which it is ignorant or the charity is not contained in the universe.

By contrast with this illusory reasoning, the position of ancient traditions is marked by simple good sense. Because we are incapable of creating something out of nothing and because spiritual life exists in the human condition but not in earthly nature, which gives no example of it, or in the universe as we observe it, or in the conditions of our animal life, therefore its models must have been taught to human societies by suprahuman instructors or by true suprahuman inspiration or revelation. Otherwise, humans would be absolutely foreign to universal reality, an entirely incomprehensible mystery. Thus we can see that the affirmation of the existence of spiritual powers does not necessarily situate them outside the cosmos, as is too often claimed.

Well before modern evolutionist theories, the brilliant Ibn Khaldun perceived the general ascension of the cosmos and the existence of various levels of relations between living beings and universal life: "Let us contemplate the universe of creation!"[8] writes Khaldun. He begins with the mineral kingdom and rises progressively, in an admirable manner, to the vegetable and then the animal. The last mineral "plane" (*ufuq*)[9] is linked to the first vegetable plane: herbs and plants without seeds.[10] The last vegetable plane—palms and vines—is linked to the first animal plane, that of slugs and shellfish, which have no sense other than touch. The word *relation* (*ittisâl*) signifies that the last plane of each kingdom is poised to become the first plane of the subsequent kingdom.

> The animal kingdom (*âlam al-hayawân*) then develops, its species increase, and in the gradual process of Creation (*tadarruj at-takwîn*), it ends with man, gifted with thought and reflection. The human level is attained starting with apes (*girada*), where we find sagacity (*kays*) and perception (*idrâk*), but which have not yet arrived at the stage of reflection (*rawiyya*) and thought. From this point of view, the first human level comes after the world of the apes: our observation stops there.[11]

These conceptions of Ibn Khaldun suffice to show that traditional philosophy is not necessarily infantile or naive, as is claimed by its scientist adversaries who have never bothered to read the texts of the ancient authors whom they judge without knowing them. Furthermore, this question remains: May a number of theories that are considered modern and revolutionary have been inspired, in many cases, by ancient works that were not cited by their plagiarists? I know several examples of this, even in the realm of physical and mathematical theory. Contrary to appearances, the discovery of a truly new idea is as rare as the discovery of an unexplored continent.

Unlike Darwin, Ibn Khaldun never ceased to reason when he could no longer observe facts, and this, whether or not rationalists like it, is the legitimate usage of reason. He writes:

Now in these different worlds we find different influences. The sensible world is influenced by the movements of spheres and elements. In the universe of Creation, there are influences of movements of growth and perception. All this shows that there is something that exercises an influence and is distinct from bodies. It is something spiritual (*rûhâni*) in connection to creatures, because the various worlds are in relation to their existence. This spiritual element is the soul (*nafs*), which perceives and moves. Above the soul, there must exist something else that is in relation to it, which gives it the power of perception and movement, and whose essence is pure perception and absolute understanding (*ta'aqqul*): This is the world of angels. Thus the soul must be ready to divest itself of humanity (*bashariyya*) for angelicism (*malakiyya*) in order suddenly to become part of the angelic species. This is what takes place when the spiritual essence of the soul has truly attained perfection.

The soul is in connection with the neighboring level, like all other planes of existing things, both upward and downward. Downward, it is linked to the body: that which procures its sensory perceptions, preparing it for effective comprehension. Upward, it is linked to the level of the angels. This is where it acquires scientific and supernatural perceptions: The consciousness of events that take place exists in the atemporal intellects of the angels. All this is a result of the order of the universe, whose essences and powers must depend on one another. . . . The possibilities of sensory perception are progressive, up to the most elevated: rational thought or power (*nâtiqa*).[12]

If we study this text closely, it becomes evident enough that Ibn Khaldun's evolutionism corresponds to a conception of order, and that it can be justified scientifically by a general theory of positive or negative entropy. Humans and animals feed on negative entropy—order—in order to compensate for their positive entropy (disorder) that provokes the emergence of every system of events in a given spatiotemporal sector. Order, in fact, is nutritive, not just energy and atoms—because one calorie has the same value as another, and an atom of iron ingested is, in itself, nothing more than an atom of iron from the exterior environment. Biological order is the true substratum for the nourishment of the living, because it provides order built on order and not order built on disorder, as in the statistical mechanism of physical order.[13]

These phenomena exist on the level of the body, but also in the level of the soul and psyche. The order on which the soul feeds also provides order built on order, but in two ways and under two distinct aspects: in its passive relations with the body and its history—according to past impressions—and in its active relations with the spirit and its creative activity—according to its future models. Thus the symbolic function is exercised following a double polarity, unconscious on the one hand, supraconscious on the other, the former determined and realized, the latter in the course of determination and realization.

IMPRESSION AND MODEL

In the animal kingdom, images and objects appearing and perceived early on seem to imprint themselves on certain young vertebrates, especially nidifugous and altricial birds. Around 1873, Spalding observed that chicks were just as likely to seek out the company of a duck or a human as that of a hen. In the late nineteenth century, Whitman noted that wild turtledoves hatched by domestic turtledoves preferred, as adults, to mate with other domestic doves rather than with their own species. In 1935, Lorenz proposed a general theory of these phenomena of formation of relationships of filial attachment or sexual orientation, which, far from being innate, are acquired in the course of the animal's individual history. Lorenz chose the term *imprinting* (*Prägung*) for this "acquisition of an object orienting instinctive social reactions."

This is distinguished from other forms of learning by many characteristics. Imprinting can take place only during a brief, critical period of an animal's life and in a specific physiological state of the young animal's development. After this period has passed, everything functions as if there were an innate knowledge, irreversible and completely rigid. This imprinting is solidified before behavioral—and especially sexual—reactions are established. The motor scheme of imprinting corresponds not to a recognition of the particular characteristics of the imprinting object, but to the general characteristics of the category to which the object belongs.

This last point seems the most important in its connection to the inductive function of analogy. Speeman had already observed that if we remove tissue from the ventral region of a triton embryo at an early stage in cell division and graft this tissue onto the region of the neural gutter, a piece of spinal marrow grows, and vice versa, by a sort of analogical agreement with the substrate. But after the critical moment has passed, the characteristics of the place of origin cease to be interchangeable.

We should also note that a substituted artificial model allows the phenomenon of imprinting to be achieved just as firmly as a natural imprinting subject. Between thirteen and sixteen hours after hatching, a young duckling, in about ten minutes, can be analogically induced to form an attachment to a stuffed toy that moves and makes sounds when the toy is enclosed with it in a circular cage. The irreversibility of the imprinting does not seem as clearly established as Lorenz assumes, but it is no less certain that the initial analogical induction always brings about a phase of regression and return to juvenile behaviors in other circumstances similar to those of the first imprinting. Adult subjects who are imprinted and then raised socially are as much disrupted by the apparition of the initial model as young subjects are; their sexual behavior proves it. There is no doubt that imprinting has profound effects, and that there is an experiential period set aside for its artificial or natural realization.

Analogous attachment to the imprinting object is very extensive in terms of the similitude of the relations that ultimately determine the choice and sexual pursuit of a partner. In 1966, P. P. G. Bateson showed that a chick raised in isolation would even become attached to the outline of the walls of its own cage, and might later pursue an object of similar appearance. In 1976, Jean-Marie Vidal observed in a remarkable article that "isolated roosters try to mate with their food dish or trough, which they sometimes prefer to a partner of their own species. Moreover, most roosters thus raised direct their aggressive and sexual behavior toward certain parts of their own bodies."[14]

This observation may strike us as highly significant, because it allows us to assume that the rooster, "using specific stimulations emanating from its own body," can acquire "certain information that it integrates into the process of identification of the object of its sexual reactions."[15] Jean-Marie Vidal adds that these roosters orient their sexual behavior toward a partner resembling them, even if it is a male, and that in such cases, their attempts at mating are oriented in an inverse position.

Lorenz emphasized another equally significant point, namely that imprinting corresponds not to the acquisition of a stimulus-response association, but to the acquisition of a versatile object, bringing about multiple responses, in particular a repertoire of social behavior. Attachment to the mother is not only nutritive, but it is also territorial, both in young birds and in primates.

We should at least remember that these complex experiments are still in the course of interpretation, and that the distress of the young creature, animal or human, becomes all the more intense when there is no object for imprinting or contact or when the object is prematurely lost. Spitz observed a high mortality rate among hospitalized infants who were deprived of objects of attachment. This is also the case for young chicks raised in isolation, despite the degree of material comfort of their cages and the satisfaction of their needs for warmth, food, and drink. Analogical attachment to territory and to certain zones of a biotope probably arises from the same affective factors as original imprinting. Therefore, anything that damages the topographic, familial, and social environment has an unimaginable effect of inner distress upon living beings in a state of growth, and its consequences run the risk of being irreversible.

11

THE DIVINATION AND
SYMBOLIC INTERPRETATION
OF THE COSMOS

ORACULAR AND DIVINATORY
HERMENEUTICS

All initiatory and religious traditions have admitted the necessity for interpreting the language of the gods, either in archaic, divinatory, and oracular forms or in the complex expressions of teachings transmitted by sacred texts. The priestly caste as a whole constitutes an organ of communication between humans and gods, and was therefore necessarily invested with power and given the task of collecting, preserving, and explaining the instructions, warnings, advice, visions, prophecies, and signs received by diviners and prophets. In "traditional" civilizations, the stratification of the priestly body historically reflected the distinction and specialization of religious activities. In an era before this distribution of functions, however, all priests had access to the various degrees and, under certain conditions, to the divinatory techniques that were taught—along with the calendars, medicine, and the writing and reading of hieroglyphs—to all those who dedicated themselves to the practice of worship.

This is the prehistoric legacy of the hunting economy. It can be observed as clearly in archaic divinatory rituals from Mesopotamian *extispicy* to that of the Aztecs of the sixteenth century, whose ancestors were also hunters. Anyone who has read Sahagún's classic descriptions in his famous "History of New Spain" (the *Codex Florentinus*) cannot help but be struck by the significance of prophecies and omens in the everyday existence of individuals, including the king.

In the decades leading up to Cortés's invasion in 1519, the king of Texcoco, Nezahualpilli (d. 1516), knew of a prophecy given by his divine priests announcing the imminent arrival of strangers who would take possession of the Valley of Mexico. In 1507, at the ceremony that marked the beginning of a new cycle with the ritual lighting of a new fire, disturbing natural prodigies and sinister omens were observed, as related by Sahagún. Around midnight, every night for a year, a strange tongue of fire could be seen rising in the east. The temple of the god Huitzilopochtli was devastated by fire; lightning without thunder destroyed the sanctuary of the god Xiuhtecutli. Immense waves lapped the shores of Lake Texcoco, and water reached the doors of Mexico City. A sister of Montezuma, believed dead and buried for four days, came back to life and was taken back to the palace and told the terrified king that, while dead, she had seen foreigners who were coming to destroy the empire.

Monsters appeared. They were brought to the king, but disappeared when he came to look at them. Bird catchers brought in a volatile gray gull that looked like a crane. On its head was a circular mirror pierced with a hole, resembling the mirrors used by diviners, and in it could be seen the sky and stars on an obsidian background as black as the lunar landscapes we have seen on television. When Montezuma examined the mysterious image brought by the bird, he saw a troop of armed men advancing, riding on stags. The priests were summoned to explain the meaning of this prophecy; they just arrived when the prophetic bird took flight.

The interpretation came forcefully to Montezuma: Quetzalcoatl, the "feathered serpent," had come as prophesied, during the One-Reed year, and reconquered the territory and city from which he had been expelled by the warrior god Tezcatlipoca. According to the Aztec calendar, because the last One-Reed year had been 1467, the next must necessarily be fifty-two years later, in 1519. Astrologers conjectured that this would be the Nine-Five day, corresponding to April 22, 1519. This was exactly the date on which Cortés's ship set sail for present-day Veracruz.[1]

MESOPOTAMIAN DIVINATORY HERMENEUTICS

Divination was of the highest importance in Babylonian culture. *Haruspicy*—the examination of the entrails of a sacrificed animal, particularly the liver but also the lungs and spinal column—is the most ancient and most constant of all divinatory practices. It appears to have preceded astrology, and it probably derives from magical rites in prehistoric societies dominated by the hunting economy.

The extraordinary complexity of the divinatory techniques of haruspicy is generally unknown. Jean Nougayrol[2] showed that Babylonian haruspicy did not ignore a single mark or characteristic of the parts constituting the sacrificed animal. The technical vocabulary of divination of a functional type, comparable to our cerebral toponymy, included six thousand various signs that had to be distinguished. Because the general vocabulary was too limited to note them, specialized language was the material of unwieldy clay books in which were engraved the codes necessary for interpretation. Under these conditions, a hypothesis seems justified: The emergence of writing signs was a simplification derived from archaic divinatory signs.

On this subject, we can note here the indications given by Jean Nougayrol himself.[3] Because the examination was methodical, the divinatory signs were doubly versatile, both in terms of some of their particular modalities and in their general goal. As for particular modalities, to determine their values, those who interpreted had to apply to them a grid of categories: presence, state, position, placement, number, size, shape, color, association, and so forth. The shape was often summarized by a reference, silhouette, or sketch. As for goal, the interpreter had to know the general goal of the consultation; the consultant; the nature of the action envisaged; whether this was a matter of a healthy man or an ill one; a friend or an enemy; what the social situation was; and so forth.

Haruspices used two methods: either pure observation without a preconceived idea, taking into account only any striking or dominant anomalies and interpreting them qualitatively; or consultation, preceded by many rites and a carefully composed question. Noted were all marks on the liver and other viscera deserving attention. With the first method, one principal sign was observed; with the second, between ten and twenty. In order to read the answer—in order to interpret the whole—all these signs were stripped of their qualitative value, retaining only their negative or positive, unfavorable or favorable value. Their sum, which was in a way algebraic, corresponded to the question posed. Great collections of prophecies were first consulted, for after this quantitative evaluation, the qualitative meaning of each sign observed had to be found, comparing it to those preserved in traditional codes.

Not all the rules of interpretation are known. Yet we do know some of them from later commentaries, and it is believed that these were applied from the beginning. For example, the right was the side of the consulter; the left, that of his enemy. Consequently, a favorable sign on the right was good for the consulter, but on the left, it was good for the enemy (unfavorable for the consulter). Each area presented its own difficulties of right-left distribution. Another rule was that of number: Two similar signs confirmed the meaning of one sign, but three nullified it. Certain principles were obvious: That which harmed or diminished was evil, that which increased or strengthened was good. Others were highly complex, especially the rules for combinations of elementary signs producing signs that were decisive, inversive, related, and so forth. Also, each sector of observation had its own particular value.

Nougayrol, like other archaeologists, noted the role of linguistic participation in the interpretations, especially the importance of wordplay, phonetic similitudes, and assonances. This is a very important point, because psychological observations show that these phenomena play a role in the subconscious. We may well wonder whether this shifting of images encouraged the emergence of paranormal faculties of prediction, considering that in dreams, time itself is profoundly perturbed in its usual successive unwinding, the "before" and "after" no longer being separated as clearly as in the waking state. What has happened is then dreamed or has been dreamed as what "happens" or may "happen." The subconscious sees no difference here in terms of what is essential: the realization of desire or fear.

These probable psychological aspects aside, Mesopotamian divination was no less founded upon processes of technological rationalization and on acquired experience. Historical prophecies were preserved with the utmost care, and they were sometimes used as models. The same sign from the past was believed to precede a like event in the future. Here, as we can see, the analogy extended even to the structure of time and its language. When the signs did not correspond to the prophecy, the haruspex declared that they had been incorrectly read. Also, we must not forget that ambiguity of signs was normal in cuneiform writing. The best Assyriologists, Jean Nougayrol opportunely reminds us, cannot read isolated signs without having an imaginary or real context as a basis. Likewise, the hepatoscopic divinatory sign must be read in a different manner depending on its position, location, dimensions, associations—that is, according to its context. This is a much more general rule than that of the techniques of Babylonian haruspicy. It extends not only to all divinatory arts, but also to all sacred hermeneutics. Only a god is capable of reading and writing the signs directly, without the least physical or logical obstacle, as confirmed by this Babylonian prayer to the sun god, the archetypal master of divinatory mystery:

> *You read the tablet beneath its envelope (without*
> *opening it)*
> *And (without opening it) you write the signs*
> *In the belly of the Sheep.*

ANCIENT ENIGMAS AND ORACLES

Littré calls the *enigma* a "definition of things in obscure terms, but which, all together, designate their object exclusively, and are given for divining," and says the word comes from the Greek *ainigma*—from *ainissestai,* "to speak in enigmas," from *ainos,* "discourse, words." The English word comes directly from medieval Aristotelian philosophical vocabulary; in fact, for Aristotle, *ta enigmena* meant "things said or indicated in veiled words."

The origin of the Greek word itself can be found in *ainos,* "speech, discourse," but also "sentence, adage," and in a "comparison" with the verb *mainomai* or its derivative *mainas,* in the form *eikemainas,* "comparable to that which is said by the Maenad," or by the Bacchante in the Dionysian mysteries. In the enigma, the prophet and sibyl, "possessed by the gods," announced the mystery. This is why the first character of the enigma was sacred. Only by an extension of this primitive meaning, everything that was said was later stated analogously in profane language, which required the deciphering of the actual object of discourse or speech. Because this object was essential, the term *enigma* was masculine before it became feminine. Rabelais, Montaigne, and Massillon all wrote of *un énigme.*

The enigma can also be connected to the oracle in its traditional forms. The "wholly other" being the archetypal character of the sacred, an "all different" speech of its profound meaning is not a simple allegory or apologue or parable. It requires an interpretation no less sacred than its mysterious expression. This is why the priests alone were authorized to interpret the ancient oracles, and why, at the beginning of the oracle of Delphi, it was the priestess herself who bore the title Pythia, or Pythoness. This name was later given to other interpreters of oracles dedicated to Apollo: for example, the oracle of the Branchides at the temple of Didymeon in Ionia. Later, it was applied to the women who predicted the future, such as the famous Pythoness of Endor. But the usual name for a prophetess was a sibyl.

The first was the sibyl of Delphi. Diodorus Siculus called her Daphne, others called her Artemis. Chrysippus said that she lived before the Trojan War. The second was the Erythrean sibyl, who predicted to the Greeks that they would capture and burn the city of Priam. The third was called the Cimmerian or Italic sibyl, according to Moevius in his *Books of the War in Africa* and Piso in his *Annals.* The fourth was the sibyl of Cumae, called Amalthea, Herophilia, or Demophilia by historians, who sold the famous *Sibylline Books* to Tarquin the Elder. The fifth lived on the Isle of Samos; she was called Euriphilia by Eusebius and Bytho by Eratosthenes. The sixth, born in the town of Marpene in the Hellespont, was called the Hellespontic sibyl for this reason, and lived in the time of Solon. The seventh, a prophetess in Libya, was the Libyan sibyl. According to St. Justin, the eighth, the Chaldean or Persian sibyl, was the daughter of the historian Berossus. This detail is important archaeologically because it allows us to assume that the *Sibylline Books* handed down archaic Mesopotamian traditions. The ninth sibyl, living in Ancyra, was known as the Phrygian sibyl. Finally, the tenth, called the Albunean or Tibertine sibyl, delivered her oracles at Tibur or Tivoli, on the Teveron.

When the sibyl of Cumae brought Tarquin the Elder nine scrolls of predictions that she said concerned the future of Rome, the king refused to buy them, finding exorbitant the sum she requested. The sibyl then threw three of these documents into the fire. When Tarquin again refused, she burned three more, then offered to sell the last three to the monarch for the same price she had wanted for the complete collection. Struck by this strange behavior and perhaps frightened of the harmful magical consequences of refusing, Tarquin consented to pay for these partial revelations, valuable as they appeared to be, and had the three volumes placed in the capitol, hiring a separate group of dignitaries to guard them. This collection was destroyed in 84 BC when the capitol burned. The senate dispatched ambassadors to Greece and Asia to attempt to gather a new collection of the vestiges of the sibylline oracles. A thousand prophetic verses were thus collected, examined, and deposited in the temple of Jupiter. By a strange misfortune, the second collection, like the first, fell prey to flames, under Nero in AD 68. After this loss, it is believed that the compilation that has been handed down to us—dating, at the earliest, to the second century AD—has little in common with the original books.

DECIPHERING THE SIGNS OF THE WORLD

In his treatise entitled *De divination,* Cicero distinguished two broad areas of divinatory techniques: the divination known as intuitive or natural, and inductive, reasoned, or conjectural divination. The first consists of inspiration that may seize certain privileged people, seers, priestesses, and prophets; the second consists of the observation and interpretation of sacred signs indicated on earth or in heaven by the gods. In Greek civilization, the sibyls and oracles played a considerable role in relations among cities. In other cultures, for example in Etruria and in Roman civilization, reasoned or inductive divination was much more important than the first kind, just as it had been earlier, in Mesopotamia.

Etruscan divination is marked by the revealed[4] character of the primordial religious deposit, a collection of sacred books, fragments of which have been passed on by Greek and Latin authors. These *Libri etrusci* appear, according to Cicero (*De divinatione,* I, 72), to have been divided into three parts: "*quod Etruscorum declarant et haruspicini et fulgurales et rituales libri.*" The first part relates to the study of the entrails of victims, and as indicated earlier, its origin appears to be in Mesopotamian techniques. The second part covers the problems of interpretation of lightning storms, and mentions the rites necessary for their expiation. The third part presents the traditions relating to human destiny, to the afterlife, and to the prodigies—*ostenta,* sacred signs—that allowed for the deciphering of phenomena as the sacred signs of the language of the gods.

The techniques of Etruscan extispicy as a whole were not different from those of Babylonian divination. Yet *kauronoscopy,* the study of lightning, holds a great deal of interest for the science of symbols because it provides a significant example, in the words of Raymond Bloch, of "an entirely casuistic interpretation" of a precise and complex theology.[5]

According to Seneca (*Quaestiones Naturales,* II): "The science of lightning forms three parts, observation, interpretation, and conjuration." The Etruscan diviners appeared to the Romans as being capable not only of diverting lightning (*exorare*) but also of attracting it to earth (*elicere*). We can get an idea of the duration of their reputation if we consider that in AD 408, according to Zosimus, the haruspices still offered to protect Rome against Alaric by striking the invading army with lightning.

The Etruscans divided the sky into four parts determined by the cardinal points, and subdivided each part into four equal sectors. Regarding this, we may observe that this numerological symbolism proceeds in fours and sixteens instead of threes and twelves, as in the zodiacal division. This was a different system from our division of the circle; it is also found in the divination of the Chinese I Ching and in ancient divination using tarantulas. The Etruscan observer would face south, and the sections to the left would present favorable signs, because propitious deities resided on the side from which the light of day comes, the east. Prophecies indicated in the sections on the right, toward the west, the side of sunset and nighttime, were unfavorable. Referring to the indications given by Pliny, Cicero, Servius, and Festus, an observer would take into account the north-south axis and place eight favorable regions on the left and eight unfavorable ones on the right—the signs being better or worse depending on their proximity to the north, considered the archetypal seat of the superior deities. We may well wonder whether such a bipartition might evoke the luminous, terrestrial world of the living on the left and the dark, celestial world of the dead on the right. Georges Dumézil proposed this hypothesis concerning the divinatory liver "of pleasure,"[6] and it seems all the more justified given that we cannot separate the practices of interpretation of lightning from Etruscan beliefs relative to the existence of a land of the dead and a sacred topology of the hereafter.

Moreover, our knowledge of the theory of lightning is very incomplete and filled with later Greek speculations. The gods of the sixteen regions probably formed the most ancient system ever founded upon a symbolic numerology derived from the quaternary, as indicated earlier here. But in the later classification by Martianus Capella, from the fifth century AD, there are twelve great gods and seven deities whose symbolism is connected to the astrological system and numerology. This superposition of the ternary on the quaternary makes the interpretation of the original Etruscan pantheon very difficult.

Etruscan theology attributed to various divine people the power and right to make known to humans their intentions and their will through the intermediary of lightning, or rather the sacred language of lightning. According to Seneca: "Lightning does not cause explosion due to a collision of clouds, as we believe. Accordingly, there is a collision only in order that the explosion may take place. Because they are all connected to the deity, they believe not that the lightning bolts announce the future because they have been formed, but that they are formed because they must announce the future."[7]

Thus, according to the logic and reasoning of the Etruscans, the phenomena of nature are simple signs through which divine powers speak to humans in order to apprise them of their duties, revealing to them their future and the transcendent designs that correspond to their destiny. The archetypal science, from this perspective, is therefore the hermeneutics of the language of the gods, rather than divination itself, as is generally stated. This is why the science of symbols cannot avoid questioning the sacred divinatory practices, not as the correct or incorrect operations of prediction, but in their relationship to a vision of the world other than our own—another logic, the logic of analogy between natural and supernatural, visible and invisible, obvious and hidden. This is a fundamental hermeneutics of the various levels of qualitative order of a finished and closed system of the universe conceived as a cosmos inseparable from the Logos that expresses it.

It is curious to note, for example, that in the sacred language of lightning, the meaning of the prophecy sent by the gods varies according to the intent of the human observer. If the observer forms only one project, the lightning is conciliatory: *fulmen consiliarum*. If he has begun to achieve it, the lightning either authorizes him to accomplish it or prohibits him: *fulmen auctoritatis*. If he has no intention, the lightning invites him to action: *fulmen monitorium*. Thus it can warn him or announce to him a fateful event or an event that can be diverted or changed by the appropriate rites.

Moreover, the interpretation of the prophecy depends on the hour and on the color and material effect of the lightning bolt, as well as on the identification of the gods who have sent the lightning or, rather, who wield it. Jupiter alone supposedly had three distinct types of lightning, or *manubiae*. Despite this privilege, before launching a second manubia, more effective than the first, he had to consult the assembly of counselor gods (*dii consentes*), and before launching a third, he had to submit to the decision of the mysterious veiled and superior gods (*dii Involuti, superiores*).

Thus, the Etruscan haruspices were theologians, but they also had to practice magic, both to avoid lightning and to attract it for their ritual ceremonies. As an archetypal sacred element, lightning implied a contact that was dangerous for anything profane, whether individual or group. The haruspex alone was supposedly capable of protecting people from it by means of expiations that purified them of the material traces of the passage of the gods. Lambs were sacrificed, and lightning was buried, according to ritual, as Lucian relates in the *Pharsal:* "Arruns collect the fires dispersed by the lightning, and bury them, murmuring somber formulas, and dedicate the place to the god who protects them."[8]

The Romans had a "sacred fear" of these Etruscan beliefs and a horror of the lightning sign, the archetypal prophecy. The ground consecrated to the lightning became untouchable: Horace (*Ars Poetica,* 471–72) writes that those who disturb such a place will go mad. A man struck by lightning must be buried on the spot, and he cannot be given funereal honors.

ANALOGICAL RELATIONSHIPS BETWEEN
THE SECTORS OF THE COSMOS

In Chinese civilization, we find other proofs of the philosophical and religious importance of the symbolic language of divination. In the Chinese culture, the classic book viewed as the oldest and most profound is the I Ching, the Book of Changes. In the areas of cosmology and metaphysics, the Confucianist and Taoist traditions—as well as others—refer to it often. Its practical applications for predicting the future have been known at least since the ninth century BC and the Chou dynasty. It is not certain that this oracular usage, attributed to King Wen, ancestor of the Chou, corresponds to the first use of this collection of sixty-four symbols, known as the *koua,* which we call hexagrams because they are each made up of six lines, either joined or broken. The positions of Fo-hi and King Wen, who appeared as early as the second millennium BC, show that the developed system of sixty-four koua is based on a primitive or radical scheme of eight trigrams arranged like a wind rose.

Chinese philosophers often designated the universe with the term *yu-yeou,* "space-time." In fact, these two categories (space and time) are directly interdependent in Chinese thought. Each of the four seasons is thus one of the four directions: Spring corresponds to east, summer to south, autumn to west, and winter to north. The idea of the center brings in a fifth temporal analogy: the middle of summer, corresponding to the element earth, the color yellow, the number 5, and the heart. East corresponds to wood, green, 8, and the spleen; south, to fire, red, 7, and the lungs; west, to metal, white, 9, and the liver; and north, to water, black, 6, and the kidneys.

The five elements, *wou hing,* are not gross substances, but rather subtle energies, breath-powers, *k'i.* They are linked to the seasons and likewise progress cyclically. Their relationships to the five viscera come from the fact that the universe was considered a great complex organism: the heaven-earth (*t'ien-ti*), and between these two poles of a single living unity, man (*jen*) was an intermediary (*t'ien-ti-jen*). This did not regard any human, however, but had to do with the archetypal man, the king or soothsayer who "resembles heaven and earth and spreads order throughout nature."

The questions presented by the origin of the I Ching, the archetypal mysterious book, have not been resolved even by Chinese scholars, and in such an obscure area, we can propose only hypotheses that are more or less useful for research. But considering the essential importance of this traditional deposit in Chinese civilization and its obvious interest for human culture in general—because it gives evidence of a capacity for abstraction and an economy of thought that have held the attention of eminent modern mathematicians and scholars—we are justified in wondering whether there might be a universal code that reveals an entirely different logic from our own, a code whose general symbolism might be useful for explaining operations and structures.

On the specifically divinatory level, the ancient Chinese processes were mostly those of divination by the turtle shell (*pou*) and yarrow stalks (*che*). The former technique, prior to the Shang era, was preceded by the consultation of cracks in the burned bones of various animals, mainly the shoulder blades of oxen or deer, a technique known generally as *scapulimancy*, when the simple appearance of a shoulder blade or other flat bone is examined, or *pyroscapulimancy*, for the interpretation of signs that appear after heating or cooking.

This technique is known to have been used in northern Asia and in North America, on the Labrador peninsula, by the Naksapi, reindeer and caribou hunters of the northern tundra.[9] It has been clearly established that these divinatory rites were associated with dreamlike experiences that were valuable as prophecies for future hunts. Cooper writes that scapulimancy, like ritual bear funerals, represents a cultural trait unifying the arctic and subarctic regions of North America with the Eurasian taiga.[10] This divinatory process characterizes the northern civilization of European and Asiatic hunters. According to Eisenberger,[11] the process never emerged in the southern United States or in Central America or South America.

We noted earlier the importance of the discoveries at Drachenloch concerning the worship of bear skulls and bones in caverns by early humans. It is clear enough, under these conditions, that the roots of arctic, subarctic, and Eurasian scapulimancy can be found in the oldest magical and religious traditions that are archaeologically known. We may also observe that among the Naksapi, the bear's kneecap itself constitutes an oracle: It is placed upon a heated stone, and questions are asked of it. If it moves, the response is affirmative; if it stays put, the decision is negative—the hunters will not find any game.[12]

Chinese pyroscapulimantic divination is certainly connected to a prehistoric hunting economy. Although it was used during the Shang and Chou periods and even into the Han, fragments have been discovered that predate the Shang era and have no inscriptions. It appears that turtle shells were considered a more noble material than mammal bones starting with the accession of King P'an-Keng at Yiu, until the end of the dynasty (1384–1110 BC).

One very important detail: The diviners used only the ventral shell, which is flat and square—the symbol of the earth. The dorsal shell, round and concave and therefore the symbol of the sky, did not play a role in their ritual operations. The animal was captured at a specific time of the year, always autumn under the Chou. According to the ancient Chinese philosopher Kouan Tseu the animal was then consecrated by sprinkling it with the blood of four oxen. A long incision was made on the internal surface of the ventral shell, then across from this incision, a circular hole, not going all the way through, was created. After this, a glowing poker was applied to the hole, and cracks formed on the other side in the form of a T—hence the image of these cracks in the character *pou,* which designates this divinatory method.[13]

These rites suggest a new economic and sociocultural phenomenon in contrast with the previous state of the prehistoric civilization of hunting. This phenomenon is the appearance of the first clearing of forests by fire and the landscaping of the terrain. Marcel Granet notes that the god of the blazing winds, Shen-nong—the god of deforesting fires—was also the god of laborers. His bull's head evoked the earth. He was conquered by the first mythical sovereign, Huang-ti. The god Ch'e-Yeou, inventor of weapons and the great founder and blacksmith, eater of minerals, had a head of copper and a forehead of iron.[14] Behind these transparent myths, there shines through the existence of rival brotherhoods. Their hierarchical organization was established little by little through a centralization of power connected with a distribution of power into sectors whose virtues opposed each other and alternated in the form of winds. Each social group thus corresponded to an area of the universe, of nature, and to a magical function capable of setting the world of humans in its proper place, between earth and heaven. This balance is essentially of a harmonic order. This is why the eight winds together preside over music and dancing.

The turtle shell is penetrated by heat and speaks through the fire according to a certain order, thus expressing the effective divisions of the earth in relation to the way of heaven. Chouang-tseu gives a significant indication concerning this. He states that after seventy-two perforations, there will be no more free space on the shell. M. Kaltenmark observes that "this number evidently has a symbolic value, but in fact, the shells were used for a maximum of about sixty operations. These followed a certain order determined by the natural divisions of the shell, especially by the median line that divides it into a right part and a left part."[15]

Chouang-tseu's allusion may well be connected to the characteristic number of brotherhoods, according to the *Shan hai King* (LV, 357). There will be no more room left on earth, as on the turtle shell, when distribution among the brotherhoods is total. Then the tao of heaven will no longer circulate. Under these conditions, the eight winds will retreat, and thereafter the number 64 will yield the necessarily always incomplete perfection required by the true order of the universe in space-time (the effective hierarchy): 8×8. Now, spontaneously, heaven produces beings and things, earth nourishes them, the four seasons progress regularly, the five elements replace one another triumphantly in an endless cycle. The *yin* and *yang* alternate, and everything goes forth of its own accord starting from the primordial retreat. Hence the justification of Chouang-tseu's fundamental conclusions on the *wuwei,* the "inaction" that is, on the contrary, the true mode of efficacy of the highest immortals.

Thus the divinatory symbols, according to the *Hi-ts'eu,* evoke the ten thousand beings—that is to say, the totality of things. But they can do this only by reason of the voluntary retreat of the ten thousand and first. This is why, in the manipulation of the bundle of fifty yarrow stalks, the *Hi-ts'eu* (section 9) declares:

> The numbers of the Great Expansion [of heaven and earth] make 50; but 49 are active [only forty-nine of the fifty stalks are used; the one set aside represents supreme unity]. They are then divided into two [groups], which are the image [*siang*] of the Gods [the yin and yang, heaven and earth, continuous line and discontinuous line]. One stalk [stalk from the group on the right] is taken from the right and is placed [between the little finger and ring finger of the left hand] to represent the Three [powers: heaven, earth, man].

In the case of the Chinese traditions of the Yi-king, therefore, the divinatory language cannot be reduced to simple techniques of correct or incorrect prediction of the future. Because it is founded upon a symbolic vision of the universe, nature, and humans, it not only integrates all their visible and concrete analogical relations in space-time, but—more subtly than scientific language, which is founded upon the logic of identity—it also evokes and suggests the invisible, incomprehensible, yet supremely efficacious unity of the transcendent principle of their origin and their end.

12 MYTH AND RITE

The term *myth* embraces two principal meanings, which are generally opposed: fable or fiction and the exemplary model or primordial revelation of suprahuman origin, transmitted by sacred tradition. Earlier, we discovered that after Xenophanes and his critique of the mythology of Homer and Hesiod, the progressive desacralization of Greek culture emptied the mythos, little by little, of all its suprahuman content—initiatory, religious, or metaphysical. "Opposed as much to the *logos* as, later, to the *historia*," Mircea Eliade writes, *mythos* ended up denoting everything "that cannot really exist. Judeo-Christianity, for its part, rejected as lies and illusion all that was not justified or validated by one of the two Testaments."[1]

For some sixty years, the research and work of ethnologists, psychologists, sociologists, and historians of religion have allowed for a better understanding of the nature and function of myth in primitive societies: Bronislav Malinowski writes:

> Studied alive, myth . . . is not an explanation in satisfaction of a scientific interest, but a narrative resurrection of a primeval reality, told in satisfaction of deep religious wants, moral cravings, social submissions, assertions, even practical requirements. Myth fulfills in primi-

tive culture an indispensable function: it expresses, enhances, and codifies belief; it safeguards and enforces morality; it vouches for the efficiency of ritual and contains practical rules for the guidance of man. Myth is thus a vital ingredient of human civilization; it is not an idle tale, but a hard-worked active force; it is not an intellectual explanation or an artistic imagery, but a pragmatic charter of primitive faith and moral wisdom.[2]

THE MORAL VALUE OF
THE MYTH

We may well wonder about some points in Malinowski's classical conception of myth, especially myth's role in safeguarding and enforcing morality and satisfying social submissions. Here are just two examples: the Greek initiatory myth of the mysteries of the voyage of Iacchus to Eleusis and the Japanese myth of Ama-no-Uzume or Uzume, the celestial deity of the Sarume priestesses.

These two mythical traditions, specialists unanimously agree, are not derived from one another, but their ritual concordance is no less obvious, and shows the primordial value of the archaic magical-religious initiatory rite in relation to mythical expression, essentially variable throughout various cultural areas.

In other words, without a ritual context, without existential participation in its dynamic process, the myth becomes a fable, and the sacred impulse of intention becomes a cultural, social, moral, and profane impulse of narrative; the word of the gods is reduced to a human language, thus alienating humans from the universal solidarity between suprahuman and human forces required for the permanent re-creation of a symbolic meaning of the cosmos—that is to say, an experiential augmentation or superreality that transfigures the cosmos. From these two examples, we can see with what intensity there takes place the transfiguration of the simplest gestures to the level of a re-creation of the meaning of the universe and the degree to which, in ancient agrarian civilizations, the supernatural was profoundly engaged in processes of fertility and the fertilization of nature.

THE JAPANESE MYTH OF THE
UNVEILING OF UZUME

Written sources of Japanese myths go back no further than the seventh century AD. They were assimilated into ancient speeches dictated by an old woman, Hieda no Are, who knew them by heart, and were preserved in the *Kojiki,* written in 712 by order of Empress Gemmyō.[3] This tradition is often linked to the traditions of the Katari-be, a society of priest-bards who preserved the primordial deposit of sacred hymns and ancestral music. The mythic episode of the goddess Uzume is part of the sung legendary cycle of Amaterasu, the great goddess of the clans of the south, celestial ancestor of the imperial dynasty and suprahuman ruler of the sun and all of nature. She is credited with the invention of agriculture, landscaping, planting, and the fertilization of fields. She is also connected to the celestial liturgy that must be repeated on the terrestrial plane by the emperor in order that the new harvest may be favorable. Likewise, she rules the art of weaving[4] in heaven, and her priestesses imitate her, weaving sacred garments on earth.

If the reigning emperor is the descendant and heir of the great goddess Amaterasu, it should be observed that this goddess, before sending to Japan her grandson Ninigi, progenitor of the future dynasty, entrusted the task of preceding him to Uzume, who had danced in front of Amaterasu at the beginning of time. The Sarume priestesses are descended from a Great Ancestor, Sarume-no-Kimi, directly related to the cult of Uzume. This, by all appearances, was a feminine priesthood of a matriarchal nature lasting through the ages. It never ceased to fulfill a sacred function in religious ceremonies, above all in those celebrated in late autumn, on the day of the full moon, the Mitama-Shizume.[5]

The goddess Uzume is said to have invented the flute and the *koto,* a kind of zither. In the ceremony instituted in her honor, these two instruments are played and a choir of a hundred female singers accompanies the gestures of the priestess. She inverts a tub, sits upon it, and strikes it ten times with a pestle, making it resound. The ritual requires her to voice a loud cry eight times, which the ceremonial transcribes thus:

Ashime! O-ô-ô-ô! O-ô-ô-ô! O-ô-ô-ô!

This cry is followed by an incantation of eight stanzas, beginning:

On heaven and on earth,
The pestle is made to resonate.
It is made to resonate.
The Gods, like me,
Hear the pestle.[6]

The goal of these cries and blows is to draw the attention of the gods, who have retreated into the hollows of heaven and must be made to descend upon earth.

The recitation of the second stanza goes along with the unveiling of a sacred object: the great eight-handed sword brought from heaven by the god Nigi-hayahi:

To the priestesses who will want the Great Sword
That is at the temple Furu of Iso no Kami,
To those who will want it, we will present it![7]

During the third stanza, the bows and arrows of the divine hunters are brought out. Uzume, by striking the strings of the bows, was inspired to invent the zither, which has the ability to make the powers of divine spirits descend.

The fourth stanza mentions Amaterasu, the great goddess. It relates to a magical ceremony of incantation and capture of solar souls. After repeating the ritual cry, the following words are pronounced:

> *We want to take the souls*
> *Of the opulent Goddess of the Sun*
> *Who deigns to rise!*[8]

The priestesses are then invited to crown themselves with "rampant herbs," in imitation of Uzume in her dance and the immortal genies who give the earth its verdure:

> *Ornament your hair with rampant herbs,*
> *Be like the immortal genies*
> *Of the mountain Anashi.*[9]

The final stanzas accompany the *furu* rite (*furu* from the verb meaning "to shake"). In a great box enveloped in woven bark, ten talismans brought from heaven by the god Nigi-hayahi are shaken: four magical jewels, two mirrors, a sword, a "snake's scarf," a "wasp's scarf," and a "mysterious being's scarf."[10]

The gods, through this rite, return to earth:

> *To the box of souls,*
> *Suspending the woven bark,*
> *Let the Souls come in.*
> *The Gods whose august souls have risen*
> *Now deign to return.*
> *Carrying the box of souls,*
> *We make to return*
> *The souls who have departed.*[11]

After this incantation, the numbers one through ten are recited ten times. Each time, a member of the Nakotomi family, one of the sacred families in charge of worship at the court, ties a knot of souls, thus magically fastening the return of the gods.

This important ritual from the Mitama-Shizume ceremony in fact conceals within the subtle fabric of advanced Japanese culture a much more simple primitive rite—one whose objects are the dance and the unveiling of the goddess Uzume, banishing the darkness of time, purifying nature, and resurrecting light and life.

The myth of the solar goddess Amaterasu is significant in this regard. Forced to retire after the sacrilegious acts of her brother, the impetuous Susanoo—who destroyed the rice fields and soiled with his excrement the temple where the new grain was offered—and frightened by this filthy rampage, Amaterasu "entered into the Rocky Cave of Heaven, blocked its entrance with a rock, and remained hidden there. Then the darkness of an eternal night reigned over all the universe."

The eight hundred myriad deities gather in a dried-up riverbed and ask the god Omoikane to find a way to conquer the darkness. They then make a magic mirror and hang it, along with other talismans made of bark and hemp, on a tree in front of the cave, where the sun goddess is hidden. Another god, Ama-no-Koyane, chants a long incantation. But then, the goddess Uzume finally intervenes.

She wraps her arms in the lycopodium moss of the heavenly Mount Nagu, known as the Shadow of the Sun of Heaven. With her hair decorated with a creeping plant and holding a bouquet of bamboo leaves, she overturns a large round bucket that has been used as a canoe—*an uke*—and climbs onto it. Dancing on it and causing it to rumble beneath her feet, possessed by divine power, she casts off all her clothes, exhibits her breasts, and offers up her genitalia for all to see. The eight hundred myriad gods all burst out laughing.

Straight away, the great goddess, pushing aside the stone blocking the entrance to the cave, inquires as to the cause of this laughter. "We are rejoicing," the gods answer, "because we have among us a goddess who has prevailed over you!" The magic mirror is shown to the solar goddess, and a rope is dangled behind her. Immediately, new light fills the sky and illuminates the earth. The cosmic order having been reestablished, Susanoo, the cause of all this trouble, is punished. His mustache and beard are clipped and his fingernails are torn out, and he is banished from heaven.

THE GREEK MYTH OF THE
DANCE OF BAUBO

In Greece, a cultural recovery of the primitive rite and the original myth has been observed, similar to what was observed in Japan. The Homeric hymn to Demeter, probably composed in the first half of the sixth century BC for a contest of bards at Eleusis, praises the goddess and her myth in elegant and highly refined literary forms.

The great goddess, founder and legislator of agricultural life, is distraught and angered because her daughter has been taken from her by the god of the underworld. After fasting in heaven for nine days, she descends upon earth with the appearance of an old Cretan woman. Received at Eleusis by King Keleos and Queen Metanine, she is hired as a nurse for the queen's newborn, and is given a bed to rest in:

> *But Demeter, bringer of seasons and splendid gifts,*
> *Refused to sit upon the splendid seat.*
> *She remained silent, her lovely eyes downcast,*
> *Until the diligent Iambe offered her*
> *A solid stool, and set upon it a silver fleece.*
> *She sat there, and her hands veiled her face.*
> *Long silent, she sat in grief upon the stool,*
> *She spoke not a word, and made no gesture,*
> *Not laughing, tasting neither food nor drink,*
> *She stayed exhausted, mourning for her daughter*
> *With the broad girdle, until the diligent Iambe*
> *With much buffoonery and mockery,*

> *Caused the virtuous sovereign to smile,*
> *To laugh, and to be of good humor.*

The goddess, having cheered up, consents to eat and accepts the *kykeon,* a brew made from semolina and wild mint; and once the deity has laughed and eaten, the earth becomes fertile once again.

The significance of the myth appears to lie in the fact that, before the invention of agriculture, humans often had to fast like the goddess herself. But this historic and rational interpretation does not explain what the poet did not tell us: How exactly did the diligent Iambe manage to console this mother, distraught at the cruelest of misfortunes?

Some light was thrown on these pagan mysteries by Clement of Alexandria:

After having received Demeter, Baubo [i.e., Iambe] gave her the *kykeon.* When Demeter refused to take it, not wanting to drink because of her sorrow, Baubo, irritated as if she had been despised, unveiled her sex and showed it to the goddess. At this sight, Demeter opened up; after seeing this spectacle, she consented to take the drink. Such are the mysteries of the Athenians! Or as Orpheus said:

> *At these words, she drew back her robes*
> *She showed in entirety*
> *The indecent contours of her body.*
> *And the infant Iacchus appeared*
> *(She shook him with her hand) laughing,*
> *Beneath Baubo's skirts.*
> *When the goddess had laughed to her heart's content*
> *She accepted the polished bowl containing the kykeon.*[12]

This text from Clement of Alexandria gave archaeologists an unsolvable problem regarding the interpretation of the appearance of the infant Iacchus, until 1895–96, when Wiegand and Schrader excavated at Priene. In the local temple of Demeter, built in the fourth century BC, bizarre statuettes were found. Without torsos or heads, they depicted only the belly of a woman, with the lines of a face drawn just above the genitals.[13] In 1901, Hermann Diels declared that these were statuettes of Baubo—a name that, according to Empedocles, meant the "belly" (Baubo and later Bamno, according to Hesychius).

The face drawn on the belly was that of the infant Iacchus. Arnobius writes on this subject: "She gave a more groomed aspect to her most intimate part, and made it smooth, like a boy whose hair is not yet rough or shaggy."[14] Arnobius also paraphrases the Orphic fragment cited by Clement of Alexandria: "At these words, Baubo hitched up her robe from the bottom and presented to the eyes the lines appearing on her lower belly. Baubo shook them in the hollow of her hand, and they formed a child's face; she slapped them and contracted them pleasantly."[15]

According to Paul Perdrizet, Baubo performs a belly dance in front of Demeter. At each of her contortions, the figure Baubo has drawn around her navel appears to laugh.[16]

Thus, in their basic forms, the Greek myth and the Japanese myth are very close to each other if not identical. But we can find their common roots starting at the level of agrarian fertility rites, probably protohistoric, which were covered and veiled by a highly different mythology, depending on the cultural area where the mythology was finally developed.

Under these conditions, the moral content of the myth in the sense understood by Malinowski seems to be almost null, at least in terms of our current value system. On the other hand, we can see at what point these myths and rituals are profoundly linked to the general economy of human relations with nature. In this sense, a prehistoric hunting economy would necessarily present very different mythical and ritual aspects from those of pastoral and agrarian economies. Yet the continuity of initiatory and religious traditions necessarily had to integrate archaic concepts whose roots were too deep to be extracted from the human spirit.

Thus a general phenomenon of mythic superposition corresponds to the phenomenon of totemic superposition discussed earlier. The versatility of the symbol is therefore not an inexplicable fact: It has preserved all the levels of human experience, from their remotest origins into modern times. Therefore we have, in the science of symbols, a psychic archaeology perhaps even more vast and more important than material archaeology. The hieroglyphs of this monumental inner architecture, if we were able to decipher them, would allow us to understand history in all its true dimensions, external and internal—that is, not opposing myth and history, but discerning in both the warp and weft of the complex and subtle fabric of time.

THE PRIESTESSES OF ELEUSIS
AND THE SACRED FAMILIES

We have the title and a few words of a plea voiced in the name of the priestess of Demeter in a suit she filed before the hierophant of Eleusis. Paul Foucart rightly concluded that part of the discourse here was "on the subject of myths relating to the arrival of the Goddess and those who received her, because these were the legends from which the sacred families of Eleusis derived the rights they claimed."[17]

The priestess of Demeter belonged to an ancient sacred family, the Philleidai, designated by the name of the woman in which the priestly function was chosen by drawing lots. The priestess lived in a special house maintained at the temple's expense and located within the sacred enclosure. She was the guardian of the primordial rites, and it was she, and not the hierophant or the daduchus, the chief of the other sacred families, who was the eponym of the sanctuary; it was she who gave her name to the holy works. Even in the imperial era, each statue of Eleusis bore the name of a priestess of Demeter and a date that corresponded to the date of her consecration. It was the priestess, and not the hierophant, who presided over an ancient winter ceremony in which animals were sacrificed in the areas reserved for the gods, the *haloa*. One hierophant,

Archias, immolated a victim at this feast, and he was condemned for his impiety.

The feast of the haloa, scholars unanimously agree, was centered on a secret ceremony of the initiation of women, a primitive version of the initiation conferred upon both sexes by the Great Mysteries. Very little is known about these rites—only that cakes were made in the shape of sexual organs, that jewels and images of this kind were worn, that the women discussed freely various subjects, and that a meal was served to them at which wine flowed abundantly. Breaking fast and permitting obscenity had important symbolic significance for an agrarian civilization: They magically reanimated the fertile powers of the fields and the earth.

In the Great Mysteries, the priestess of Demeter played an essential role. Suidas* tells us that, like the hierophant and the daduchus, she was "the one who initiates the mystics."

She performed pantomimes with the hierophant, who seized her and led her to a dark retreat, the nuptial union of Demeter and Zeus. The torches were then extinguished, and the crowd of mystics "awaited her salvation from what was happening in the shadows between these two people."[18] Hippolytus adds these details: "The hierophant is not mutilated like Attis, but he is made a eunuch by means of hemlock, and has renounced all carnal generation. At Eleusis, at nighttime, amidst innumerable fires, he celebrates the great and ineffable mysteries; he raises his voice and cries these words: 'The August has given birth to a sacred boy, Brimō Brimos!' meaning 'the strong!'"[19] Very probably, the sacred dance of Baubo was meant to correspond to the final phase of these fertility rites. The priestesses of Eleusis, like those of the goddess Sarume, were entrusted with eminent priestly functions for which Baubo and Uzume were the mythical prototypes.

The magical scope of these Greek and Japanese rites is unquestionable, and it should be noted that in both cases, the mystical-religious

---

*Suidas was the compiler of a Greek lexicon-encyclopedia in the tenth century AD.

ceremonies were connected to music, dance, poetry, and song. In fact, it was Baubo-Iambe who invented the *iamb,* the three-beat step of the ancient waltz. The link between iambic poetry and the cult and mysteries of Eleusis has been recognized by archaeologists. The iamb was accompanied by two musical instruments, and these light dances corresponded to songs in which mockery, sexual allusions, and double entendres were required by sacred tradition.

As in Japan, in Greece ritual cries had considerable liturgical importance. During their procession from Athens to Eleusis, the mystics cried "Iacchus!" and redoubled their ardor upon approaching the sanctuary. An entirely magical efficacy was attributed to this cry. According to Herodotus, shortly after the Battle of Salamis, Demaratus, the former king of Sparta, and an Athenian who had passed into the service of the Persians saw a cloud of dust rising from the direction of Eleusis, which appeared to be the result of the footsteps of thousands of men and from which issued a clamoring in which the Athenian recognized the mystical name Iacchus. He explained to Demaratus that this was a voice from the gods coming to the aid of the Athenians and their allies. This cry was believed to be capable of destroying with its breath anything that might sully the surroundings of Eleusis.

Iacchus, the laughing child evoked by this cry, gave his name to the nineteenth of the month Boedromion, the day of the procession of the mystics escorted by the epheboi, spears in their fists, shields at the ready, crowned with myrtle. Strabo called him "the demon of the mysteries of Demeter." Aristophanes dedicated the following stanzas to this ideal chief of the procession:

> *Iacchus, O Iacchus! . . .*
> *Thou that dwellest in the shadow*
> *Of great glory here beside us,*
> *Spirit, Spirit, we have hied us*
> *To thy dancing in the meadow!*
> *Come, Iacchus; let thy brow*

> *Toss its fruited myrtle bough . . .*
> *Up, Iacchus, and awaken!*
> *Come, thou star that bringest light*
> *To the darkness of our rite,*
> *Till thine old men leap as young men, leap with every*
>   *thought forsaken*
> *Of the dullness and the fear*
> *Left by many a circling year:*
> *Let thy red light guide the dances*
> *Where thy banded youth advances*
> *To be merry by the blossoms of the mere!*[20]

THE POETIC TRANSMISSION OF MYTH

The preceding examples suffice to show the importance of poetic expression in ritual formulas and in the symbolic recapitulation of primordial cosmogony and mythology.[21] This is a matter not of an aesthetic finality, but of a magical efficacy of the repetition of sacred words to which creative power is attributed. For archaic societies, if life could not be restored, if its flux was irreversible, it could at least be brought back to itself and, in a way, revealed by the memory of pouring forth from its source. This return is a mythical and symbolic commemoration of the primordial word, charged with an inexhaustible fertile energy and transcending time.

The words by which Io fashioned the Universe—that is to say, by which it was implanted and caused to produce a world of light—the same words are used in the ritual for implanting a child in a barren womb. The words by which Io caused light to shine in the darkness are used in the rituals for cheering a gloomy and despondent heart, the feeble aged, the decrepit; for shedding light into secret places and matters, for inspiration in song-composing, and in many other affairs, affecting man to despair in times of adverse war. For all such the ritual to enlighten and cheer includes the words (used by Io) to dispel darkness.[22]

Here, the myth serves as a model, a type magically effective and applicable to every new genesis, to the procreation of a child, to the re-creation of an equilibrium, and to a harmonious order between heaven and earth, whether in a matter of social crisis or of damage done to an individual's life by doubt, melancholy, or despair. Primitive humans appeared to sense the homology of genetic structures and the analogy of relationships among the biological, the psychological, and the sociological as existential situations relevant to the same dynamics of the primordial genetic unity of the cosmos and the Logos. In leading the signal and the signification back toward the significator itself, the recitation of ritual formulas reinserts, so to speak, history and time past into the heart of the eternal witness, who experiences them but also transcends them in the end and in the beginning of every cycle of things and beings.

Thus the cosmogonic myth is recited on the occasion of a death, whether physical or initiatory, as well as at the birth of a child. For example, among the Osage, a North American tribe, a man who has "spoken with the gods" presents himself at the house of the woman who has given birth and recites to the newborn the story of the creation of the universe and the earthly animals. The infant cannot be suckled without first observing this rite. Later, when the child wants to drink water, other words must first commemorate the origin of this element, and when the child is weaned, he hears the story of the creation of grains and other plants necessary for life.[23]

In collective ceremonies and at important community events, myths are always reactualized. This is especially the case upon the accession of a sovereign. The coronation of the Indian king, the *rajasûya,* includes a re-creation of the universe. The various phases of the ritual correspond "to a regression of the future sovereign to the embryonic state, his gestation for one year, then his mystical rebirth as 'king of the world,' simultaneously identified as *prajâpati* (the God of All) and the cosmos."[24]

Mircea Eliade noted that the primitive cosmic renewal performed at the coronation had considerable consequences in the later history of humanity. Mobile ceremonies were removed, little by little, from the immovable liturgical framework of the ancient sacred calendar, and the king became, in a way, the only one responsible for the stability, fertility, and prosperity of the cosmos. Universal renewal, no longer connected to the great cosmic rhythms, was mythically transferred to historical events and people.[25]

Poetic transmission itself has undergone profound changes in that it has been linked to myth and not to history, to the magic of rhythms and their powers necessary for the reactualization of oral traditions rather than to the song of words and the emotional forces that they can evoke and transmit. Thus it has been observed that the quantity of the syllable, short or long—an entirely musical notion—very rapidly ceased to be distinguished in Gallo-Roman poetic literature around the third or fourth century AD, as the Roman Empire was ending.

Latin verse had no rhymes and was based on rhythm. Even Latin stress, a substitute for rhythm, ceased to be observable around the eighth century. Thereafter, the emphasis uniformly falls on the last syllable in Latin words introduced into poetic texts in the Roman language. One of the causes of this transformation was the simplification of liturgical singing, performed voluntarily by the church in order to prevent a return to pagan ceremonies, as Georges Lote showed.[26]In AD 393, St. Augustine, combating the Donatist heresy among the African populace, decided to write a poem that "rejected all prosodic and tonic links. It had no regard for measure or stress, so that in the verses, the syllables are merely counted."[27]

Here, it was not the rhythm but the syllabism that became a mnemotechnical tool adapted for the teaching of illiterate people, the essential point being to determine how many syllables could be remembered by the ear without being grouped by a break. The congregation of the faithful thus invigorated, maintained, and taught by participation in sung services through associating syllabism with liturgical and musical emotions. Later, there was progressive secularization of Latin and Roman verses: A new development under the influence of ancient songs from popular dances, pagan in their origin, was integrated into Roman poetry between the eighth and tenth centuries.

Two centuries later, the total participation of the faithful in the sung liturgy progressively ceased, and the development of music resulted in singers being entrusted with the performance of the parts of the service in which, formerly, all the people of God had taken part. This first separation between learned music and poetry and their popular expressions was further accentuated by the development of writing and poetry that was read and understood only by an audience rich enough to purchase expensive manuscripts. From then on, means of diffusion and also tastes and interests never ceased to diverge between two poetic cultures that were henceforth strangers to one another—that of the literate and that of the illiterate—and between two social classes, the rich or their clientele and the poor.

Under these conditions, poetic activity, in the genetic and cosmogonic sense of its mythical, primordial expression, was no longer understood independently from its literary formulation and its aesthetic criteria or even its emotional and sung language. Thus it was communicated either in the form of poems, more and more subtly developed, whose interpretations were accessible only to a very limited group of educated readers, or in the form of popular songs that forcefully expressed the primary colors of psychic landscapes with the most immediate intensity possible: violent chromatic contrasts, like postcards and calendars illustrated with rhetorical flora surrounding images of the same double mirror with no name and no face.

The consumption of these two cultural forms corresponds quantitatively to the increasing numerical difference between two populations: one diminishing constantly just as the other grew to such a degree that the universal triumph of song over poem was easily predictable. This was a more general phenomenon, resulting from the fact that intellectual production, whether of art, poetry, or even philosophy or science, was never totally independent from the concrete conditions of the economy in a society entirely dominated by a mythology of production.

This has been the case in our society since the Renaissance, and in this sense, we can connect the increasing decadence of poetic activity in contemporary Western societies to the fact that historicism and its development have situated art in produced history and not in the genetic perspective of the eternally creative and re-creative myth of its expression. For Hegel, for example, art constitutes one of the phases of the history of the mind: It is born, it grows, and it must die in that it is another imperfect but enjoyable form of possession of the world. First, object and pleasure; then, critique and judgment; and finally, science— each is merely a stage in the gaining of consciousness of the world, and as such, this limit must necessarily be surpassed by the progress of reflexive culture and the production of forms that make manifest the development of the idea.

In fact, this conception of art and poetry, which, according to Hegel, is the archetypal aesthetic form, must be situated in its relationship to the bourgeois philosophy of the symbol as it has been expressed since the Renaissance—principally in the Kantian and Hegelian systems, as well as through the main representatives of German philosophy.

This general evolution has been pointed out in other areas by numerous authors. In his dictionary of eleventh- to sixteenth-century French architecture, Viollet-Le-Duc (1814–79) presented the essential problem of the progressive loss of poetic and symbolic meaning among the populace since the Renaissance:

> The fabliaux so often depicted in our sculptures and paintings of the thirteenth, fourteenth, and fifteenthth centuries are, in most cases, a moral teaching intended to be imprinted upon the memory through the eyes.[28] But these representations must not be confused with symbolic figures, which are of a higher order and require a certain amount of metaphysics in order to be understood. There is no need to repeat all the resources that medieval symbology offered

to artists or the fact that, all in all, medieval symbology was more poetic than these banal representations of ornaments and figures—without meaning for the populace—with which we have covered our monuments since the Renaissance. Thus it is no surprise that the indifference held toward all these sculptures, allegorical though they may be, has replaced, among the populace, the interest once associated with symbols whose meaning everyone could decipher. Thus art among us is now only addressed to dilettantism and has ceased to penetrate into all lives, great and small. And thus, beneath the reign of the classicism of convention, besides the amateurs, there are only barbarians.[29]

This is not a phenomenon isolated from the other conditions of political, juridic, philosophical, scientific, and technical evolution. And if the economy is not the only active cause of all these conditions that react upon each other as well as upon their economic basis, then at least it constitutes an axis of convergence around which, like a magnet, the fields of force of a society gather in a manner much more visible than in other directions. A mythology of production, economically indispensable for the political class in power, cannot reconcile its values with those of traditional societies for which contemplation and not action was the goal of every true human civilization.

13 THE BOURGEOIS PHILOSOPHY OF THE SYMBOL

THE HEGELIAN PHILOSOPHY OF THE SYMBOL

Is combat between nature and spirit the law of the world? Can we assume, as Hegel claims, that "the concept of the spirit, as a genuine totality, is . . . implicitly only this, namely to divide itself as object in itself and subject in itself in order through this opposition to arise out of nature and then, as its conqueror and as the power over it, to be free and serene in contrast with it"?[1] Is this principal moment, this decisive element, anything other than a new scene in the representation we unceasingly give of our own image? "Looked at historically or in reality this transition is the progressive transformation of man in a state of nature into a system of established rights, i.e., to property, laws, constitution, political life."[2]

Is it, in fact, a matter of anything other than the development of the spirit? It is a matter of a decisive and real historic moment, certainly, but is it one that relates only to the consciousness of a social class, finally free and victorious because it came to conquer all others after three centuries of ideological battles and political conflicts? The bourgeois philosophy, in the sense Ernst Bloch used this expression,[3] began in the Renaissance, grew during the Age of Enlightenment, and blossomed into the French

Revolutionary ideal and Kant's rationalism. But it found its most profound and most lasting expression in Hegel's philosophy and in historicism, which was its principal consequence. According to Hegel, it was not only the *idea* that constituted the basis of things, the essential element of the real, but also the historical progress of the *production*[4] of forms that realized it and objectivized it. "The Idea as such is only truly Idea as developing itself explicitly by its own activity," Hegel writes:

> At every particular stage on which the Ideal treads the road of its unfolding there is immediately linked with every *inner* determinacy another *real* configuration. It is therefore all one whether we regard the advance in this development as an inner advance of the Idea in itself or of the shape in which it gives itself existence. Each of these two sides is immediately bound up with the other. The consummation of the Idea as content appears therefore simultaneously as also the consummation of form.[5]

This thesis is indispensable for the coherence of all Hegelian aesthetics and for his analysis of the symbol in general, with which the second part of Hegel's *Aesthetics* begins: "The symbol," writes Hegel, "in the meaning of the word used here, constitutes the beginning of art, alike in its essential nature and its historical appearance."[6] This approach to the problems of symbolism is already contestable. But here is the general explanation Hegel gives for it:

> Symbol as such is an external existent given or immediately present to contemplation, which yet is to be understood not simply as it confronts us immediately on its own account, but in a wider and more universal sense. Thus at once there are two distinctions to make in the symbol: (1) the meaning, and (2) the expression thereof. The first is an idea or topic, no matter what its content, the second is a sensuous existent or a picture of some kind or other. Now the symbol is *prima facie* a *sign*. But in a *mere sign* the connection which meaning and its expression

have with one another is only a purely arbitrary linkage. In that case this expression, this sensuous thing or picture, so far from presenting *itself*, brings before our minds a content foreign to it, one with which it does not need to stand in any proper affinity whatever.[7]

This Hegelian concept of the sign was repeated a little more literally by Ferdinand de Saussure, the father of linguistics, a century later. "So," Hegel adds, "in languages, for example, the sounds are a sign of some idea, feeling, etc. But the predominant part of the sounds in a language is linked purely by chance with the ideas expressed thereby . . ."[8] (Here, the sign and the thing signified are indistinct from each other.)

It is a different thing when a sign is to be a *symbol*. The lion, for example, is taken as a symbol of magnanimity, the fox of cunning, the circle of eternity, the triangle of the Trinity. . . . Therefore in these sorts of symbol the sensuously present things have already in their own existence that meaning, for the representation and expression of which they are used; and, taken in this wider sense, the symbol is no purely arbitrary sign. . . . Yet nevertheless it is not to bring *itself* before our minds as this concrete individual thing but in itself only that universal quality of meaning [which it signifies].[9]

We will doubtless observe that the examples given by Hegel to support his definitions are not initiatory and religious symbols, but philosophical and aesthetic allegories, an abusive assimilation that is Kantian in its origin. In the pages he devotes to allegory, Hegel, seemingly unintentionally, allows the true reason for this initial confusion to appear:

F. von Schlegel has observed that every work of art must be an allegory. Yet this saying is true only if it is to mean nothing but that every work of art must contain a universal idea and an inherently true meaning. Whereas what *we* have here called an allegory is a mode of representation subordinate in both form and content, only imperfectly corresponding to the essence of art. For every human event and imbroglio, every relationship, etc., has some sort of universality in itself which can also be extracted *as* universality; but such abstractions we have otherwise already in our minds, and with them in their prosaic universality and their external indication, to which alone allegory attains, art has nothing to do. Winckelmann also wrote an immature work on allegory in which he assembles a mass of allegories, but for the most part he confuses symbol and allegory.[10]

In fact, Hegel at once undertakes a reductive critique of allegory and an amplifying critique of the symbol in art in order to transfer into the aesthetics of form and the metaphysics of ideas—into anthropology, or rather into the theoanthropology that he conceives—everything that previously connected allegory to the sacred art and that connected symbols to theology.[11] This is why, on at least this point, Kant and Hegel agree: Bourgeois philosophy must ultimately found its own religion of humanity. The contrast with Friedrich Schlegel is all the more significant considering that this philosopher's mystical and religious tendencies exercised a profound influence over the theologian Schleiermacher. Moreover, Hegel took care to explain that Winckelmann confused not only symbol with allegory, but also allegory with iconology, proposing a definition for the symbol that was very close to the Hegelian notion of a relationship between an image and a general idea.

We cannot help but be struck by the extraordinary broadening of anthropology, especially of the function of art in general as Hegel conceives it:

The determinate being of God is not the natural and sensuous as such but the sensuous elevated to nonsensuousness, to spiritual subjectivity, which instead of losing in its external appearance the certainty of itself as the Absolute, only acquires precisely through its embodiment a present actual certainty of itself. God in his truth is therefore no bare ideal generated by imagination; on the contrary, he puts himself into the very heart of the finitude and external contingency of existence, and yet knows himself there as a divine subject who remains infinite in himself and makes this infinity explicit to himself. Since therefore the actual individual man is the appearance of God, art now wins for the first time the higher right of turning the human form, and the mode of externality in general, into an expression of the Absolute. . . . The different moments, which constitute the totality of this worldview as the totality of truth itself, now, therefore, find their appearance in man.[12]

Thus, according to the new theoanthropology of bourgeois philosophy, the human being is no longer the image of God or one of his shadows among infinite others, but is the true manifestation of the divine, and through him the absolute is revealed to the relative and in the relative. Under these conditions, how could humans not have all rights, including that of destroying nature and destroying our kin if the mind and the idea require it at certain moments in history?

No civilization has proposed such an obviously anthropocentric interpretation of the human condition as the bourgeois philosophy of theoanthropology as Hegel immoderately develops it. How can we not understand the ferocious words of Léon Brunschvicg: "What good is it to be Hegel, to carry within oneself the universe of logic and history, art and religion, if only to see, in a passing emperor, the mind of the world on horseback?"

THE KANTIAN PHILOSOPHY OF THE SYMBOL

Kant's little-known work *Dreams of a Spirit-Seer*—one of the "classics of rationalism," as F. Courtès puts it[13]—deserves to be placed in the first rank. It is rare to see a great philosopher deigning to descend to the level of "obscurantist mysticism" or "illuminist charlatanism" in order to battle windmills and mirages. In academic circles, this work is held to be so obviously invalid that even declaring to be an adversary of it, we risk being intellectually dishonored: If you fight with cudgel-wielding peasants, you may get your sword dirty. Certainly, Kant had an excuse: He was still far from being famous. "Hence," F. Courtès discreetly notes, "this unconscious phase of noble recklessness, which caused him to attack Swedenborg: He did not yet know how to keep his distance."[14]

We should not exaggerate this charitable proximity: In this book, Kant still manages not to say a word about Swedenborg's scientific career or the high technical quality of his "memorials on finance" or his role as state engineer or the misfortunes of his solitary old age or even the trials of his country, Sweden, which was isolated from Europe and left to itself with its archaic phantoms.

These circumstances, these biographical facts, held no interest for Kant. In his view, Swedenborg was merely one kind of visionary among others. Debunking him simply meant washing his hands of mystical experiences, metaphysical reveries, fictive societies, and imaginary voyages. In Königsberg, Prussia, reason knew where it was to be found: in the city that crowned the kings of Prussia—albeit recently, considering this family of social climbers had bought everything, land and crown, within the space of a generation. Hence their tendency to enter into military alliance with those who offered the best price. In the witty words of F. Courtès, in Königsberg "despotism had its troops of geniuses, its quartermaster's office, and its agents whereby it was enlightened just as true warriors are by sighting the cavalry."[15]

We can never know what can happen with visionaries—all the more because they are usually obsessed with playing the role of the oppressed. "Our Kant" (*"unser Kant"*) was completely capable of "working to set right so many enthusiastic minds,"[16] in the words of Borowski, the court sacristan's son. From the first lines of the title, heavy Kantian artillery is set loose: *Dreams of a Spirit-Seer Illustrated by Dreams of Metaphysics.* This says it all. The tone is set: "The land of shadows is the paradise of dreamers. Here, they find an unlimited country where they may build their houses ad libitum. Hypochondriac vapors, nursery tales, and monastic miracles provide them with ample building material."[17]

None of this is true. Kant proves it: "As usual where it is not our business to search—he found nothing. This is indeed by itself a sufficient reason for writing a book . . ."[18] But it is a strange reason: "Thence originated the present treatise, which, we flatter ourselves, will fully satisfy the reader; for the main part he will not understand, another part he will not believe, and the rest he will laugh at."[19]

In fact, Kant was expressing a bourgeois philosophy quite different from the one that first appeared during the Renaissance, as Ernst Bloch so aptly showed. The erstwhile "citizens of liberated cities" henceforth acquired history, gained power, and formed knowledge that reflected the conditions and operations of the values and guarantees indispensable for the functioning of a merchant economy that was also already a manufacturing and speculative one. During the medieval era, access to international fairs and foreign markets required long and often perilous travels. After the founding of the first European bank by the Medicis in Florence, considerable financial operations could be undertaken by various intermediaries without personal physical risk. The increasing abstraction of economic exchange was even reflected in the evolution of philosophical and scientific language.

Descartes explained the most difficult problems in the clearest manner, in a language that was in no way different from that of the honest man of his time. For Kant, the art of obscuring evidence started to become the criterion of the philosopher's mind. The bourgeoisie thus achieved one of the most lasting forms of its ideal: deceiving people about imminent concrete realities under the cover of distant, abstract imperatives. Descartes is still roaming; Kant stays right where he is. In Königsberg, people did not take risks—not in business or in thought.

We think just as we weigh: with a scale and some weights. Kant states this clearly, thus immediately placing rationalism among the attributes of mercantile reason:

The inaccuracy of scales used for commercial measurements, according to civil law, is discovered, if we let the merchandise and the weights exchange pans. So the partiality of the scales of reason is revealed by the same trick, without which, in philosophical judgments, no harmonious result can be obtained from the compared weighings. . . . I confess that all stories about apparitions of departed souls or about influences from spirits, and all theories about the presumptive nature of spirits and their connection with us, seem to have appreciable weight only in the scale of *hope,* while in the scale of speculation they seem to consist of nothing but air.[20]

Thus reason and even speculation change their meanings. Reason, the power of universal knowledge, the questioning of substantial ends, is transformed by rationalism into a practical capacity for functional coordination between means and ends. Its criterion is nothing more than efficacy. Its fundamental logic is not that of analogy, which guarantees nothing. It is reduced to the ideal of identity and its methods, because without them, no calculation is possible, no value is guaranteed for the product. Speculation must therefore yield something palpable— at least a socially exchangeable interest. This instrumental reason, in its various forms—positivism, pragmatism, scientism, the idolatrous cult of technological output—is, everywhere from Kantism to contemporary systems, nothing more than the flattening of the world and nature that Marcuse so rightly called "false unidimensional consciousness."

Thus Kant, believing that we wish in vain to extend the feeble measure of our strength to so many adventurous projects, declares that we must "do without such vain investigations"[21] and use our intellectual faculties to greater advantage for the things remaining. Here we can already see the dawning of the principle of the economy of thought, which today still constitutes the ideal of the contemporary technocracy.

Thus philosophy, according to Kant, changes entirely in its meaning and range. Germanized from birth and Prussianized by Hegel, historicized and then socialized by the post-Hegelians, salvaged by political power in the form of the watchdogs so justly denounced by Paul Nizan, the adventurous quest for the truth, as it was conducted by those great ancient and medieval hunting dogs, has become something totally foreign. What use now are those subtle indexes of the unknown that are symbols? Mystery yields nothing—not even the satisfaction of understanding it. What good is it to use our nose and paws in vain when so much tasty meat is displayed in all the world's shop windows? In his conclusion, Kant cites Voltaire: "Let us look after our happiness, go into the garden, and work."[22]

In a commentary, Swedenborg had already responded to this vegetative philosophy of rationalism:

> That a "tiller of the ground" is one who is devoid of charity, however much he may be in faith separated from love, which is no faith, is evident from what follows: that Jehovah had no respect to his offering, and that he slew his brother, that is, destroyed charity, signified by "Abel." Those were said to "till the ground" who look to bodily and earthly things, as is evident from what is said in [Genesis 3:19, 23], where we read that man was "cast out of the garden of Eden to till the ground."[23]

Kant, the "Cain" of Königsberg, reduced the symbol to a specific function of the rational type, a hypotyposis, a method for making an argument concrete, expressing sensibly that which is abstracted or thought. Hypotyposis takes place in two ways: either schematically, when "the corresponding intuition is given" to "a concept comprehended by the Understanding," or else symbolically, adding to a concept of reason "an intuition . . . with which accords a procedure of the Judgment analogous to what it observes in schematism."[24]

In fact, the examples given by Kant show that he does not clearly distinguish symbol from allegory: "Thus," he writes, "a monarchical state is represented by a living body, if it is governed by national laws, and by a mere machine (like a hand-mill) if governed by an individual absolute will."[25] Thus the symbol, in the Kantian sense, is a natural relationship of convenience and mutual pleasure of the collective and aesthetic type: "Now I say the Beautiful is the symbol of the morally

Good, and that it is only in this respect . . . that it gives pleasure with a claim for the agreement of every one else."[26]

Despite the indigence of Kant's conceptions of the symbol, they do present the fairly obvious advantage of proposing a purely anthropological development of its interpretations. This is why, through Hegel himself, Kant's influence in this area is exercised even today over a substantial part of European cultural and social symbolism as illustrated by numerous authors.

In Hegel, we can continually observe a separation from Kantian rationalism on the level of the conception of myths, perhaps under the influence of the works of Friedrich Creuzer, whom Hegel cites with a great deal of esteem. According to Hegel, myths contain an immediate philosophy and general ideas. The things that manifest and are manifested in myths form a concrete unity. The Greek gods are not symbols; they are subjectivities sufficient unto themselves. In fact, Hegel transferred a religious concept of the symbol—reduced to a moment of the immediate or nonreflected natural consciousness according to which the subject is not separated from the object—to the plane of philosophical ideas and free, reflective subjectivity. Idealistic Hegelian dialectics gave the unifying and conciliatory movement between the conceptual and the real an entirely mystic efficacy, as we can see in this characteristic statement: "The idea is the truth in and of itself, the absolute union of concept and objectivity. Its ideal content is nothing other than the concept in its determinations; its real content is nothing but its presentation, which it assumes in the form of an exterior existence."[27]

In Goethe's interpretation, symbolism is no less rationalist than for Kant and Hegel; symbols are considered principally in terms of the perspective of classical Greek art and neoclassicism à la Lessing or Winckelmann. Allegory is considered to be the direct representation of the general by the particular, while the symbol expresses the general character of the particular. But Goethe admits that the symbol is "the living and instantaneous revelation of the unexplorable."[28] Through the symbol, the idea changes into image and thus acquires limitless and ineffable activity. This identification of the symbol with the image has exercised considerable influence over "vital" German philosophy, especially that of Lessing, Klages, and Jaspers. As for Schelling and the Romantics, what we might call the "surrationalist" current of Western philosophy attributed an importance to symbols that appears, in many respects, to arise from a conception no less amplificatory than the philiosophy of their adversaries was reductionist. Retaining only the enigmatic and mysterious properties of indirect symbolic communication from Hegelian philosophy, Kierkegaard and Nietzsche, despite the differences between their Christian and Dionysian orientations, came under the influence of the aforementioned current—which lasted through Nietzsche and Max Scheler as far as Martin Heidegger.

Considering idealist thought from Plato to Hegel as a thought of ideas—that is, of that which makes the hidden visible through the activity of the subject—Heidegger showed that this was a matter of a reversal of relations with being. Submitting it to the subject through the objectivity and visibility of its philosophical and metaphysical attributes, the abuse of the ratio, both as reason and as calculation and measure, has discolored and effaced the glow that emanates spontaneously from things and nature. Thus, instead of attaining the real, humans, becoming dominating and voluntary technicians, have descended by degrees toward the midnight of the world's ages, and the gods have fled. What are these gods? Symbols. The conversion, the return (*kehre*) therefore consists of the idea of the secret: that which is expressible only indirectly through words that are said in the manner of silence, in not wanting, "even excluding the desire not to want."

Here, then, is a new avatar for the symbol in modern thought: It is deified. This bizarre process of the bourgeois philosophy of the symbol can be described in two words: *hypotyposis,* according to Kant, and *apotheosis,* according to Heidegger.

Of these two opposite points in the oscillation of the philosophical pendulum, the former corresponds to a period of expansion of the economic and political power of the Western financial and merchandising bourgeoisie and the latter to the interior crises and world conflicts that this bourgeoisie was incapable of avoiding or resolving. The unconscious sentiment of these historical setbacks was manifested, as in any neurotic crisis, by a sort of fever of symbolization, which, as we know, continued to agitate Hitler's Germany during the years leading up to the World War II. Never was the sinister sorcery of the symbolic image exploited in a more perfectly premeditated, systematic fashion or in a more collectively efficacious manner than by Nazism.[29]

Moreover, in many respects, we may connect certain aspects of the end of the medieval epoch with aspects of the present time. In particular, we may compare the consequences of the great plague epidemics with those of our world wars. The current trend in studies of death directly linked to an obsession with sexuality and to the renewal of superstitious practices and witchcraft is only one of many factors suggesting singular convergences with the dominant themes of the fifteenth-century mentality. Likewise, the period of the space race appears to correspond to the era of great oceanic voyages, so much so that it does not take a prophet to predict that the most important discoveries in space will take place within the next twenty years.

The apocalyptic themes, the melancholic and pessimistic burden of our epoch, are magnificently barbaric. Our barren imaginations, our fascination with obituaries marking the "death of man" following the "death of God"—all these indicators of the decline of the "modern" world, and above all its increasingly heavy and opaque solidification— are so many pathological signs of the exhaustion and saturation of the great ideological themes from whose soil the postmedieval bourgeois civilization sprang forth at the beginning of the Renaissance. But just as it was possible in the fifteenth century to predict the emergence of a new mind and to turn away from dead things in order better to contemplate things being born at the same time and place, so various indicators permit us to believe that a future society will be capable of putting an end to the battle between nature and the spirit.

This conflict, despite Hegel's bellicose delusions, is not a law of the world—unless it is for the philosophy of a society dominated by a dualistic and conflicting vision of relationships of exploitation between predator and prey. Any conception of a historical development founded upon such a vision of the world, whether bourgeois or proletarian, can recognize only one principle: Might makes right is the law of the jungle, not the law of civilization.

The nature of humans is such that we can avoid neither the infra-human nor the suprahuman, because we take part in these two realities, which are both present in the universe. This essentially mixed character of our condition does not necessarily imply an alternation, but it requires a mediation between the inferior and the superior, a double movement that causes us to rise and the other to descend. The transfiguration of nature is therefore inseparable from the incarnation of the spirit. To lose consciousness of one is to condemn ourselves to the increasing abstraction and finally the alienation of the other. The symbol, by reason of its forever concrete foundation in analogy (and hence in all true poetic activity), is the archetypal means for the transfiguration of things and beings. Therefore, saying that our society has lost the meaning of the symbol or, indeed, the meaning of the vital value of poetry is simply observing our society's delirium of ideological abstraction.

Historically, we know that at the root of this neurosis there lies the increasing abstraction of the economic process, beginning in the Renaissance, and a mythology of production necessary for the abusive exploitation of humans and nature. It is futile to oppose these two fundamental errors with a demand for revolution, which will merely rebuild them in new, no less repressive forms. This is why all dogmatic systems endeavor to reduce symbolism to insignificance and poetic activity to purely literary games. As Dan Sperber has so rightly pointed out: "Because symbolism is one of the anthropological foundations of liberty, power in all its forms obstinately strives to contain it. Traditional exegesis and its modern avatar, semiology, reflect these attempts at repression: Scientific criticism implicitly leads to political criticism. Rethinking symbolism also means reconsidering the ideological frameworks of our sensibility."[30]

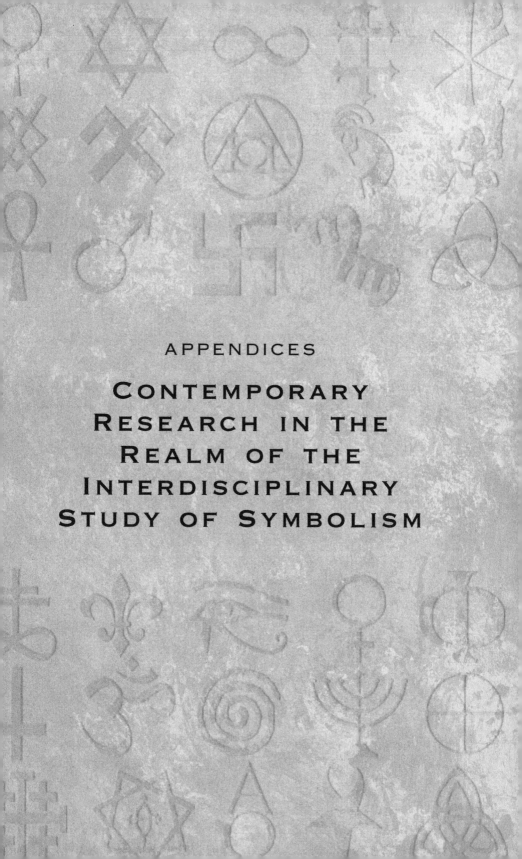

APPENDICES

CONTEMPORARY RESEARCH IN THE REALM OF THE INTERDISCIPLINARY STUDY OF SYMBOLISM

1
A Letter from Ms. Claire Lejeune Concerning the History of the Journal *Cahiers Internationaux de Symbolisme**

Dear René Alleau,

You wanted me to write a brief history of the venture known as *Cahiers Internationaux de Symbolisme* (International Journals of Symbolism). Essentially, the history of the Society of Symbolism begins with this journal, whose first issue was published in 1962.

But it had a prehistory (in which you played a part), lasting more than ten years, in the course of which its activities were restricted to the organization of conferences in Paris, Geneva, Vienna, and Basel.

What need did it satisfy? Here is what its founder, Dr. Moïse Engelson of Geneva, writes today on the subject:

> One of the events in my existence was the discovery that the meaning of life was *understanding* and that this word designated a mutual integration of the two principles constituting thought: conscious-

---

*[Written in 1975. —*Ed.*]

ness and phenomenon. This having been established, it is evident that the point of impact between these two principles, in order to become intelligible, must undergo reduction to a *common denominator,* which may be designated with the term *symbolism.*

This quest for symbolism as a common denominator of the subject and object of consciousness (as a power of the word) goes back to the very origins of human intelligence, and turns out to be—in innumerable so-called initiatory societies—the "hub of the Rota." But most of these secret societies do nothing more than grow and cultivate the "venerable garden," without ever practicing the *opening* into the permanent metamorphosis of the contemporary world. Like religions, they do nothing but reproduce endlessly the prestigious rites of bygone days, instead of forcing them to make the Phoenix's sacrifice: death as a condition of permanent regeneration.

It was with this quest in mind that the Society of Symbolism was founded in 1950, undertaking to attempt to open the cages, the various "fences" by which thought was enclosed, hemmed in either by the individual himself or by the coercion of constituted powers, jealously guarding their hegemony.

The fortunes of the Society of Symbolism, whose major function between 1950 and 1960 was the organization of interdisciplinary conferences, were subject—as are those of every pioneering enterprise—to great fluctuations: The conferences organized oscillated between the best and the worst, to the point where the *Cahiers Internationaux de Symbolisme* were established not to promote this preferential philosophical system, but to serve as a place for the expression of all forms of integrative thought, in the course of a continual, incessant transmutation.

The first text in issue no. 1 of the *Cahiers* is the message Gaston Bachelard addressed to us at the conference we organized under his leadership at the UNESCO palace, in June 1962, on "The Foundations of Symbolism in Light of Multiple Disciplines."

Allow me to reproduce the whole of this text, which appears to us today as having marked the birth of the *Cahiers:*

The organizers of the Conference on Symbolism have done me the honor to ask me to preside over your debates. My poor health prevents me from joining you. But I wish to tell you how certain I am of the success of your efforts.

Dr. Engelson gives a new impetus to your investigations. He knows the virtues of the union that we receive from all symbolism. The symbol centralizes the forces that are in man and the forces dispersed throughout all beings in the world. In your research on structure, you are sure to find the coherence of structuring forces that operate simultaneously in the psyche and the cosmos. The past, the immense past of the symbol, suddenly becomes present and alive when it is meditated upon as a creative force. Thus the symbol is more than a drawing; it is a program. Through works such as yours, we will enter into the realm of open symbolism. Through you, through your work, the symbol has a future, and the psychology of the symbol is an optimistic psychology because it is a psychology of creation.

Open symbolism proves to us that man has a need to imagine, that he has the right to imagine, that he has the duty to augment the real. Your conference is a starting point. It will prove that the symbol is, at each turn, a force of concentration and a force of polemic. The symbol must convince, but it must also persuade. Hence the usefulness of vast discussions.

I hope that all your investigations and all your discussions will be minutely recorded, and that thus, you will give us a great book, a great collection that will make us aware of the future of symbolism.

There was formed a governing committee, which included, besides Dr. Engelson and myself, Gilbert Durand of Grenoble, André Guimbretière of Paris, and Bernard Morel of Geneva, and a few years later, Hans Witte of Nijmegen joined us.

It should be noted that in the early 1960s, a certain courage was required, a certain freedom of thought, to grant any sympathy to such an undertaking; the very notion of symbolism was still strictly taboo, both in rationalist positivism and in theological positivism, not to mention the curses that our desire for opening, which constituted sacrilege, brought upon us from various hard-line "traditionalists."

But some people answered our call, and we were soon surrounded by an academic patronage, without which we would not have been able to round the perilous cape of the 1960s . . .

Conferences were held annually, in Paris, Brussels, and Geneva; and sometimes in Lausanne and Neuchâtel. It was a work of friendship and generosity, a time of a kind of happy artisanal research, subsidized by a patronage that was embodied almost exclusively by Dr. Engelson.

1969 and 1970 were difficult years, due both to the climate that prevailed in academic circles and to the difficulties inherent in our own administration. In 1970 I became ill, and because I alone had the charge of editing and administering the *Cahiers,* this caused a rupture in our rhythm of publication. But perhaps this brief eclipse was simply the sign of a necessary change in administrative structure.

This was also the epoch of the development of the young University of Mons. A project was born from an alliance between the privately funded interdisciplinary research center that we had become (which had ten years of active experience and twenty published journals) and the governmental powers of Belgium, or, more specifically, between the Scientific Research Department of the National Ministry of Education and the University of Mons. This project solidified, around the beginning of 1971, into the Interdisciplinary Center for Philosophical Studies at the University of Mons [French abbreviation: C.I.É.P.H.U.M.]. This center was responsible for, among other things, the organization of conferences and seminars, as well as the publication of *Cahiers Internationaux de Symbolisme.*

In this new infrastructure we found our second wind and formed the new, active friendships that such an enterprise requires in order to stay alive. In the spring of 1976, *Cahiers* nos. 31 and 32 will go to the presses.

When we are the all-purpose laborer for a publication—as I was, right from its birth—we have a prospective viewpoint, by dint of the love we put into it. The retrospective viewpoint is rarer, due to lack of time. And yet the critical approach we must be able to bring periodically to the work in progress can be born only from the dialectic exercising of the prospective and retrospective points of view.

If I set about reflecting upon all this now, at the end of the year 1975, it is because you have convinced me, and I have received your invitation not only as an opportunity to increase the audience of the *Cahiers,* but also as an occasion to evaluate the situation.

Do the *Cahiers* have a philosophy? If they do, I think it could be defined using Gaston Bachelard's words: "Your conference is a starting point. . . . Through works such as yours, we will enter into the realm of open symbolism."

This was reaffirmed by our late great friend Ferdinand Gonseth every time he spoke among us—and these were great moments in our meetings. If we have a philosophy, it must consent to this "open philosophy," to this philosophy of listening in which Mr. Gonseth, before his passing, so lovingly instructed us.

The foundation of the *Cahiers Internationaux de Symbolisme* is certainly not a "philosopher's stone," not secret membership in one or another esoteric tradition, but, paradoxically, *openness.* We have never had any kind of cliquish or exclusive structure arising from engagement either in subjectivism or in objectivism. This is not our goal. Rather, our aim is to avoid being tied down by contemporary modes of thought while at the same time remaining attentive and aware—all things being marked and modified (not codified) by their more or less significant, more or less ephemeral existence.

The *Cahiers* remains a place of resonance, a place of interferences in which we can learn, in which the multidimensional present of the symbol is woven. I believe I can affirm today that it has effectively become the publication that Bachelard wanted it to become fourteen years ago—a publication *that makes us aware of the future of symbolism,* that is, of the never completed birth of our reality, our presence in the world.

This is why it is not, strictly speaking, a matter of a "history" of the *Cahiers Internationaux de Symbolisme.* It is the place for a network of histories, more or less evident, more or less secret, which certain circumstances of time and place lead into the light of day, illuminating the current consciousness that these same circumstances obscure and potentialize. . . . Forgotten history is often only repeated "futurized" history, delayed history, history that must return to the belly of the night—to the kingdom of Hermes—in order for its sun to ripen there, the symbol being the womb of all things possible.

Thus, without a doubt, the *Cahiers* is a sort of discrete memory for symbolism populated by future readings, a nursery of the outlandish battling with a dogmatic structure in which the future of the word is already inhibited and codified, kept safe in the immobile sanctuary of the Origin, in the deification of the one-dimensional.

In its tranquil manner, without having recourse to the violence of advertising, the *Cahiers,* through good times and bad, pursued its labor of opening, its work of permanent revolution, serenely awaiting the joy of being read.

Claire Lejeune

2 GENERAL SYMBOLOGY AND THE EXPLORATION OF THE IMAGINARY*

For half a century, the enormous progress of techniques of visual information on the one hand (photography, cinema, television, processes of illustration and printing, etc.), and, on the other hand, discoveries made by psychoanalysis have returned the image to the highest level of investigations in anthropological research. The second half of the twentieth century saw the triumph of what we might call, along with André Malraux and René Huyghe, "the civilization of the image," and André Leroi-Gourhan—with less optimism than McLuhan—asked whether in the destiny of man, the image was in the process of supplanting "gestures and words." The gesture having been abandoned to machines, the word—and its roots in writing and printing—is now giving way to a language (mode of expression and communication) in which the visual image occupies the primary position. Information in all its forms, from scientific work to "mass media" and entertainment, is becoming more and more visual: Scientific documentation, journalistic and literary information,

---

*Text from a presentation given at the Center for Multidisciplinary and Interuniversity Research on the Imaginary and the Symbol, abbreviated to Center for Research on the Imaginary (C.R.I.) by its founders. This text is published with their authorization.

advertising, propaganda, and the diffusion of ideas all use visual resources increasingly. This technological and societal movement in the very foundations of information requires, epistemologically and methodically, the establishment of a multidisciplinary research organization—because the old "disciplines—anthropology, psychology, the literary sciences, sociology, history, and so forth—are still founded upon a system of regulation that is a matter of concepts and not of images. The traditional disciplines of the university reveal themselves under the influence of—among other things—the irreversible discoveries made in psychoanalysis, depth psychology, structuralist comparativism, and cultural anthropology, tributaries to 80 percent of the problematics of the imaginary.

The establishment of a Center for Anthropological Research devoted to the Imaginary—that is, to the empirical totality of images and systems of images—was therefore necessary. The humanities and social sciences faculty at Grenoble were pioneers in this regard, being one of the first groups to focus upon imagination, image, symbol, and so forth.

Starting in 1956, there was direct collaboration between the French literature department and the philosophy department, then the psychology and sociology departments. Professors Léon Cellier and Gilbert Durand held seminars centered on questions of image, myth, and symbol in literature and anthropology. This trend would become increasingly well defined: In 1962, Professor L. Cellier joined the patronage committee and G. Durand joined the director's committee of *Cahiers Internationaux de Symbolisme,* a publication of the Society of Symbolism that was organized during several years of conferences within a wide area (Paris, Brussels, Geneva). Above all, Professors Cellier and Durand devoted a great portion of their work and their articles to the subject of the imaginary. From a long list of important works that have been translated into five or six other languages, we will cite only these examples: *L'Épopée romantique* (1954; republished in 1971 under the title *L'Épopée humanitaire et les grands mythes romantiques*), *Mallarmé et la Morte qui parle* (1959) by L. Cellier, *Les structures anthropologiques de l'Imaginaire* (1960, second edition 1964, third edition 1969), *Le décor mythique de la Chartreuse de Parme* (1961, second edition 1971), and *L'imagination symbolique* (1964) by Gilbert Durand—not to mention the numerous articles published by L. Cellier and G. Durand in *Cahiers Internationaux de Symbolisme* and by G. Durand in the volumes of *Eranos Jahrbuch*. Finally, the problems of the imaginary met with great success among young seekers: Many doctoral theses and numerous degrees were oriented toward these subjects both in French literature and in foreign languages and civilizations, as well as in the various departments of the humanities. Moreover, since its founding, the C.R.I. has attracted the interest of highly distinguished French and foreign scientists, who now form a permanent scientific council.

THE FOUNDING OF THE CENTER FOR RESEARCH ON THE IMAGINARY

On December 20, 1966, the Faculty Council for Literature and Humanities at Grenoble unanimously backed Professor G. Durand (chair of sociology and cultural and social anthropology, director of the College of Literature at the University of Chambéry) and Professor L. Cellier (chair of French literature) in their creation of an Interdisciplinary Center for Research on the Imaginary. This development was perfectly integrated into the perspectives of the Reform of Higher Education, which advocated a program establishing Study Centers for interdisciplinary research. On March 13, 1967, a preparatory meeting took place at the College of Literature at the University of Chambéry, gathering some thirty researchers belonging to various disciplines. The Center for Research on the Imaginary—with its provisional subtitle, Cooperative Group for the Study of the Imaginary and the Symbol: Contribution to the Humanities—was founded, and its leadership was unanimously bestowed upon Professor Gilbert Durand.

The center was properly established in the course of a certain number of meetings. In October 1967, a calendar was established comprising the names of about sixty researchers, among them professors of French literature, comparative and foreign literature, and psychology; doctors from psychiatric hospitals; psychologists and sociologists; and doctoral and master's students from many disciplines.

After this first phase, which proved the interest and scientific relevance of such an institution (the opportunity for interdisciplinary coordination offered by the center, the success encountered with teachers and young seekers alike), a vigorous struggle was necessary in order to pass through a second, crucial stage: obtaining official recognition and a minimum of material aid. There were many difficulties. Only after trying multiple approaches did the director of the C.R.I. and his late colleague Paul Deschamps succeed in the official establishment of the center, which was finally granted by the Minister of National Education. This establishment was announced by ministerial decree on June 10, 1968. The minister recognized the founding of a Center for Cultural Anthropological Research with the subtitle Center for Research on the Imaginary.

Since the beginning, the center, brought to life by Professor G. Durand, director of the defunct C.L.U. of Chambéry, had been working effectively in Chambéry with the personnel of the C.L.U.—particularly, in collaboration with a technician and a technical agent allocated to the center by the C.L.U. Thus the center was physically based at Chambéry, and within the framework of the Law of Orientation, its higher learning center obtained autonomy under the title of Academic Center of Savoie. The statutes of the U.E.R. for Literature, Humanities, and Social Sciences at Chambéry then established the Center for Multidisciplinary and Interuniversity Research of the Imaginary and the Symbol (abbreviated as the Center for Research on the Imaginary) as a research center connected with this same U.E.R.

Finally, to conform with the stipulations in Article 13 of the Law of Orientation of Higher Education, on November 7, 1968, the Center for Research on the Imaginary prepared an outline for statutes that, together with the statutes of the U.E.R. of Literature, would obtain general approval following an identical procedure.

THE FUNCTION OF THE C.R.I.

The center consisted of a library, which currently contains three thousand books and is growing steadily. This library collects multidisciplinary works (ethnology, psychology, sociology, religion, the arts, literature, etc.); copious materials from cultural anthropology; and specialized works on images, myths, symbols, and so forth. This reference library, which also loans out books against a deposit, is open exclusively to members of the C.R.I. It is the indispensable infrastructure for research, and thanks to its files—organized analytically, alphabetically, thematically, and so forth— researchers can obtain large amounts of information very rapidly.

The C.R.I. is essentially a multidisciplinary grouping of academics and professionals from diverse backgrounds, and its primary mission is to form new contacts between people who, in their personal research (master's theses, etc.), have thus far been working alone but in similar areas. It encourages the exchange of bibliographical, theoretical, and methodological information, and allows for an "opening" of research, helping scholars to get out of the rut of solitary work and to pass beyond the strictly disciplinary walls of academic study.

The C.R.I.—at least in its current state—does not have its own full-time team of independent or contractual researchers. It is a superstructure embracing and coordinating specific researchers employed professionally by various entities. Nevertheless, research at the C.R.I., although unpaid, is organized and systematic. Thus research is *program oriented,* revolving around subjects chosen by all the researchers together finding a specific echo with the various sectors of research works in progress. At the basis, we stick to nine general themes: the view, the mask, colors, refuge, the fall, monsters, interconnections and redundancies, allegory, and ascension. To these we must add the image of the body and the myth of the messenger and the voyager. The programming of research along major themes (not excluding the possibility of identifying subthemes or derived themes) takes place on three levels. The first level is academic teaching, where an effort is made, as far as possible, to coordinate certain certificates (especially the C2 in the Imaginary established at Grenoble and Chambéry and the C3 in the Sociology of Fine Arts and Culture at Grenoble), as well as the subjects of the master's and doctorate theses. Thus entire seminars of master's students are established and grouped around the same topic, which each one examines in terms of a different author or area. On the basis of these works, we can envisage the establishment of syntheses suitable for integration into the body of research, constituting an important contribution to the advancement of the study of humans and civilizations. Because of this method, research by students (graduate research, theses, etc.) escapes the isolation to which it is traditionally confined, and most important, it escapes the ignorance that necessarily results from this isolation. Thus research can become truly fruitful. The second level of this programmed research is the work of the C.R.I. itself: Conferences and publications follow this thematic program systematically. Third, this programmed research facilitates solitary research, guiding each scholar's exploratory efforts. These efforts solidify into a categorization project (analytical files by author, image files). The development of such files is fundamental for the center because it forms a concrete and precise basis for the cooperative that the center is designed to be.

During the academic year, the C.R.I. holds approximately monthly meetings at which scholars evaluate their investigations on fundamental topics and share their methods of approaching the imaginary. These meetings generally consist of a series of small presentations, which crystallize interest and allow for discussion in which different points of view are compared and fruitful exchanges are established. Seven years of functional experience will allow for a stricter organization of the programming and the heuristic process in years to come. Two types of meetings are planned. The first, in small specialized workshops that take place about two or three times per month, will establish the specialized foundations for research. These workshops will be mobile (i.e., they can move from one year to the next depending on the imperatives of the general topic of research chosen in the general assembly), and will be led by specially qualified Masters of Research. The second type of meeting will be a general "crossroads" assembly in which the annual or biennial research programs will be established, and in which the results of workshop projects will be compared. Four meetings of this type will take place each year, and as in years past, they will result in printed reports.

Besides these regular meetings, the C.R.I. organizes annual Days of Study, which, although private, are open to all people who are seriously interested in the subject of the imaginary. These days consist of conferences followed by discussions, and they are attended by people from French and foreign universities.

DIFFUSION OF RESEARCH
AND PUBLICATIONS[1]

The reports from these meetings are regularly published after each general meeting and are sent to all members of the C.R.I. with all accompanying documents (bibliography, texts, etc.). The C.R.I. also plans for the publication (in offset) of a complete directory.

The center publishes annually a substantial collection (300–400 pages) under the title *Circé,* appearing as part of *Éditions des Lettres modernes* (Minard) in Paris. *Circé* is essentially devoted to studies of thematics, alternating with numbers on methodology. Most of the articles are written by the center's core researchers, but some are composed by exterior people connected with the C.R.I. through their area of research and their interests. *Circé* comprises a series of long main articles of about fifty pages each, followed by a second, shorter part ("Research and Projects") that includes summaries of works in progress and reports on papers and Days of Study at the C.R.I. Given the success of this publication, the C.R.I. and its editor plan to create a collection reserved for theses and works of greater breadth.

People are authorized to become members of the C.R.I. if they have already published known works on the subject matter, if they are currently conducting research for master's or doctoral theses, or if they are pursuing related work in any university or in their sector of professional activity. The candidacy of each prospective member is submitted for evaluation to the center's management for eventual presentation by or patronage of two researchers. Anyone wishing to become a member of the center must make his or her request personally, in writing, to the director and the general secretariat.

Registration in the C.R.I. is annual, and the activities of the C.R.I. follow the pattern of the French academic year.

EVALUATION AND FUTURE PERSPECTIVES

The Center for Research on the Imaginary did not wait for the events of May 1968 to consider itself a comanaged, multidisciplinary organism that shattered the walls of narrow specialties and proclaimed "the powers of the imaginary." The C.R.I. is original and specific on three levels: (1) on the level of internal functioning; (2) on the level of the object of research and methods; and (3) on the level of its relationship to research in the humanities in general and, more particularly, with research relating to the imaginary.

The very life of the center is founded upon the active participation of each member, considered—from the tenured professor to the master's student—as a researcher and also as a full-fledged administrator. All the problems of the C.R.I. are always discussed in general assembly. Its interdisciplinary nature is effective, forming direct relations among literary scholars, linguists, psychologists, sociologists, psychiatrists, and so forth, who benefit from fruitful collaboration, all starting from the privileged launching pad that is the imaginary. The scientific hierarchy is respected, for the highest criterion is the quality and strength of work.

Some people may be surprised—or even indignant—at the term *imaginary,* which the center has decided to keep in its name. This is intended to convey the idea that its research is prohibited from falling back into the strict specializations implied by other related terms, such as *image, imagination, mental imagery, iconology, symbolism,* and so forth. The C.R.I. intends to establish a truly fundamentally interdisciplinary research, all at once mobilizing methodological and epistemological resources, normal and pathological psychology, art history, the history of religion, aesthetics, literature, literary criticism, ethnology, mythology, iconology, and so on. The C.R.I. wishes to work on the anthropological level, in the broadest, interdisciplinary sense of this word, as stated by Claude Lévi-Strauss: Its aim, across the various methods and different strategies of the necessary specialized disciplines, is a comprehensive fundamental synthesis of the basic hominid energy that contemporary anthropology as a whole has ultimately recognized in the universe of imagination.

Thus, the research of the anthropologist of the imaginary ultimately aims at an understanding of the final structures of hominid behavior. This understanding appears more important than ever, considering the scientific knowledge of nature acquired by modern man and the enormous—and sometimes terrifying—technical power that has emerged from it. Research on the imaginary envisages man transcending fatally reductive ethnocentric and epistemocentric classifications, seeing him in terms of what is more fundamental and at the same time more concrete—dare we say—in terms of his nature. Furthermore, it is conducive to therapeutics, or at least to pedagogies that go beyond the inevitable routines of the disciplinary division of anthropological research. For these reasons, it is applicable to a new humanism on a turn-of-the-twentieth-century scale. The Center for Research on the Imaginary is the first institution to have opened a positively revolutionary path within the ancient and venerable French university system, battling against prejudices and centuries-old blockades just as has been done by other revolutions, whether short-lived or resulting in utopian innovations. The C.R.I. is aware that its example has been followed and that it is not the only entity working in this direction. It has established a network of exchanges and relationships with organizations and people working with its same perspectives. Thus, it has direct relations with the International Society of Symbolism, the Interdisciplinary Center for Philosophical Studies at the University of Mons (current publisher of *Cahiers Internationaux de Symbolisme*), the International Society of Techniques of Mental Imagery, the Ch. Baudouin International Institute of Psychology and Psychotherapy, the C. G. Jung Study Group, the Research Group on Symbols at the University of Genoa, the Center for Research on Symbology at the University of Quebec in Montreal, the Eranos Foundation in Ascona, the Society for Scientific Research on Symbols in Köln, the Center for Studies and Research on Advertising at the University of Grenoble, the Center for Advanced Studies of Medieval Civilization at the University of Poitiers, and the research seminaries at universities in Dijon, Reims, Bordeaux, and Paris (the Sorbonne).

The center also has a large membership among foreign scholars, and consequently has "correspondents" in various parts of the world, including Switzerland, Germany, Spain, Australia, Algeria, Belgium, Denmark, the Netherlands, Morocco, Iran, Italy, Israel, Japan, Korea, Romania, Togo, the United States, and Russia.

BIBLIOGRAPHY OF THE WORKS AND PUBLICATIONS OF THE MEMBERS OF THE C.R.I. RELATING TO RESEARCH ON THE IMAGINARY

INDIVIDUAL WORKS FROM THE C.R.I.

Achard, Y. *Le langage de Krishnamurti*. Paris: Le Courrier du Livre, 1970 (doctoral thesis).

Albouy, P. *Mythes et mythologie dans la littérature française*. Paris: Armand Colin, 1981.

Baudin, H. *La science fiction*. Paris: Bordas, 1971.

Bellet, R. *Mallarmé: l'encre et le ciel*. Seyssel: Champ Vallon, 1987.

Bies, J. *Athos—Voyage à Sainte-Montagne*. Paris: Éd. Dervy, 1980.

———. *Littérature française et pensée hindoue*. Paris: Klincksieck, 1973.

———. *Passeport pour les Temps nouveaux.* Paris: Éd. Dervy, 1982.

Bonardel, F. *L'hermétisme.* Paris: Que sais-je?, P.U.F., 1985.

Bosetti, G. *Le mythe de l'enfance dans le roman italien contemporain.* Grenoble: ELLUG, 1987.

Bourgeois, R. *La flèche et le but.* Grenoble: Éd. Université III, 1984.

———. *L'ironie romantique.* Grenoble: P.U.G., 1974.

Bril, J. *À cordes et à cris.* Paris: Clancier-Guenaud, 1980.

———. *Lilith ou la mère obscure.* Paris: Payot, 1981.

———. *L'invention comme phénomène anthropologique.* Paris: Klincksieck, 1973.

———. *Origenes et symbolisme des productions textiles: de la toile et du fil.* Paris: Clancier-Guenaud, 1984.

Brunel, P. *L'évolution des morts et la descente aux enfers.* Paris: S.E.D.E.S., 1974.

———. *Le mythe d'Électre.* Paris: Colin, 1971.

———. *Le mythe de la métamorphose.* Paris: Colin, 1974.

———. *Théâtre et cruauté ou Dionysos profané.* Paris: Méridiens, 1983.

Burgos, J. *L'enchanteur pourrissant de Guillaume Apollinaire.* Paris: Minard, 1971. (This work won the 1972 critical edition prize.)

Cambronne, P. *Recherche sur les structures de l'Imaginaire dans les "Confessions" de saint Augustin.* Paris: Études Augustiniennes, 1982.

Cazenave, M. *La subversion de l'âme, mythanalyse de l'histoire de Tristan et Iseut.* Paris: Seghers, 1981.

Cazenave, M., and R. Auguet. *Les empereurs fous.* Paris: Imago, 1981.

Cellier, L. *Gérard de Nerval, l'homme et l'œuvre,* 3rd edition. Paris: Hatier, Boivin, 1974.

———. *L'épopée humanitaire et les grands mythes romantiques.* Paris: S.E.D.E.S., 1971.

———. *Parcours initiatique.* Neuchâtel: La Baconnière and P.U.G., 1977.

Centeno, Y. K. *A Alquimia e o Fausto de Goethe.* Lisbon: Arcadia, 1983.

Centeno, Y. K., et al. *A viagem em Os Luisiadas de Camoes: Simbolo e mito.* Lisbon: Arcadia, 1980.

Cesbron, G. *Édouard Estaunié, romancier de l'être,* followed by "Récits spirites." Geneva: Droz, 1977.

Chalas, Y. *Vichy et l'imaginaire totalitaire.* Arles: Actes-Sud, 1985.

Charon, J. E. *L'esprit, cet inconnu.* Paris: Albin Michel, 1977.

Christinger, R. *Le livre du soleil.* Paris: Denoël, 1974.

———. *Le voyage dans l'imaginaire.* Geneva: Éditions du Mont-Blanc, 1971.

Christinger, R., P. Solier, F. Siegenthaler. *Récits mythiques et symbolisme de la navigation.* Paris: Dervy-livres, 1980.

Christinger, R., J. Eracle, P. Solier. *La croix universelle.* Paris: Dervy-livres, 1980.

Crespi, F. *Méditation symbolique et société.* Paris: Méridiens-Klincksieck, 1983.

Czyba, L. *La femme dans les romans de Flaubert, mythes et idéologie.* Lyon: P.U.L., 1984.

Dauge, Y. A. *Le barbare.* Brussels: Éd. Latomus, 1981.

———. *Virgile, Maître de Sagesse.* Milan: Arche, 1984.

David, M. *Letteratura e psicanalisi.* Milan: Mursia, 1967.

———. *La psicanalisi nella cultura italiana,* revised and expanded 3rd edition. Turin: Boringhieri, 1970.

Dorfles, G. *L'intervalle perdu.* Paris: Méridiens, 1984.

———. *Mythes et rites d'aujourd'hui.* Paris: Klincksieck, 1975.

Dubois, C. G. *Celtes et Gaulois au XVIᵉ siècle.* Paris: J. Vrin, 1972.

———. *La conception de l'histoire de France au XVIᵉ siècle.* Paris: Nizet, 1977.

———. *L'imaginaire de la Renaissance.* Paris: P.U.F., 1985.

Duborgel, B. *Imaginaire et pédagogie.* Paris: Le Sourire qui Mord, 1983.

Ducret, A. "Œuvre d'art et sens commun: l'apport de Lévi-Strauss." In *Art et Société.* Brussels: Éd. Les Éperonniers, 1989.

Durand, G. *Figures mystiques et visages de l'œuvre; de la mythocritique à la mythanalyse.* Paris: Berg International, 1979.

———. *La foi du cordonnier.* Paris: Denoël, 1984.

———. *L'âme tigrée. Les pluriels de psyché.* Paris: Denoël, 1980.

———. *Le décor mythique de la Chartreuse de Parme, les structures figuratives du roman stendhalien.* Paris: J. Corti, 1983.

———. *Les structures anthropologiques de l'Imaginaire.* Paris: Presses Universitaires de France, 1969.

———. *L'imagination symbolique.* Paris: P.U.F., 1984.

———. *Science de l'homme et tradition.* Paris: Berg International, 1979.

Durand, G., M. Cazenave, J. Le Goff, et al. *Mythe et histoire.* Paris: Albin Michel, 1985.

Durand, Y. *L'exploration de l'imaginaire.* Paris: Éd. L'espace bleu, 1988.

Durand, Y., and J. Morenon. *L'imaginaire de l'alcoolisme.* Paris: Éditions Universitaires, 1972.

Faivre, A. *Accès à l'ésotérisme occidental.* Paris: Gallimard, 1987.

———. *Les conférences des Élus Cohens de Lyon 1774–1776. Aux sources du rite écossais rectifié.* Braine-le-Comte, Belgium: Éd. de Baucens, 1975.

———. *L'ésotérisme au XVIIᵉ siècle en France et en Allemagne.* Paris: Seghers, 1973.

Felman, S. *La "folie" chez Stendhal.* Paris: J. Corti, 1971.

Gagnebet, C. *À plus hault sens: l'ésotérisme spirituel et charnel de Rabelais,* 2 vols. Paris: Maisonneuve et Larose, 1986.

Gallais, P. *Dialectique du récit médiéval, Chrétien de Troyes et l'hexagone logique.* Amsterdam: Rodopi, 1982.

———. *Genèse du roman occidental, Essai dur Tristan et Iseut.* Paris: Éd. du Sirac, Tête de feuilles, 1974.

———. *Perceval et l'Initiation.* Paris: L'Agrafe d'Or, Éd. du Sirac, 1973.

Glowczewski, B., and J. F. Matteudi. *La cité des Cataphiles.* Paris: Méridiens, 1983.

Godinho, H. *O Mito e o estilo, introdução a une mitoesti listica.* Lisbon: Arquivos Nacionais, 1982.

Hillman, J. *Le mythe de la psychoanalyse.* Paris: Imago-Payot, 1977.

Lerède, J. *La suggestopédie.* Paris: Que sais-je?, P.U.F., 1983.

———. *Les troupeaux de l'aurore.* Boucherville, Quebec: Les Éditions de Mortagne, 1983.

Libis, J. *Le mythe de l'Androgyne.* Paris: Bern International, 1980.

Maffesoli, M. *Essai sur la violence banal et fondatrice.* Paris: Méridiens, 1984.

———. *La conquête du présent.* Paris: P.U.F., 1979.

———. *L'ombre de Dionysos.* Paris: P.U.F., 1979.

Marigny, J. *Le vampire dans la littérature anglo-saxonne.* Paris: Didier Érudition, 1985.

Mathias, P. *La Beauté dans les* Fleurs du Mal. Grenoble: P.U.G., 1977.

Milner, M. *Entretien sur l'homme et le diable.* Paris: Monton, 1965.

———. *La fantasmagorie. Essai sur l'optique fantastique.* Paris: P.U.F., 1982.

———. *Le Diable dans la littérature française de Cazotte à Baudelaire, 1772–1861,* 2 vols. Paris: Corti, 1960.

Miranda, M. *La société incertaine.* Paris: Méridiens, 1986.

Morin, M., and C. Bertrand. *Le territoire imaginaire de la culture.* Quebec: Hurtubise, 1979.

Nicolescu, B. *Nous, la particule et le monde.* Paris: Payot, 1985.

Paques, V. *L'arbre cosmique dans la pensée populaire et dans la vie quotidienne du Nord-Ouest américain.* Paris: Éd. Musée de l'Homme, 1964.

Pelletier, F. *Imaginaire du cinématographe.* Paris: Méridiens, 1983.

Pennacchioni, J. *La nostalgie en image.* Paris: Méridiens, 1983.

Perrin, J. *Les structures de l'Imaginaire schelleyen.* Grenoble: P.U.G., 1973.

Petit, M. C. *Galdos y la fontana de oro, genèse de l'œuvre d'un romancier.* Ediciones Hispanoamericanas, 1972.

———. *Les personnages féminins dans les romans de B. Perez Galdos.* Lyon: P.U.L. II, coll. Les Belles-Lettres, 1972.

Pessin, A. (in collaboration with M. Maffesoli). *La rêverie anarchiste 1848–1914.* Paris: Méridiens, 1982.

———. *La violence fondatrice.* Paris: Champ Vallon, 1978.

Pessin, A., and H. Torgue. *Villes imaginaires.* Paris: Champ Urbain, 1980.

Pimenta, A. *A (mas)cara diante da cara.* Lisbon: Presença, 1981.

Reckert, S., et al. *A viagem entre o real e o imaginario.* Lisbon: Arcadia, 1981.

Sachs, V. *The Game of Creation.* Paris: M.S.H., 1982.

Sachs, V., ed. *Le Blanc et le Noir chez Melville et Faulkner.* Paris: Mouton, 1974.

Sansonetti, P. G. *Graal et Alchimie.* Paris: Berg International, 1982.

Sansot, P. *La France sensible.* Paris: Champ Vallon, 1985.

———. *Les formes sensibles de la vie sociale.* Paris: P.U.F., 1986.

———. *Poétique de la ville.* Paris: Klincksieck, 1971 (master's thesis).

———. *Variations paysagères.* Paris: Klincksieck, 1980.

Sauvageot, A. *Figures de la publicité, figures du monde.* Paris: P.U.F., 1987.

Servier, J. *Les forges d'Hiram ou le genèse d'Occident.* Paris: Grasset, 1976.

———. *L'homme et l'invisible.* Paris: Imago, 1980.

Sironneau, J. P. *Sécularisation et religions politiques.* Paris: Mouton, 1982.

Solie, P. *La femme essentielle.* Paris: Seghers, 1980.

———. *Psychanalyse et imaginal.* Paris: Imago, 1980.

Tacussel, P. *L'attraction sociale. La dynamique de l'imaginaire dans la société monocéphale.* Paris: Méridiens, 1984.

Thomas, J. *Structures de l'Imaginaire dans l'Énéide.* Paris: Éd. Belles Lettres, 1981.

Tristan, F. *Houng, les sociétés secrètes chinoises.* Paris: Balland, 1987.

Tuzet, H. *Le cosmos et l'imagination.* Paris: Corti, 1965.

Vierne, S. *Jules Verne.* Paris: Balland, 1986.

———. *Jules Verne et le roman initiatique, contribution à l'étude de l'Imaginaire.* Paris: l'Agrafe d'Or, Éd. du Sirac, 1973 (master's thesis).

———. *Jules Verne, mythe et modernité.* Paris: P.U.F., 1989.

———. *L'île mystérieuse de Jules Verne.* Paris: Hachette, 1973.

———. *Rite, roman, initiation.* Grenoble: P.U.G., 1973 (complementary thesis).

Wunenberger, J. L. *La fête, le jeu et le sacré.* Paris: Éd. Universitaires, 1977.

———. *Le sacré.* Paris: Que sais-je?, P.U.F., 1981.

———. *L'utopie ou la crise de l'imaginaire.* Paris: Delarge, 1979.

COLLECTIVE WORKS FROM THE C.R.I.

Charon, J. E., ed. *Imaginaire et réalités.* Paris: Albin Michel, 1984.

———. *L'esprit et la science.* Paris: Albin Michel, 1984.

Dubois, Cl. G., ed. *Imaginaire du changement.* Bordeaux: P.U.B., 1984–85.

Durand, G., and S. Vierne, eds. "Le mythe et le mythique." In *Actes du colloque de Cerisy.* Paris: Albin Michel, 1987.

Maffesoli, M., ed. *La galaxie de l'imaginaire, dérive autour de l'œuvre de Gilbert Durand.* Paris: Berg International, 1980.

Pitta, D. Perin Rocha, ed. *O imaginario e a simbologia da passagem.* Recife, Brazil: Massangana, 1984.

Verjat, A., ed. *Les valeurs heuristiques de la figure mythique d'Hermès.* University of Barcelona: GRIM, 1985.

Vierne, S., ed. *Espaces et imaginaires.* Grenoble: P.U.G., 1979.

———. *Essai sur l'imaginaire musical.* Grenoble: ELLUG, 1984.

———. *Itinéraires imaginaires.* Grenoble: ELLUG, 1986.

———. *Le retour du mythe.* Grenoble: P.U.G., 1980.

———. *Sciences et imaginaire.* Grenoble: ELLUG, 1985.

JOURNALS OF THE VARIOUS
DIVISIONS OF THE C.R.I.

C.R.I., University of Grenoble III. *Iris.*

C.R.I., University of Burgundy. *Cahiers du Centre de recherches sur l'image, le symbole et le mythe.*

C.R.I., University of Bordeaux III. *EIDOLON.*

C.R.I., University of Angers. *Cahiers de recherches sur l'imaginaire.*

G.R.I.M., University of Barcelona. *Anthropos.*

University of Savoie. *Annales du Centre de recherches et d'applications psychologiques et sociologiques.*

3 "THE UNIVERSE OF THE SYMBOL"

BY GILBERT DURAND

It is naturally expected that someone who, like myself this evening, has the formidable honor of starting off a week of study devoted to the symbol will give peremptory definitions. I will be disappointing in this regard, refusing to give such unequivocal definitions, precisely because, on the one hand, the challenge of the subject we are approaching is inherently many-sided, and on the other hand, because it always appears suspect to me to want to begin at the end. Thus, rather than operational definitions—which I have already outlined and even presented in a table in a little book[1]—I wish to give only operative designations, collected according to the symbolic and mythological usage of twenty years of research.

Certainly, in order to satisfy everyone, we may depart from the classic definition of the *symbol* as authors from Creuzer to Lalande to Jung have given it for the last century:[2] three characteristics delimiting the understanding of the notion—first, the *concrete* aspect (sensory, pictorial, figurative, etc.) of the *signal;* then its *optimal* character (this is the best way to evoke—make known, suggest, reveal, and so forth—the *signification;* and ultimately this latter is *something impossible to perceive* (see, imagine, understand, etc.), directly or otherwise. In other words, the symbol is a system of indirect knowledge in which the signification and the signal more or less nullify the "break"—rather in the way that Jacques Derrida set up the *gramme* against the Saussurean break.[3] The symbol is a borderline case of indirect knowledge in which, paradoxically, this knowledge tends to become direct, but on a different level from that of biological signals or logical discourse. Its immediacy aims for the plane of *gnosis* as if in an asymptotic movement. This gives an idea of the privileged usage given to the symbol by all types of mysticism and all paths of enlightenment. But we must be cautious here, especially when facing an audience of theologians, who give meanings to symbols and signs that are diametrically opposed to those given to them by anthropologists.[4] And perhaps the theologians are right—for what we anthropologists call a *symbol* is simply the famous "sign of recognition" (*symbolon*), using two halves of a broken object; yet what is demanded of the symbol is entirely different from what is demanded of the unequivocal mechanism of the symbolon. The symbol is required to "give a meaning," namely beyond the realm of communication, and to give us access to the world of expression.[5]

Once we take these precautions into consideration, I will endeavor to give here the results of twenty years of work, the aim of which was to establish operatively the problematic vocabulary for events such as the one that is beginning this evening. I would like to outline—summarily, of course, for this is only a conference—the three dimensions of the symbol such as I was led to them after long experience and experimentation, closing in on them and putting them to work. I will cover the first two dimensions fairly quickly. They were established, at least in my view, at least fifteen or twenty years ago, and I will content myself with noting that I have written about them. The third dimension, however, appears to me to be more current, underlying the problematics of myth, in favor of which I will allow myself to deviate slightly from the realm of this talk.

I will call the first dimension of the problematics of symbols the *mechanical dimension,* meaning simply that since the dawn of research on the symbol, there have appeared a group of notions that, both in their static organization and in their functioning (cinematic, so to speak), define a psychic apparatus. To these notions, I devoted the introduction[6] to the outcome of many years of reflection on symbols. I then introduced the possible functioning categories of the symbol and outlined the modalities of symbolic disqualification—that is to say, the procedures by which a symbol is stripped of its specific powers and falls back into the category of sign, allegory, metaphor, metonymy, parable, and so on.

Three categories still seem to me to constitute the symbolic apparatus. The first is the scheme, which I have metaphorically called *verbal,* because in natural languages the verb is what "expresses action." This category is the most immediate for figurative representation, and arises directly— with the help of reflexive connections in the large human brain—in the unconscious reflexes of the living body. Schemes are the main referential for all gestures possible for the species *Homo sapiens.* This is what Bergson perceived in the segregation of the *Homo faber* within us. But by placing the scheme at the root of symbolic figuration, I separate myself from the Jungian theory that ultimately places a reservoir of elaborate archetypes in a collective unconscious, and likewise I separate myself from reductions of the symbolic figure, both Freudian (reduction to the symptom of a unique libido obsessed with the digestive and genital orifices) and Lacanian (reduction of this prelinguistic language to the syntaxes and wordplay of a natural language). Along with Mauss, I firmly believe that the first language, the word, is corporeal expression. And I do not wonder—like Faust, who must have read Derrida—whether it was the word *or* the action that was at the beginning, because the word is a specific action, not only on the level of the verbs "to plug," "to fill," "to stuff," "to engulf," and so on, but also on the all-important level of the motivity of the limbs, walking erect, and, first and foremost, the hands. The penis is not the only verbal thing! Mimicry, dances, gestures—what Husserl called the "prereflexive"—are principial in relation to speech— and all the more so in relation to writing.

Receiving only second place are the famous archetypes.[7] And in turn, these "primal images, universal to the species" are divided into the categories of the metaphorical discourse that we have just outlined, into epithets and substantives, depending on whether they relate to sensible or perceptive quantities, such as high, low; hot, cold; dry, wet; pure, deep; and so forth, or else objects perceived and denominated substantively: light, darkness, abyss, child, moon, mother, cross, circle, numbers, and so on. Archetypes are on the path of perceptive differentiation and exogenous distancing.

Finally, archetypes are also specified under the qualifying influence of purely exogenous incidents: climate, technology, geographic area, fauna, cultural state, associations by contact, phonetic assonances and consonances, and so forth. This is the place of the symbolic apparatus that we may call a *symbol* in the strictest sense. For example, the archetype of the East that is so popular in this little peninsula of Asia formed by Asia Minor and Europe—the symbolic procession of the sun rising over mountains or desert lands, which we connect to the golden color of the sand, was a different color for the ancient Mexicans:[8] turquoise, connected with the sun rising over the humid Gulf of Mexico from which the rainy winds blew; and the light of the morning star was replete with symbols of plant fertility.

We could also demonstrate how the *natural languages* add derivations and semantic idioms to the symbolic apparatus via their phoneticism or when they are graphically written. The apostolic foundation of the church upon Simon the Rock originates in wordplay, in the near-homonymy of *sema/soma* ("prison/body," in Greek), from *shiva/shavâ* ("god/cadaver," in Sanskrit), the Arabic calligraphy of *bâ* and *alif* (*bâ*, B, first letter of the inaugural eulogy of the Qur'an, *Bismillâh*)[9] attesting, along with many others, to the derivative and creative power of the symbols of the natural languages.

But these derivations are the limited mechanism beyond which the general definition of the symbol given at the beginning of this study no longer applies. As we engage more and more in cultural particularisms and in the situations and events of history, the symbol loses its plurivocity and becomes a syntheme,[10] the archetypal sign sometimes surviving but the meaning losing its equivocalness, for the signal is detached more and more from the signification. The symbol of the cross, so archetypal, appearing everywhere in the ornamentation of Christian churches, risks an initial historical and sentimental particularization when it is specified in *crucifixus,* and ultimately falls into the state of the sign (in the sense understood by anthropologists!): the sign for addition, which is entirely unequivocal in mathematical language.

This decline in symbolic content, this kind of entropy forever making the letter cover and hide the spirit, hints at a cinematics of the symbol: Symbolism functions only when there is distancing, but without breaks, and only when there is plurivocity, but no arbitrariness. This is because the symbol has two requirements: It must take measure of its inability to make us see the signification in itself, but it must also engage belief in its total pertinence. Symbolism ceases to function, either due to distancing in the perception, in the direct representations of the animal psyche, or due to plurivocity in the processes of synthemization or through breaking in the case of the arbitrariness of the sign that is so dear to Saussure.

But these are limited cases, difficult for the animal species *Homo sapiens* to realize, and this leads us to consider the genetic dimensions of the symbol.

This internal agency of the symbolic apparatus leads to genetic reflections on the formation of the symbol not only in the infant, as examined by Piaget, but also in the animal kingdom—if we assume the correctness of evolution—as examined by contemporary ethnologists, most specifically Jacob von Uexküll.[11]

Were we to try to summarize the works of contemporary biologists, we might say that what distinguishes the behavior of *Homo sapiens* from that of other animals is the fact that his psychical activity, with rare exceptions, is indirect (or reflexive)—that is to say, it never has the immediacy, the certainty, or the unequivocality of instinct.

The reason of the rational animal and the sapience of *Homo sapiens* are merely consequences of this neuro-psychological mediateness. The defeat of Bergsonism is marked by the fact that the immediate given of consciousness can be only infrahuman unconsciousness. The anatomic and physiological indicator of all this is the fact that in *Homo sapiens* a third brain subsumes the two brains that are histologically and physiologically viewed as distinct:[12] the mammalian brain (the rhinencephalon, the limbic brain) and the vertebrate brain (the paleoencephalon). In simpler terms, this means that due to this large human brain, the most crocodilian aggressiveness (as Laborit called it) and the most limbic affective emotiveness are interpreted—that is to say, doubled in their reflexive effects, representations, fantasies, ideologies, and so forth—by their being taken charge of by the neoencephalon. As Ernst Cassirer[13] admirably put it, all human activity and all human intelligence is simply the totality of diversified "symbolic forms." In other words, the symbolic universe that we have the formidable honor of presenting tonight is nothing less than the entire human universe!

The progress of consciousness should not be confused with technological progress, as Léon Brunschvicg merges them, but should be integrated into an increasingly advanced genetics of the symbol. This is absolutely not—as is believed by those with highly ethnocentric perspectives, such as H. Laborit and Jacques Derrida[14]—a matter of suppressing the two prehominid brains, and even the *logos,* in favor of a logical-mathematical rationality. It seems both the biologist Laborit and the philosopher Derrida forgot about the fundamentally aggressive character of the carnivorous primate that is *Homo sapiens.* It is a sin of the angelic aspirations of Western humanism, which wishes to see itself only in terms of successes such as computers and economic planning. Anthropological humanism, on the other hand, modestly recognizes that "none of what is infrahuman in me is foreign to me!"—not even the carnivore in us, who is our second nature.

I along with some ten other scholars with various specialties have edited a voluminous collective work—the *Atlas des Mondes Imaginaires*—

whose organization, authorized by this scientific Aeropagus, attests to this genetics of *Homo signifer,* this progress of consciousness that is the process of symbolic pervasion. At the lowest level—outside of this Atlas—at the Pavlovian level, so to speak, the symbol appears in the animal world in the form of complexes of signals. The famous tick studied by Uexküll does not symbolize; its signifying universe is made up of three unequivocal dimensions. But for a dog, and apparently for every animal with a brain—or at least for birds—a postural mimicry, a reflexive attitude, shows how the reflex, which is instinct, can be diverted—albeit rarely—from its direct original functioning. The higher animal has attitudes of circumspection. Pavlov's dog passes from the signal to the sign, and it is not unreasonable to believe, along with the biologist Adolf Portmann,[15] that animals also perform representations established for the species: *Urbilder.* But the specific, monumental quality of symbolization is incontestably the property of this special, bizarre, carnivorous primate, this "naked ape"[16] that is man. Perhaps because the gap between desire and reality is greater in the human primate, humankind is fated to neoteny, to immaturity, like its simian cousins. Be that as it may, it is in *Homo sapiens* that we see the plenary blooming of the process of mediate thought, enclosing various fields of signification by means of a sign. But this symbolization takes place progressively.

In the stage of childhood[17]—the stage that Jean Chateau, Piaget, and above all Bernard Andrey have called the stage of "restricted imagination," because the imaginary is at once intensified, stereotyped, and repressed by the great psycho-physiological immaturity of the human child—the slowly developing processes of distancing from the world that allow for symbolizing reflection are highly predetermined by educational institutions, parental validation, and even games.

Likewise, in the mentally ill, contrary to current opinion, the imaginary is distorted, and the distancing necessary for the symbol is disorganized by existential intrusions. Obsessive or delirious monopolization prevents consciousness from mediating.

Only with acculturation did the *Atlas of the Imaginary* appear fully, and then only by degrees, from the simple symbology and derived mythology of utopian literature and constructions to engagement in the very flesh of cultural exchange. It was with art, philosophy, and religion—as Hegel predicted—that symbolic consciousness attained its highest level of functioning. The work of art, the philosophical system, the religious system—and additionally, the system of social institutions—constitute paradigms of high symbolic frequency. This means that the figures they convey and from which they are woven can serve as inexhaustible "renewals"—as Ricœur said—interpreted or translated (sometimes incorrectly!) without the meaning being exhausted. To summarize this, we might say, labeling as mythological these higher constructions of the imaginary, that mythology is the exemplary perfection of the genesis of the symbol. We will find this importance for mythology when we explore the dynamics of the symbol. For the moment, let us examine the supreme place we grant to culture, at the apex of symbolic genetics. This justification for acculturation is not meant to imply that we take a culturalist position, even though we have recently been falsely accused of base reflexological psychologism. In fact, between the culture (which can be dead, in the sense of a completely dead language such as Etruscan or Egyptian before Champollion) and the reflexological nature that escapes the conscious, there is an anthropological path, a "trace"—as Derrida called it—accessible only as a scientific reality of anthropology.

The human animal, with its large brain, is functionally cultivatable, so to speak. This is what radically differentiates the human child or the mentally ill person from an ape or a dog: for humans, society—and its consciousness, which is culture—is a symbolic form, doubly necessary due to the social characteristics of the human animal, so lacking in instincts for subsistence, and due to the qualities of reflexive mediation of its large brain. This phenomenon of the overlapping of natural behavior and cultural conditions is permitted by the general phenomenon of human necessity[18]—the fact that the human brain comes into the world immature and incomplete. Whereas a young chimpanzee completes its cerebral growth in the first twelve months after its birth, the human brain requires a minimum of six years—and more often ten or twelve—to develop. In other words, there can be no brain development without cultural education. Far from needing to view culture in the singular—because our instincts are too blurry to subsume the whole species within a single social behavior—the anthropological path pluralizes and singularizes cultures without forgetting the biological nature of humans, which, for science, is by no means a "forgotten paradigm."[19] Animal nature and singular culture are no more separable for the large human brain than the brain's own primitive strata are separable. When Lévi-Strauss masterfully showed that "men have always thought just as well,"[20] thus refuting ethnocentrism and colonialism, we can infer from this—though it seems the great anthropologist did not dare to cross the line—that *Homo sapiens* has a biological nature, not at all empty, but instead full of potentialities, and that these potentialities can apply in infinite realizations. These realizations, cultures, are the privileged and specific characteristic of humans, but they are not the cause, the dominant factor, of our representations.

It is in this sense that we believe that the culturalist solution—as in Hegel's, Spengler's, and Comte's perspectives—monolithically reduces the pluralism of cultural solutions for the human instinctive deficiency to totalitarianism and cultural monism, and is therefore distorting because it is partial, and partial because it is ethnocentrically partial. Certainly, Spengler, like Hegel, showed that the highest instance of consciousness coincides with cultural apogees (philosophy, art, religion), but none of them—especially not Hegel and Comte, who add decided ethnocentrism to their monism—defines culture as a system of regulation or functioning of instances that are antagonistic and contradictory because they compensate for one another. If cultures are the crowning of the genetics of the human symbolic apparatus, then for us, it is not a matter of reducing these cultural derivations to a totalitarian solution such as ethnocentrism—especially not the ethnocentrism of our Western pedagogy and ideology.

I believe that this divergence of mine from the entire Western totalitarian model (less tentative than that of Derrida, who rejects the "nonpertinence" of cultural totalitarianism but retains the logical-mathematical dualism of our Western cultural model) is manifested in the method of scientism and our pedagogy, in the hedonistic truth of liberalism or in socialism. I believe that only this decided divergence allows for the explanation of the dynamism of the symbol. The analytical procedures that allow us to understand the evolution, change, and recurrences of the symbolic apparatus are invested in *difference*.[21]

And this difference, for anthropologists like myself, is called myth. It therefore appears not only in the area of writing, because myth is speech before being written, but is also within the natural language that translates the myth, because the myth must in turn be translated. It is also in the mythological metalanguage of which Lévi-Strauss writes,[22] in that "presemiotic" language in which the gestures of rite, cult, and magic relay the grammar and vocabulary. Myth is the ultimate discourse in which is constituted the antagonistic tension fundamental to all discourse—that is to say, to all development of meaning. Nietzsche[23] saw brilliantly—unlike his culturalist successors—that the myth, which constitutes Greek thought, is a tale of antagonism between Apollonian and Dionysian forces. Lévi-Strauss emphasized this dilemmatic characteristic of the myth, a logical tool for diachronically conciliating semantic entities that could not overlap synchronically. But we can thank Max Weber[24] for the most explicit thesis on this polytheism of values from which arises a paradoxical determinism inducing nonbivalent logics. And when, some twenty years ago, I observed that the anthropological structures of the imaginary were classed into three irreducible isomorphic series, I stated in turn that there is no homogeneous continuity—contrary to what the Freudian doctrine of the libido claims—between the three structural regimes, simply because there is no homology between the anatomical and physiological supports of these regimes. The works of Freud's successors, that of Adler and Rank in particular, assumed that there was only one libido.[25] Here Adler agrees perfectly with contemporary assumptions in cerebral anatomy and physiology that detect an area localizing aggressiveness in the paleoencephalon. Certainly, at the time, in order to characterize one of these three structural regimes, I incorrectly used the term *synthesis,* which might have suggested that synthetic structures were the result of a totalizing dialectic such as that of Hegel or even Ricoeur or J. P. Richard. Now, for me, it is not, nor has it ever been, a matter of a synthetic resolution after the manner of Hegel. And if, today, I wanted to give a name to this category of structures, I would hesitate between a Lévi-Straussian term such as *diachronic structures* and a Derrida-style term such as *disseminating structures,*[26] because this is a matter of both structures that integrate time—and consequently the tempo of the story—and structures that indicate "an irreducible and generative multiplicity." Now the myth, being a tale, ultimately fits into this structural group, but above all, it irreducibly and generatively subsumes all three structural regimes. It is liable for a logic of antagonists such as that which Stéphane Lupasco[27] studied and which Derrida called *conflictorielle* [conflictual].

Certainly, there is also an internal mechanism in the mythical tale whereby (just as the symbol distends semantically into synthemes) myth distends into simple parable, fairy tale, or fable, and finally into literary tale[28] or even becomes encrusted with existential or historical events, thus exhausting its pervasive meaning in the symbolic forms of aesthetics, morality, or history. The myth is made from the symbolic content of the symbols in the story it tells: archetypes or profound symbols or even simple anecdotal synthemes.

But what we must remember here is the ultimate nature of the myth in explicative procedures of integration. It was Freud's idea to seek out Oedipus, Jocasta, and Diana in ancient Greek mythology as the ultimate paradigms for situations that no dialectic reasoning—such as Plato's—can explain. The myth—the diachronic dissemination of sequences (mythemes) and symbols, the ultimate, asymptotic system for the integration of antagonisms—is the ultimate discourse; and this ultimate discourse, in the final analysis, expresses the war of the gods.

I hope that this expression—like that of polytheism, which I borrow from Weber—will not scandalize the Christian theologians to whom I am addressing myself! In the mouth of a philosopher such as Plato or an anthropologist like me, it is merely a sign of humility: Human wisdom, like human science, must stop at that limit beyond which theologians and mystics debate. Certainly, in placing the war of the gods at the root of anthropology, we do not intend an easy return to the legendary philosophies of Heraclitus and Empedocles. It is the most recent biology that indicates to us that at the root of the hominid, there is a fundamental contradiction[29] between the behavior of a primate—that is to say, a frugivore or insectivore—and that of a land-dwelling carnivore. For the contemporary biologist, "leaving the Garden of Eden" assumes a quasi-scientific meaning. The fate of the hominid, *Homo erectus, Homo faber,* and *Homo sapiens,* is to be constitutively torn between the frugivorous, tree-dwelling realm of its primate structure and the carnivorous, land-dwelling realm of its behavior as a large, hunting meat-eater. The war of the gods is forever proclaimed in *Homo sapiens* by the irrepressible antagonism between Mars and Venus, Apollo and Dionysus, between what some have termed the principle of pleasure and the principle of reality. But as soon as there is a theogony, there are within us the constitutive powers of the ultimate, the extreme symbolic elements beyond which we can say nothing more, and which, for the sake of convenience, we call "the gods." Gods and war of the gods are the limits of our human destiny and of all humanism. Consequently, they are the ultimate domain of anthropology. Certainly, there are "pagan" polytheisms that illustrate our thesis most candidly: the *Iliad* and the Bhagavad Gita show us that the gods fight with us, within us. But I have also shown to what extent, in monotheisms as strict as Islam,[30] the polytheism of values—dulia rather than latria—is constitutive of religious discourse itself. Ever since there was an economy of salvation, mediation, the war of the gods emerged in the Abrahamic tradition and was converted into terms of nostalgia, the Fall, sin, rebellion, exile, but also into terms of redemption. And this dissemination of mythical powers constitutes

C. G. Jung's profound analysis in his admirable *Answer to Job*. But it also constitutes the *Romantic Epic* explored by Léon Cellier.[31]

When I say that myth constitutes the dynamic of the symbol, I wish not only to express that it helps symbols subsist through the discursive drama[32] that it animates, through the conflagration of the antagonisms and dialectical deepenings (in the Socratic sense of the term!) with which it nourishes symbology. I wish to say, above all, that in the duration of cultures and individual human lives—which some people call by the confusing term *history,* but that I, like Goethe, prefer to call *Schicksal* ("destiny")—the myth, so to speak, distributes the roles in history and allows us to decide what makes the historic moment, the spirit of an epoch, a century, or a time of life.

This reverse Euhemerism is certainly most shocking for Western ethnocentrism, in which the hypostasis of history as a final explanation is founded upon poorly assimilated Christianity and upon the progress of technology and the means of production. The myth is the last referential with which history can be understood, with which the historian's trade is possible, and not vice versa. The myth goes before history, bears witness to it, and legitimizes it, just as the Hebrew scriptures and their figures guarantee the historical authenticity of the Messiah for a Christian. Without mythic structures, no historical intelligence is possible. Without messianic expectation—which is mythical—there is no Jesus Christ; without myth, the battles of King Philip and Waterloo are only various facts.

As testimony—and here I must summarize these proceedings—I need only the activation of symbols at the end of the thirteenth century and the beginning of the fourteenth century in Europe, which allowed, amid a certain mythical messianism, for the literary and ideological revival of the old myth of Prometheus and the historical incarnation of this myth in Napoleon Bonaparte. With regard to the myth of Napoleon, his rise and his decline, I can only refer to the suggestive works of Jean Tulard.[33] But this myth of Napoleon, "the supreme captive on the rock," is plausible only because it itself arises from the enormous resurgence of the myth of Prometheus throughout the pre-Romantic and Romantic period.[34] Whether the martyred Titan is connected to the Passion of the Christ, as with Maistre, or contrasted with religion and churches, as with Shelley, it was the same myth that obsessed the Romantic soul between 1780 and 1865, from Goethe, Byron, Ballanche, Hugo, and Michelet, to Quinet, Louis Ménard, Marx, and Louise Ackermann, finally shattering in the Nietzschean heritage of the *Prometheus* of Spittler, Gide, Élémir Bourges, André Suarès, and d'Aragon. And here we see Sisyphus and above all Dionysus,[35] progressively replacing Prometheus, invading the mythological scene as Prometheus's ideological favor declines. The Destine of the West is this same mythological fabric in which heroes, Titans, and gods do battle. Above all, this is not a matter of reducing Prometheanism to the parricide of 1792 or the conquests of the Industrial Revolution of the 1840s: Prometheus was there from 1780 on, well before regicide, well before the first steam engine was used in Fulton's steamboat in 1807. The French Revolution and the technological advent of steam power were, to say the least, synchronous with the myth of Prometheus. Certain epochal myths—that is to say, myths that explain an epoch—do not die out along with the epoch that secretes them: Unamuno revealingly showed that "quixoticism" did not require a historical incarnation for the Knight of the Sad Countenance, and that Don Quixote is still living in our century, so far removed from knightly prowess.[36]

The dynamic of the symbol that constitutes the myth and consecrates mythology as the mother of history and destiny clarifies the genetics and mechanics of the symbol a posteriori, because it replaces the symbolic element, the ritual gesture of mytheme in this metahistory, *in illo tempore,* giving it its optimal meaning. The symbol does not refer to history, to the chronological moment of such-and-such a material event, but to a constitutive advent of its meanings. For a long time, for example, our historical blinders caused us to misunderstand the tale of the famous origins of Rome. Georges Dumézil[37] has masterfully shown us that the entire story of the founding, *ab urbe condita,* only ensured its power and its eternal nature because it was the mythical paradigm of all the history, ideology, and destiny of Roman society.

Here I have all too briefly sketched the outline of this universe of symbols, which ultimately appears as the empire of humans, as the world of parables and paradigms that constitute the human spirit in its grandeur and its relativity, its finiteness, and its aspirations. I have given the great definitions that arise from an attentive operation on the symbolic image over the course of more than twenty years, and I have arrived at these mechanics, genetics, and dynamics of that essential activity of *Homo sapiens* (or, if you will, the Adam Kadmon, because it is the same thing) which is symbolic thought. All that now remains for me—as an anthropologist honored to be invited here by theologians—is to delight (as I hoped to do in 1959 after the publication of the conclusions of the Conciliar Commission on the liturgy, when the Dominicans asked me to determine "The Status of the Symbol and the Imaginary in the Present Day"[38]) in seeing theologians and ecumenical councils exorcising the funereal vigils of the death of God, turning away from the fashionable agnosticism and the iconoclastic insolence of positivism and becoming truly catholic—recognizing that every revelation, even that which is most situated in history, in order to fulfill its soteriological and eschatological role, must be anchored in what transcends history, in what always was, forever and everywhere, the basis of the human condition.

And if I may be allowed to make a wish for this conference, as well as for all the future of Western theology, I will say that I wish you, dear colleagues, a demystifying return to the decisions of the Second Council of Nicaea; I wish you an iconophilic theology, a humble theology because it rests upon this human condition—this intermediary world, neither angel nor beast—a theology that remembers, above all, that humans are made "in the image and resemblance of God."

NOTES

INTRODUCTION

1. See bibliography.
2. Gilbert Durand, *Les structures anthropologiques de l'imaginaire* (Paris: Presses Universitaires de France, 1969). Translated into English as *Anthropological Structure of the Imaginary* (Brisbane: Boombana Press, 1999).
3. Ibid., 51.
4. Georges Dumas, *Nouveau traité de Psychologie* (Paris: Alcan, 1930), 268.
5. Georg Wilhelm Friedrich Hegel, *Aesthetics: Lectures on Fine Art,* vol. 1, trans. T. M. Knox (Oxford: Clarendon Press, 1975), 399.
6. Gilbert Durand, *Les structures anthropologiques de l'imaginaire,* 51.
7. Ibid.
8. Ibid.
9. Ibid., 52, citing Carl Jung, *Types psychologiques,* 387, 454.
10. Ibid, 53.
11. Ibid.
12. René Alleau, *De la nature des symboles* (Paris: Flammarion, 1958), 17 and 38.
13. At this time I was ignorant of a crucial fact: The rhinencephalon became complexified as the neocortex, the "new brain," evolved. Evolution has modernized the ground floor while building the upstairs at the same time. In humans, neither the old brain nor the new in the normal state can function alone.
14. Léon Brunschvicg, "Double aspect de la philosophie mathématique," in *Les grands courants de la pensée mathématique* (Paris: 1948), 526.
15. Ibid., 50, citing Robert Deltheil, *L'analogie en mathématiques.*
16. Ibid., citing Malebranche.

CHAPTER 1. ORIGIN AND SEMANTICS
OF THE WORD *SYMBOL*

1. Trévoux, *Dictionnaire universel françois et latin,* vol. 7 (Paris: Comp. des Librairesres Associes, 1771), 927.

2. Ibid.

3. Jesuits of Trévoux, *Dictionnaire universel françois et latin.*

3. Ibid.

4. Ibid.

5. Ibid.

6. *Encyclopaedia Britannica* (Edinburgh: Society of Gentlemen, 1771).

7. See chapter 13, "The Bourgeois Philosophy of the Symbol."

8. Denis Diderot and Jean le Rond d'Alembert, eds., *Encyclopédie de Diderot et d'Alembert* (1780).

9. Ibid.

10. Ibid.

11. Denis Diderot and Jean le Rond d'Alembert, eds., *Preliminary Discourse to the Encyclopedia of Diderot.*

12. Ibid.

13. Diderot and d'Alembert, eds., *Encyclopédie,* vol. 10, 921. See the entry "Mystère."

14. Charles du Fresne, Lord Du Cange (1610–88). His *Glossarium ad scriptores mediae et infimae latinitatis* (1678) was completed by Dom Carpentier, Heuschel, and Favre. Here I cite the Paris edition (1846), vol. 6, 467.

15. Albert Dauzat, *Dictionnaire étymologique de la lange française* (Paris: Librairie Larousse, 1938).

16. Pausanias, *Description of Greece,* VIII, 54.

17. See *Histoire secrète des Mongols,* French translation by Paul Pelliot (Paris: Adrien-Maisonneuve, 1949): "The origin of Gengis Qayan (Khan) was Börtä Cino (the blue Wolf). . . . His wife was Qo'ai Maral (the fallow doe). In the Chinese text, *tsang-so* is annotated next to the wolf, and instead he is connected with the color green."

18. E. H. Minns, *Scythians and Greeks* (Cambridge: Cambridge University Press, 1913), 77–78.

19. Marco Polo, *The Travels* (London: Penguin, 1958), 116.

20. A. P. Elkin, *The Australian Aborigines* (London: Angus and Robertson, 1979), 166–67.

21. Ibid., 172.

22. Ibid., 172–73.

23. Ibid., 175.

24. Ibid.

25. Ibid.

26. Here we should note the existence, in the Ishmaelian mystical tradition, of the *mundus imaginalis*, the *'âlam al-mithâl* analyzed by Henry Corbin, as distinct from the "imaginary world." See bibliography.

27. A. P. Elkin, *The Australian Aborigines*, 240–41.

CHAPTER 2. SIGN AND SYMBOL

1. André Lalande, *Vocabulaire technique et critique de la philosophie* (Paris: Alcan, 1926).

2. Ferdinand de Saussure, *Course in General Linguistics*, trans. Roy Harris (Chicago: Open Court, 1986), 15.

3. [*Signifiant* and *signifié*, terms popularized by Saussure, are translated respectively as "signal" and "signification" in Roy Harris's English edition of *Course in General Linguistics*. We follow his example here, although these terms are sometimes also translated as "signifier" and "signified." —*Trans.*]

4. Saussure, *Course in General Linguistics*, 66–67.

5. Ibid., 67–69.

6. Ibid., 69–70.

7. Ibid., 118.

8. Ibid., 119.

9. Ibid., 68.

10. Ibid., 68–69.

11. Whitney is the author of *The Life of Language* (1875).

12. Saussure's unfinished article on Whitney. Cited in Michel Arrivé, *Linguistics and Psychoanalysis: Freud, Saussure, Hjelmslev, Lacan and Others*, trans. James Leader (Amsterdam: John Benjamins, 1992), 22.

13. W. Doroszewski, "Quelques remarques sur les rapports de la sociologie et de la linguistique: Durkheim et F. de Saussure," *Journal of Psychology*, no. 30 (1933): 82–91.

14. G. C. Lepschy, *La linguistique structurale* (Paris: Payot, 1969), 32.

15. Gabriel de Tarde, *L'invention considérée comme moteur de l'évolution sociale* (Paris: V. Giard and E. Brière, 1902), 5–6.

16. Saussure, *Course in General Linguistics*, 13–14.

17. Ibid.

18. Ibid., 17.

19. Ibid., 96–97.

20. Ibid., 98–99.

21. Ibid., 80.

22. Ibid., 73.

23. Edward Sapir, *Language* (New York: Harcourt, Brace, 1921), cited in *Encyclopedia of the Social Sciences*, vol. 9, 155–69.

24. Saussure, *Course in General Linguistics,* 68.

25. This word was used for the first time in 1958 in my book *De la nature des symboles* (Paris: Flammarion, 1958).

26. Jean Piaget, *La psychologie de l'intelligence* (Paris: Armond Colin, 1947). Translated into English as *The Psychology of Intelligence* (London: Routledge Classics, 2001).

27. G. S. Kirk and J. E. Raven, *The Presocratic Philosophers* (Cambridge: Cambridge University Press, 1957), 169.

28. *Thucydides*, vol. 1, 21, trans B. Jowett (Oxford: Clarendon Press, 1881), 14.

29. Mircea Eliade, *Aspects du mythe* (Paris: Gallimard, 1963), 193. Translated into English as *Myth and Reality* (Prospect Heights, Ill.: Waveland Press, 1998).

30. Rudolf Otto, *The Idea of the Holy: An inquiry into the non-rational factor in the idea of the divine and its relation to the rational,* trans. John W. Harvey (New York: Oxford University Press, 1958.

31. Claude Lévi-Strauss, *Mythologiques* (Paris: Plon, 1964), 21.

32. Ibid.

33. Karl Polanyi, Conrad M. Arensberg, and Harry W. Pearson, *Trade and Market in the Early Empires: Economies in History and Theory* (New York: The Free Press, 1957), 374.

34. Andri Martinet, ed., "Semiologie," in *Le langage* (Paris: Gamillard, 1968), 94.

35. Konrad Lorenz, *King Solomon's Ring: New Light on Animal Ways* (London: Routledge, 2002), 160.

36. Ibid.

37. Claude Lévi-Strauss, *La pensée sauvage* (Paris: Plon, 1962), 85–88.

38. Mircea Eliade, *Aspects du mythe* (Paris: Gallimard, 1963), 178.

39. Rudolf Otto, *The Idea of the Holy,* 13–14.

40. Ibid., 14.

41. C. G. Jung, *Modern Man in Search of a Soul,* trans. W. S. Dell and Cary F. Baynes (London: Routledge, 2001).

42. Ibid.

43. Ibid., 21.

44. Ibid., 22.

45. Sigmund Freud, *Totem and Taboo: Resemblances between the Psychic Lives of Savages and Neurotics,* trans. A. A. Brill (Amherst, N.Y.: Prometheus Books, 2000), 174.

CHAPTER 3. THE EXPERIENTIAL ORIGINS
OF THE ANALOGICAL PROCESS

1. George Catlin, *O-Kee-Pa* (London: Trubner and Co., 1867), 13, 28, cited in Mircea Eliade, *Myths, Dreams, and Mysteries,* trans. Philip Mairet (New York: Harper and Brothers, 1960), 206.

2. Mircea Eliade, *Myths, Dreams, and Mysteries* (New York: Harper and Brothers, 1960), 208–209.

3. C. W. Hobleq, *Bantu Beliefs and Magic* (London: 1922), 78 ff., 98 ff.

4. A. Gahs, *Kopf, Schädel und Lang Knochenopfer bei Renntiervölkern* (Vienna: 1928), 23–68.

5. Ibid., citing E. Baechler.

6. Kurt Lindner, *La chasse préhistorique* (Paris: Payot, 1950), 250.

7. Ibid., 247.

8. Raymond Ruyer, *La genèse des formes vivantes* (Paris: Flammarion, 1958), 232.

9. E. O. Willis, "Is the Zone-tailed Hawk a Mimic of the Turkey Vulture?" *The Condor* 65 (April 1963): 313–17.

10. Yveline Leroy, "Le Mimetisme Animal," *La Recherche* 45 (May 1974).

11. Or Mullerian mimicry, named after the German lepidopterist Muller.

CHAPTER 4. THE LOGIC OF ANALOGY

1. Harald Höffding, *Le concept d'analogie,* trans. R. Perrin (Paris: J. Vrin, 1931), 7.

2. See the remarkable work by François Chenique, *Élements de logique classique— l'art de penser et de juger* (Paris: Dunod, 1975), 69–72.

3. Translation: *Terminus qui convenit pluribus secundum rationem partim eamdem, partim diversum*; or again: *secundum rationem simpliciter diversam et secundum quid eamdem.* Thomas Aquinas, *Commentary on Aristotle's Metaphysics,* XI, lecture 3. Analogy is sometimes called "voluntary equivocalness" (*aequivocitas a concilio*).

4. Translation: *Terminus analogus attributionis est qui convenit pluribus propter ordinem ad unum.*

5. Translation: *Terminus analogus proportionalitatis est qui pluribus convenit propter aliquam similitudinem proportionum.*

6. In Kant's philosophy, "analogies of experience" relate solely to the principal regulators that synthesize perceptions.

7. Kant, *Critique of Judgment,* 65.

8. See Émile Meyerson, *De l'explication dans les sciences,* I, 217–34, and *Bulletin de la société française de philosophie* (February 24, 1921): 39.

9. Harald Höffding, *Le concept d'analogie* (Paris: J. Vrin, 1931), 15.

10. Karl Marx, *Capital: A Critique of Political Economy,* trans. Samuel Moore

and Edward Aveling (New York: The Modern Library, 1906), 41–48, part 1, chapter 1, section 1. See also a very clear discussion of his doctrine by Marx himself, from around 1865, in his letter to the General Council of the International Workers' Association, published in 1898 by *Devenir social* under the title "Salaires, prix et projets."

11. Ibid., 44. I have italicized the significant expressions that I will analyze later.

12. See Marx's letter cited above (letter to the General Council of the International Workers' Association).

13. Albertus Magnus, *Ethica,* in *Opera omnia,* vol. 4 (Lyon: 1651), book 5, tracts 9 and 10, 201 ff.

14. See Aristotle, *Nicomachean Ethics* (London: MacMillan, 1897), 140–42, book 5, chapter 5.

15. Albertus Magnus, *Ethica,* in *Opera omnia,* vol. 4, book V, tract 9.

16. Ibid., tract 10, 203.

17. Thomas Aquinas, *Commentaria in Ethica* (Parma edition), XXI, 172.

18. Marx, *Capital: A Critique of Political Economy,* 588: "Labor is the substance, and the immanent measure of value, but has itself no value." This, in fact, corresponds to an absolute criterion.

19. Ibid., 51.

CHAPTER 5. THE SYNTHEMATIC
FUNCTION OF SYMBOLISM

1. Nicolas Bourbaki, *Éléments de mathématique* (Paris: 1960), book 1.

2. This danger is obviously not a concern for psychologists and sociologists, who possess a profound knowledge of the logical and mathematical techniques of formalization. We know, for example, what remarkable discoveries Jean Piaget made in the domain of genetic psychology.

3. And to the act of thinking itself, as indicated by its etymology, from the vulgar Latin *pensare,* "to weigh." See Albert Dauzat, *Dictionnaire étymologique de la lange française* (Paris: Librairie Larousse, 1938), 546.

CHAPTER 6. THE ALLEGORICAL
FUNCTION OF SYMBOLISM

1. Jean Pépin, *Dante et la tradition de l'allégorie* (Paris: J. Vrin, 1970), 15–16.

2. Origen, *De principiis,* IV, 2, 4 (II), 312–13.

3. Origen, *De principiis,* Bachrens edition, 42, 332–34, bottom of page.

4. On the basis of this teaching of Origen, I have distinguished the notions of "model" and "imprint" in the typological function of symbolism (see part 5, The Type).

5. From the Greek *ana,* "above," and *agōgos,* "leading."

6. Clement of Alexandria, *Excerpts from Theodotus,* 18, 2, cited in Marguerite Harl, *Origène et la fonction révélatrice du Verbe incarné* (Paris: Seuil, 1958), 153.

7. From the Greek *tropologia,* "figured language," from *tropos-logeo,* "to speak in tropes or figures" (Origen, *Contra Celsum,* I, 15).

8. *Contra Celsum,* V, 56, 59. See Harl, *Origène et la fonction révélatrice du Verbe incarné,* 156–57: "Origen unceasingly recommended performing an interpretation of the actions of Jesus allowing us to grasp their true scope. He called this interpretation *anagoge,* or also *tropologia,* these two terms signifying 'spiritual interpretation.'"

9. Cited by Régis Blachère, *Le Coran* (Paris: P.U.F., 1966), 83.

10. Ibid., 75.

11. Ibid., 78.

12. See bibliography.

13. Henry Corbin, *Commentaire de la Qasida ismaélienne d'Abu'l-Haitham Jorjani* (Paris: Adrien-Maisonneuve, 1955), 44.

14. Ibid., 47.

15. 2 Corinthians 3:17.

16. Plutarch, *On Isis and Osiris* (Cambridge: Harvard University Press, 1936), chapter 32.

17. Ibid, chapter 40.

18. Flavius Josephus, *The Wars of the Jews,* V, 5, 4.

19. Ibid., V, 5, 5.

20. Philo, *The Special Laws,* book 1, chapter 12, 66, in *The Works of Philo Judaeus, Contemporary of Josephus,* trans. Charles Duke Yonge (London: H. G. Bohn, 1854–90).

21. Philo, *Questions and Answers on Exodus,* book 2, 79.

22. Philo, *Questions and Answers on Genesis,* book 3, chapter 3, in *The Works of Philo Judaeus.*

23. Philo, *Allegorical Interpretations,* book 2, chapters 31–38, in *The Works of Philo Judaeus.*

24. Philo, *Allegorical Interpretations,* book 2, chapter 11, in *The Works of Philo Judaeus.*

25. See "Genesis" in *La Pentateuque, en cinq volumes,* trans. the French Rabbinate, with commentary by Rashi (Paris: 1971), 187.

26. Philo, *A Treatise on the Dreams That Are Sent from God,* book 1, chapter 19, in *The Works of Philo Judaeus.*

27. *La Pentateuque, en cinq volumes.*

28. Ibid.

29. E. C. Hoskyns, *The Fourth Gospel* (London: Faber and Faber, 1947), 129.

30. François Quiévreux, "La structure symbolique de l'Évangile selon saint Jean," in *Revue d'histoire et de philosophie religieuse* (Paris: P.U.F., 1921), 152.

31. Ibid., 160.

32. Ibid., 159.

33. The Koran, trans. George Sale (Philadelphia: J. W. Moore, 1856), 480.

CHAPTER 7. APOLOGUE, FABLE, AND PARABLE

1. Émile Littré, *Dictionnaire de la langue française* (Paris: Hachette, 1863–72).

2. Ibid., entry "Apologue."

3. Jean de La Fontaine, *Fable 7*, "À Madame de Montespan" (Toronto: Dover Publications, 2000).

4. Etienne de Campos Leyza, *Analyse étymologique des racines de la langue grecque* (Bordeaux: 1874), 37.

5. See the edition published by Sylvestre de Sacy in 1816.

6. This distinction between the outside, or exterior, and the inside, or interior, is, in the most precise sense of this term, what separates the *exoteric* from the *esoteric*—what is taught openly and publicly from what is explained particularly to disciples and initiates.

7. Gershom Scholem, *On the Kabbalah and Its Symbolism* (New York: Schocken, 1969), 12.

8. See J. P. Migne, *Patrologia Graeca,* vol. 12, col. 1080 (Paris: APUD Garnier Fratres, 1857).

9. This statement of monotheism is all the more significant because it comes from a philosopher of the sixth century BC and a founder of the Eleatic school.

10. Diogenes Laertius (IX, 51); Cicero, *De natura Deorum,* book 1, chapters 23, 63.

11. Aristotle, *The Metaphysics of Aristotle,* trans. Rev. John H. M'Mahon (London: George Bell and Sons, 1896), 339–40, book 11, chapters 8, 10.

12. See bibliography, page 282.

CHAPTER 8. DEVICE AND EMBLEM

1. Roman de Renart, *Or vos en ferai le devis,* eighteenth century.

2. Cicero, *De Oratore,* book 3.

3. See, in particular, Georges Dumézil, *Jupiter, Mars, Quirinus. Essai sur la conception indo-européenne de la société et sur les origines de Rome* (Paris: Gallimard, 1941), and *Les Dieux des Indo-Européens* (Paris: P.U.F., 1952).

4. See C.N.R.S. (National Center for Scientific Research), *Cahiers d'héraldique,* no. 1.

5. Ibid.

6. An excellent study of these traditions of nobility is found in Gérard de Sède, *Aujourd'hui, les nobles* (Paris: A. Moreau, 1975).

7. Montaigne, *The Essays of Michel de Montaigne,* vol. 17, trans. Charles Cotton (Mineola, N.Y.: Dover Publications, 1996), book 3, chapter 9 (Of Vanity).

8. Cennino Cennini, *The Book of the Art of Cennino Cennini: A Contemporary Practical Treatise on Quattrocento Painting,* trans. Christiana J. Herringham (London: George Allen, 1899), 87. This treatise was written in 1437.

9. Ibid., 33–34.

10. R. A. Stein, *Tibetan Civilization,* trans. J. E. Stapleton Driver (Stanford, Calif.: Stanford University Press, 1972), 281.

11. Giuseppe Tucci, *The Theory and Practice of the Mandala,* trans. Alan Houghton Brodrick (Mineola, N.Y.: Dover Publications, 2001).

CHAPTER 9. ALLEGORY AND ICONOLOGY

1. John Chrysostom, "Commentary on the Epistle of St. Paul to the Galatians," in *A Library of Fathers of the Holy Catholic Church,* vol. 5 (Oxford: John Henry Parker, 1840), 69.

2. Thomas Aquinas, *Quaestiones de quodlibet,* VII, question 6, article 2 (15).

3. Isidore of Seville, *Quaestiones in Vetus Testamentum,* XXXIII, 207 B.

4. Johan Huizinga, *The Waning of the Middle Ages* (Mineola, N.Y.: Dover Publications, 1999), 186.

5. St. Bonaventure, *De reductione artium ad theologiam,* in *Opera Omnia,* vol. 7 (Paris: 1871), 502.

6. Chastellain, "Traité par forme d'allégorie mystique sur l'entré du ruy Loys en nouveau règne," in *Oeuvres,* VII, p. 1. Molinet, II, p. 71, III.

7. Coquillart, *Les droits nouveaux et d'Héricault,* I, p. 72.

8. Huizinga, *The Waning of the Middle Ages,* 289.

9. Chastellain, III, p. 414, cited in Huizinga, *The Waning of the Middle Ages,* 289.

10. Jean de Roye, *Chronique scandaleuse,* I, 27, cited in Huizinga, *The Waning of the Middle Ages,* 290.

11. Jean Gerson, *Opera omnia,* book 1, 203.

12. Ibid., book 2, 521–22.

13. Ernst Bloch, *Vorlesungen zur Philosophie der Renaissance* (Frankfurt am Main: Suhrkamp, 1972).

14. The archbishop of Nice, Bessarion was born in Trebizond in the late fourteenth century and died in 1472. He was a monk of St. Basil, and played a significant role in the war against the Turks.

15. Pedro Calderón de la Barca, *Obras completas III: Autos sacramentales,* ed. Ángel Valbuena Prat (Madrid: Aguilar, 1967), 1242.

16. "Queriendo que el Pueblo sepa, que no hay fábula sin misterio, si alegórica a la Luz desto se mira," "El Laberinto del Mundo," in Calderón de la Barca, *Obras completas III: Autos sacramentales,* 1558.

17. Published in Dresden in 1766 and dedicated to the "Göttingen Royal Society of Sciences."

18. Johann Joachim Winckelmann, *Versuch einer Allegorie* (Dresden: 1766), 26.

19. Ibid., 67.

20. Ibid., 70.

CHAPTER 10. THE TYPOLOGICAL
FUNCTION OF SYMBOLISM

1. Raymond Ruyer, *L'animal, l'homme, la fonction symbolique* (Paris: Gallimard, 1964), 86.

2. Karl von Frisch, *Animal Architecture* (New York: Harcourt, 1974).

3. E. Cassirer, *An Essay on Man* (Princeton, N.J.: Princeton University Press), 93.

4. Ruyer, *L'animal, l'homme, la fonction symbolique,* 94.

5. Ibid., 95.

6. Ibid., 97.

7. Susanne Langer, *Philosophy in a New Key* (Colchester, Essex, UK: Signet, 1968) 51.

8. Many thanks to M. P. Monteil, the eminent French translator of Ibn Khaldun's *Muqaddimah* (*Discours sur l'histoire universelle*).

9. Literally, "horizon."

10. If he had known more about alchemy, Ibn Khaldun would have allowed for the *genetic* ability of minerals to transform.

11. Ibn Khaldun, *Muqaddimah* (*Discours sur l'histoire universelle*).

12. Ibid.

13. This does not mean that this new "level" is "metaphysical." See Erwin Schrödinger, *What Is life? The Physical Aspect of the Living Cell* (Cambridge: Cambridge University Press, 1992).

14. Jean-Marie Vidal, "L'empreinte chez les animaux," in *La Recherche,* no. 63, 32.

15. Ibid.

CHAPTER 11. THE DIVINATION AND SYMBOLIC
INTERPRETATION OF THE COSMOS

1. These facts were reported and confirmed by an eminent Swedish scholar, A. Hultkrantz, *La divination en Amérique du Nord* (Paris: 1968). See bibliography.

2. See bibliography, page 284.

3. Jean Nougayrol, "Colloque sur le signe et les systèmes de signes," in *Royaumont* (April 12–15, 1962).

4. The Etruscan religion, unlike the Greek religion, was founded upon a revelation of sacred writings by a nymph, Vegoia or Begoa, and by an infant sage, Tages, assimilated by the Greeks into Chthonian Hermes.

5. Raymond Bloch, "La divination en Étrurie et à Rome," in *La Divination,* vol. 1 (Paris: 1968), 205.

6. Georges Dumézil, *La religion romaine archaïque* (Paris: Payot, 1974), 675.

7. Seneca, *Quaestiones Naturales,* book 2, chapter 32. In this, work, Seneca passed on fragments of a treatise by A. Caecina, *De etrusca disciplina.*

8. Lucian, *Pharsal,* I, 589.

9. See John M. Cooper, *Northern Algonkian Scrying* (Wien: Anthropos, 1927), and Frank G. Speck, *Divination by Scapulimancy* (American Philosophical Society).

10. John M. Cooper, *The Culture of the Northeastern Indian Hunters* (1946), 298.

11. Elmar Jakob Eisenberger, *Das Wahrsagen aus dem Schulterblatt,* in *Internationales Arhiv für Ethnographie* 35.

12. Frank G. Speck, *Naksapi* (Norman: University of Oklahoma Press, 1935), 107 and 162 ff.

13. See Max Kaltenmark and Ngo Van Xuyet, "La divination dans la Chine ancienne," in *La Divination,* vol. 1 (Paris: 1968), 339–40.

14. Marcel Granet, *La Civilisation chinoise* (Paris: La Renaissance, 1929), 230.

15. Kaltenmark and Van Xuyet, "La divination dans la Chine ancienne."

16. Ibid., 149.

CHAPTER 12. MYTH AND RITE

1. Mircea Eliade, *Aspects du mythe* (Paris: Gallimard, 1963), 10.

2. Bronislav Malinowski, "Myth in Primitive Psychology," in *Magic, Science, and Religion* (Garden City, N.Y.: Doubleday, 1954), 101.

3. See B. H. Chamberlain, *Kojiki or Records of Ancient Matters* (London: 1882).

4. See the attributes of Athena and Minerva in the Greek and Roman religions.

5. Under Emperor Mommu (AD 697–707). In the official annals of Japan, this ceremony is mentioned from the year 685.

6. *Nenchū-gyōgi-hisho,* cited in N. Matsumoto, *Essai sur la mythologie japonaise* (Paris: P. Guethner, 1928).

7. Ibid.

8. Ibid.

9. Ibid.

10. Ibid.

11. Ibid.

12. Clement of Alexandria, *Protreptikon,* book 2, chapter 20.

13. Th. Wiegand and H. Schrader, *Priene* (Berlin: 1904), 149–54.

14. Arnobius, *Adversus Nationes,* book 5, chapter 25.

15. Ibid.

16. P. Perdrizet, *Bronzes grecs d'Égypte de la collection Fouquet* (Paris: 1911), 42–43.

17. Paul Foucart, *Les mystères d'Éleusis* (Paris: A Picard, 1914), 218–19.

18. *Asterius,* cited by Foucart, *Les mystères d'Éleusis,* 477.

19. Hippolytus, *Philosophumena,* book 5, chapter 8.

20. Aristophanes, *The Frogs,* trans. Gilbert Murray (London: George Allen, 1908), 30–31.

21. Here I must mention Gérard Legrande's insightful study, *Sur Oedipe (Anatomie de la mythologie)* (Paris: Losfeld, 1972), in which a new and profound approach is taken to the genetic nature of the myth. On page 24, Legrande writes: "Every true myth in some way concerns birth; all birth of discourse seeks to be formulated in reference to the *mythos.*"

22. E. S. C. Handy, *Polynesian Religion* (Honolulu: Bernice P. Bishop Museum, 1927), 11.

23. Alice C. Fletcher and F. la Flesche, *The Omaha Tribe* (Washington, D.C.: Bureau of American Ethnology, 1911), 116.

24. Mircea Eliade, *Aspects du mythe* (Paris: Gallimard, 1963), 54.

25. Mircea Eliade, *Mephistopheles and the Androgyne* (New York: Sheed and Ward, 1965).

26. G. Lote, *Histoire du vers français,* vol. 1 (Paris: Boivin, 1949), 55.

27. Ibid.

28. This "mnemotechnical" application of the painted or sculpted image was a sort of visual syllabism, a song mnemonized by sight, which, so to speak, through this moral instruction of the illiterate, doubled the musical syllabism of the liturgy intended to solidify memories of mystic and religious emotions.

29. Eugène Viollet-Le-Duc, *Dictionnaire raisonné de l'architecture française du XIe au XVIe siècle* (Paris: Ve. A. Morel et Cie, 1882), 506.

CHAPTER 13. THE BOURGEOIS
PHILOSOPHY OF THE SYMBOL

1. Georg Wilhelm Friedrich Hegel, *Aesthetics: Lectures on Fine Art,* trans T. M. Knox, vol. 1 (Oxford: Clarendon Press, 1975), 465–66.

2. Ibid., 466.

3. Ernst Bloch, *Vorlesungen zur Philosophie der Renaissance.*

4. Hegel gave the mythology of production its true ideological foundations.

5. Hegel, *Aesthetics: Lectures on Fine Art,* 299–300.

6. Ibid., 303.

7. Ibid., 303–4.

8. Ibid.

9. Ibid., 304–5.

10. Ibid., 400–401.

11. Theogony must not be confused with theoanthropology. The former is an ontogeny of transcendent or suprahuman origin; the latter is necessarily immanent.

12. Hegel, *Aesthetics: Lectures on Fine Art,* 520.

13. Immanuel Kant, *Rêves d'un visionnaire,* trans. F. Courtès (Paris: J. Vrin, 1967).

14. Ibid., 7.

15. Ibid., 33.

16. "Es ist mir von ganzem Herzen um die Zurechtstellung so mancher schwärmerischen Köpfe auch in unserm Lande zu thun." Letter from Ludwig Ernst Borowski to Kant, March 6, 1790, in *Kants gesammelte Schriften,* vol. 11 (Berlin: Reuther und Reichard, 1902), 138.

17. Immanuel Kant, *Dreams of a Spirit-Seer Illustrated by Dreams of Metaphysics,* trans. Emanuel F. Goerwitz (London: Swan Sonnenschein and Co., 1900), 37.

18. Ibid., 39.

19. Ibid., 39.

20. Ibid., 85–87.

21. Ibid., 113.

22. Ibid., 122.

23. Emanuel Swedenborg, *Arcana Coelestia,* 345. Translated into English as *Heavenly Secrets* (West Chester, Penn.: Swedenborg Foundation, 1998).

24. Kant, *Kritik of Judgment,* trans. J. H. Bernard (London: MacMillan, 1892), 248.

25. Ibid., 249.

26. Ibid., 250–51.

27. Hegel, *Encyclopädie der philosophischen Wissenschaften,* V, 213, 190.

28. Goethe, *Als lebendig-augenblickliche Offenbarung der Unerforschlichen, Maximen und Reflexionen* (Weimar: 1961), book 9, 306.

29. See my study *Hitler et les sociétés secrètes.*

30. Dan Sperber, *Le symbolisme en général* (Paris: Hermann, 1974).

APPENDIX 2. GENERAL SYMBOLOGY AND
THE EXPLORATION OF THE IMAGINARY

1. See the bibliography of works in appendix 2 published by members of the C.R.I (page 242).

APPENDIX 3. "THE UNIVERSE OF THE SYMBOL"
BY GILBERT DURAND

1. Gilbert Durand, *L'imagination symbolique* (Paris: P.U.F., 1968), introduction: "Le vocabulaire du symbolisme."

2. See Georg Friedrich Creuzer, *Symbolik und Mythologie der alten Völker* (Hildesheim: Olms, 1990), and C. G. Jung, *Psychologische Typen* (Zürich: Rascher, 1921).

3. See Jacques Derrida, *Positions* (Paris: Éd. de Minuit, 1972), 40, 50.

4. See J.-L. Leuba, "Signe et symbole en théologie," in *Signe et symbole.*

5. See Gilbert Durand, "Langage et métalangage," in *Eranos Jahrbuch*, no. 39 (1970).

6. Gilbert Durand, *Les structures anthropologiques de l'Imaginaire* (Paris: P.U.F., 1960).

7. On the relationship of schemes and archetypes to biological support, see A. Portmann, "Das Problem der Urbilder in biologischer Sicht," in *Eranos Jahrbuch*, no. 19 (1950); F. Alvedres, "Die Wirksamkeit von Archetypen in den Instinkthandlungen der Tiere," *Zoll. Anzeiger*, no. 19 (1939); and K. Lorenz, "Die angeborenen Formen möglicher Erfahrung," in *Zeitschrift für Tierpsychologie* (Berlin: 1943).

8. See J. Soustelle, *La cosmologie des Anciens Mexicains* (Paris: Hermann, 1940).

9. See P. Ponsoye, *L'Islam et le Graal* (Paris: Denoël, 1957).

10. See René Alleau, *De la nature de symboles* (Paris: Flammarion, 1958).

11. See G. Schaller, *The Mountain Gorilla* (Chicago: University of Chicago Press, 1963); K. Lorenz, *Man Meets Dog* (London: Methuen, 1954); D. Morris, *Primate Ethnology* (London: Weidenfeld and Nicholson, 1967); J. von Uexküll, *Streifzüge durch die Umwelten von Tieren und Menschen* (Berlin: J. Springer, 1934) and *Bedeutungslehre* (Leipzig: Verlag von J. A. Barth, 1940).

12. See H. Laborit, *Psychologie humaine, cellulaire et organique* (Paris: Masson, 1961); *Neurophysiologie. Aspects métabolique et pharmacologique* (Paris: Masson, 1969); J. M. R. Delgado, "Aggression and Defense under Cerebral Radio Control," in *Aggression and Defense: Neural Mechanisms and Social Patterns* (*Brain Function 5*) (Los Angeles: 1965); and Van Hooff, "Facial Expression in Higher Primates," *Symp. Zool. Soc. Land.*, no. 8 (1962).

13. Ernst Cassirer, *Die symbolischen Formen,* translated into English as *The Philosophy of Symbolic Forms* (New Haven, Conn.: Yale University Press, 1996).

14. See H. Laborit, *L'agressivité détournée* (Paris: U. G. d'Édition, 1970); Jacques Derrida, *Positions,* 48.

15. See A. Portmann, "Das Problem der Urbilder in biologischer Sicht," in *Eranos Jahrbuch,* no. 19 (1950): 13 ff.; and H. Hediger, "Bemerkungen zum Raum-Zeit System der Tiere," *Schweizerischer Zeitschrift für Psychologie und ihre Anwendungen,* no. 4 (1946).

16. See Desmond Morris, *The Naked Ape* (New York: McGraw Hill, 1967); and S. L. Washburn, *Classification and Human Evolution* (London: Methuen, 1964).

17. See J. Chateau, *Les sources de l'Imaginaire* (Paris: Éd. Universitaires, 1972). I once studied "Les trois niveaux de formation du symbolisme," in *Cahiers internationales du Symbolisme,* vol. 1 (1962); see also my article "Les Structures polarisantes de la conscience psychique et de la culture," in *Eranos Jahrbuch,* no. 36 (1967).

18. See D. Morris, *Primate Ethnology,* 33.

19. See E. Morrin, *Un paradigme oublié: la nature humaine* (Paris: Éd. du Seuil, 1973).

20. See Claude Lévi-Strauss, *La pensée sauvage* (Paris: Plon, 1962).

21. See Jacques Derrida, *L'écriture et la différence* (Paris: Seuil, 1967).

22. See Claude Lévi-Strauss, *Anthropologie structurale* (Paris: Plon, 1958).

23. See F. Nietzsche, *The Birth of Tragedy.*

24. Max Weber, *The Protestant Ethic and the Spirit of Capitalism* (1905), and the lectures "Politics as a Vocation" and "Science as a Vocation."

25. See also the ethnologists who have insisted that aggressive and defensive behaviors are primordial: D. Morris and R. Morris, *Men and Snakes* and *Men and Pandas* (n.p.: Hutchinson, 1966); and M. Bastock, D. Morris, and M. Moynihan, "Some Comments on Conflict and Thwarting in Animals," *Behavior,* no. 6 (1953).

26. See Jacques Derrida, *La dissémination* (Paris: Seuil, 1972).

27. See M. Beigbeder, *La contradiction ou le Nouvel Entendement* (n.p.: Bordas, 1973).

28. See Mircea Eliade's works, and Ch. Baudouin, *Le Triomphe du Héros* (Paris: Plon, 1952).

29. D. Morris, *The Naked Ape,* 19: "The ancestral apes were forced to do one of two things: either they had to cling on to what was left of their old forest homes, or, in an almost biblical sense, they had to face expulsion from the Garden." Morris, like Yerkes, Zuckerman, and Lorenz, offers us a genetic explanation for the famous nostalgia for Paradise that Rank simply connected to the trauma of birth.

30. See Gilbert Durand, "Structure et fonctions récurrentes de la figure de Dieu," in *Eranos Jahrbuch,* no. 37 (1968).

31. See Léon Cellier, *L'Épopée romantique* (1954), republished under the more revealing title *L'Épopée humanitaire et les grands mythes romantiques* (Paris: S.E.D.E.S., 1971).

32. See Gilbert Durand, "Dualisme et dramatisation: régime antithétique et structures dramatiques de l'imaginaire," *Eranos Jahrbuch,* no. 33 (1964).

33. See Jean Tulard, *L'anti-Napoléon* (n.p.: Juilliard, 1965), and *Le mythe de Napoléon* (Paris: A. Colin, 1971).

34. See P. Albouy, *Mythes et mythologies dans la littérature française,* vol. 2, chapters 1, 3 (A. Colin, 1969).

35. See J. Brun, *Le retour de Dionysos* (n.p.: Desclée, 1969), and Gilbert Durand, "Les mythes et symboles de l'intimité et le XIXe siècle," *Romantisme (Revue de la Société des Études romantiques).*

36. See M. Unamuno, *The Life of Don Quixote and Sancho.*

37. See Georges Dumézil, *L'héritage indo-européen à Rome* (Paris: Gallimard, 1949); *Naissance de Rome* (1944); *Rituels indo-européens à Rome* (1954); and *Tarpéia* (Paris: Gallimard, 1947).

38. See Gilbert Durand, "Le Statut du Symbole et de l'Imaginaire aujourd'hui," *Lumière et Vie,* no. 16 (1967).

BIBLIOGRAPHY

GENERAL BIBLIOGRAPHIES OF SYMBOLISM

Centre de recherches en symbolique. *Le symbole*. Montreal: Éditions Sainte-Marie, 1969.

Cirlot, Juan Eduardo. Bibliography in *A Dictionary of Symbols*. London: Routledge and Kegan Paul, 1962.

Droulers, E. Bibliography in *Dictionnaire des attributs, allégories, emblèmes et symboles*. Turnhout, Belgium: Brepols, 1949.

Freud, Sigmund. *The Interpretation of Dreams*. Translated by A. A. Brill. New York: MacMillan, 1913. Important bibliography on the symbolism of dreams.

Lunker, Manfred. *Bibliographie zur Symbolkunde*. Baden-Baden: Heitz, 1964. The most important bibliography regarding symbols and general symbology.

———. *Beiträge zum Symbolbegriff und Symbolforschung*. Baden-Baden: Koerner, 1982.

DICTIONARIES OF SYMBOLS

Barbier de Montault, Xavier. *Traité d'iconographie chrétienne*. Paris: Vivès, 1890.

Beigbeder, Olivier. *Lexique des symboles*. Saint-Léger-Vauban: Zodiaque, 1969.

Benedictines of Saint-André-lez-Bruges. *Le symbolisme dans l'iconographie chrétienne*. Paris: 1937.

Benedictines of Saint-Louis-du-Temple. *Dictionnaire du symbolisme*. Paris: 1935.

Bonnefoy, Yves, ed. *Dictionnaire des mythologies*. Paris: Flammarion, 1981.

Cirlot, Juan Eduardo. *A Dictionary of Symbols*. London: Routledge and Kegan Paul, 1962.

Corblet, J. *Vocabulaire des symboles et des attributs employés dans l'iconographie chrétienne*. Paris: 1877.

Chevalier, Jean, and Alain Gheerbrandt, eds. *Dictionnaire des symboles*. Paris: Laffont, 1969.

Droulers, Eugène. *Dictionnaire des attributs, allégories, emblèmes et symboles*. Turnhout, Belgium: Brepols, 1949.

Martigny, Jos. Alex. *Dictionnaire des antiquités chrétiennes*. Paris: 1877.

Salmon, William, and Gaston LeDoux de Claves. *Dictionnaire hermétique*. Paris: Gutenberg reprints, 1979. A useful reproduction of the rare 1695 edition.

Urech, Édouard. *Dictionnaire des symboles chrétiens*. Paris: Delachaux et Niestlé, 1972.

Verneuil, Maurice Pillard. *Dictionnaire des symboles, emblèmes et attributs*. Paris: H. Laurens, 1897.

SYMBOLISM AND GENERAL SYMBOLOGY

Alleau, René. *De la nature des symboles*. Paris: Flammarion, 1958.

Allemann, Beda, et al. *Le symbole*. Paris: Fayard, 1959.

Allendy, René. *Le symbolisme des nombres*. Paris: Éd. Traditionnelles, 1984.

Andronikoff, Constantin. *Les sens des fêtes*. Paris: Éd. du Cerf, 1970.

———. *Le cycle pascal (Le sens des fêtes II)*. Paris: l'Âge d'Homme, 1985.

———. *Euchariste et symbole*. Angers: Université catholique de l'Ouest, 1985.

———. *Le sens de la liturgie*. Paris: Éd. du Cerf, 1988.

Baes, Edgar. *Le symbole et l'allégorie*. Brussels: Hayez, 1900.

Bayley, Harold, *The Lost Language of Symbolism*. Mineola, N.Y.: Dover, 2006.

Becker, Matthias. *Bild, Symbol, Glaube*. Essen: Hans Driewer, 1965.

Beigbeder, Olivier. *L'Agneau (symbolisme de)*. Paris: Presses Monastiques, 1962.

———. *L'Aigle (symbolisme de)*. Paris: Presses Monastiques, 1964.

———. *L'Arbre (symbolisme de)*. Paris: Presses Monastiques, 1968.

———. *La symbolique*. Paris: Presses universitaires de France, 1957.

———. *Le Boeuf*. Paris: Presses Monastiques, 1966.

———. *Le Cerf*. Paris: Presses Monastiques, 1962.

———. *Le Lion*. Paris: Presses Monastiques, 1961.

———. *Le Triangle*. Paris: Presses Monastiques, 1967.

———. *L'Homme (symbolisme de)*. Paris: Presses Monastiques, 1965.

Benoist, Luc. *Art du Monde*. Paris: Gallimard, 1941.

———. *Signes, symboles et mythes*. Paris: Presses universitaires de France, 1975.

Berenda, Carlton W. *World Visions and the Image of Man*. New York: Vintage Press, 1965.

Boulnois, J. *Le caducée et la symbolique dravidienne indo-méditerranéenne de l'arbre, de la pierre, du serpent et de la déesse-mère*. Paris: J. Maisonneuve, 1989.

Bryson, L., et al. *Symbols and Values: An Initial Study*. Thirteenth symposium of the Conference on Science, Philosophy, and Religion. New York: Cooper Publishers, 1964.

———. *Symbols and Society*. Fourteenth symposium of the conference. New York, 1964.

Carcopino, Jérôme. *Le mystère d'un symbole chrétien*. Paris: Fayard, 1955.

Cassirer, Ernst. *An Essay on Man*. New Haven, Conn.: Yale University Press, 1957.

———. *Language and Myth*. New York: Dover, 1946.

Castelli, Enrico, et al. *Demitizzazione e immagine*. Padua: C.E.D.A.M., 1962.

———. *Umanesimo e simbolismo*. Padua: C.E.D.A.M., 1958.

Cazeneuve, Jean. *Les mythologies à travers le monde*. Paris: Hachette, 1966.

Champeaux, G. de, and Dom Sébastien Sterckx. *Introduction au monde des symbols*. Saint-Léger-Vauban, Yonne: Zodiaque, 1966.

Chao, Yuen Ren. *Language and Symbolic Systems*. London: Cambridge University Press, 1968.

Charbonneau-Lassay, Louis. *Le bestiaire du Christ*. Paris: Albin Michel, 2006.

Child, Arthur. *Interpretation: A General Theory*. Berkeley: University of California Press, 1965.

Delanglade, Jean, et al. *Signe et symbole*. Neuchâtel: A la Baconnière, 1946.

Deonna, Waldemar. *Le symbolisme de l'oeil*. Paris: de Boccard, 1965.

Dilley, Frank Brown. *Metaphysics and Religious Language*. New York: Columbia University Press, 1964.

Duby, George. *Les trois ordres ou l'imaginaire du féodalisme*. Paris: Gallimard, 1978.

Dumézil, Georges. *Mythe et épopée*. Paris: Gallimard, 1971.

Duncan, H. Daziel. *Symbols in Society*. London: Oxford University Press, 1968.

Durand, Gilbert. *Les structures anthropologiques de l'imaginaire*. Paris: Dunod, 1992.

———. *L'imagination symbolique*. Paris: Presses universitaires de France, 1966.

Eaton, Ralph M. *Symbolism and Truth: An Introduction to the Theory of Knowledge*. New York: Dover, 1964.

Eichholz, Georg. *Tradition und Interpretation*. Munich: C. Kaiser, 1965.

Eliade, Mircea. *Aspects du mythe*. Paris: Gallimard, 1963.

———. *Forgerons et alchimistes*. Paris: Flammarion, 1956.

———. *Histoire des croyances et des idées religieuses*. Paris: Payot, 1986.

———. *Images and Symbols: Studies in Religious Symbolism*. Princeton, N.J.: Princeton University Press, 1991.

———. *The Myth of the Eternal Return: Cosmos and History*. Princeton, N.J.: Princeton University Press, 1971.

———. *Myths, Dreams, and Mysteries*. Translated by Philip Mairet. New York: Harper, 1960.

——. *Naissances mystiques*. Paris: Gallimard, 1959.

——. *The Sacred and the Profane: The Nature of Religion*. Translated by Willard R. Trask. San Diego: Harcourt Brace Jovanovich, 1987.

——. *Traité d'histoire des religions*. Preface by Georges Dumézil. Paris: Payot, 1953.

Ferry, Erwin-Sidney. *Symbolism in Flower Arrangement*. New York: Macmillan, 1958.

Festugière, Andre Marie Jean. *La révélation d'Hermès Trismégiste*. Paris: Les Belles-Lettres, 1981.

Fletcher, Angus. *Allegory: The Theory of a Symbolic Mode*. Ithaca, N.Y.: Cornell University Press, 1964.

Forstner, Dorothea. *Die Welt der Symbole*. Innsbruck: Tyrolia, 1967.

Foss, Martin. *Symbol and Metaphor in Human Experience*. Lincoln: Nebraska University Press, 1966.

Fromm, Erich. *Dromen, Sprookjes, Mythen. Inleiding tot het verstaan van een vergeten taal*. Utrecht: Bijleveld, 1967.

Frye, Northrop, et al. *Myth and Symbol*. Lincoln: Nebraska University Press, 1963.

Ghyka, Matila. *Philosophie et mystique du nombre*. Paris: Payot, 1952.

Goblet d'Alviella, Eugène. *La migration des symboles*. Paris: Thames and Hudson, 1992.

Gorceix, Bernard. *Alchimie*. Paris: Fayard, 1980.

Guénon, René. *Aperçus sur l'ésotérisme chrétien*. Paris: Éditions Traditionnelles, 1954.

——. *Aperçus sur l'initiation*. Paris: Éditions Traditionnelles, 1953.

——. *Formes traditionnelles et cycles cosmiques*. Paris, 1970.

——. *La grande triade*. Paris: Gallimard, 1957.

——. *Le règne de la quantité et les signes des temps*. Paris: Gallimard, 1950.

——. *Le symbolisme de la croix*. Paris: Gallimard, 1950, 10/18, 1970.

——. *Symboles fondamentaux de la science sacrée*. Paris: Gallimard, 1962.

Guiraud, Pierre. *Index du vocabulaire du symbolisme*. Paris: Klincksieck, 1953.

Gusdorf, Georges *Mythe et métaphysique*. Paris: Flammarion, 1953.

Izard, M., and P. Smith, eds. *La fonction symbolique*. Paris: Gallimard, 1979.

Jung, Carl Gustav. *Métamorphoses de l'âme et ses symboles*. Paris: Buchet-Chastel, 1966.

——. *The Psychology of the Unconscious*. Mineola, N.Y.: Dover, 2003.

Jung, Carl Gustav, with Charles Kerényi. *Essays on a Science of Mythology*. Princeton, N.J.: Princeton University Press, 1969.

Jung, Carl Gustav, et al. *Man and His Symbols*. New York: Anchor Press, 1988.

Kaulbach, Friedrich. *Philosophische Grundlegung zu einer wissenschaftlichen Symbolik*. Meisenheim am Glan: A. Hain, 1954.

Kepes, Gyorgy. *Sign, Image, Symbol.* New York: Braziller, 1966.

Knights, L. C., et al. *Metaphor and Symbol.* London: Butterworths, 1960.

Koch, Rudolf. *The Book of Signs.* New York: Dover Publications, 1955.

Konrad, Hedwig. *Étude sur la métaphore.* Paris: J. Vrin, 1939.

Lanoe-Villène, Georges. *Le livre des symboles.* Paris: Librairie Générale, 1927.

Laplantine, François. *Les trois voix de l'imaginaire.* Paris: Éd. Universitaires, 1974.

Lefebvre, Maurice-Jean. *L'image fascinante et le surréel.* Paris: Plon, 1965.

Lehner, Ernst. *Symbols, Signs and Signets.* New York: Dover Publications, 1969.

Lévi-Strauss, Claude. *Anthropologie structurale.* Paris: Plon, 1958.

———. *La pensée sauvage.* Paris: Plon, 1962.

———. *La potière jalouse.* Paris: Plon, 1985.

———. *La voie des masques.* Geneva: Skira, 1975.

———. *Mythologiques* I, *Le cru et le cuit.* Paris: Plon, 1964.

———. *Mythologiques* II, *Du miel aux cendres.* Paris: Plon, 1967.

———. *Mythologiques* III, *L'origine des manières de table.* Paris: Plon, 1968.

Malrieu, Philippe. *La construction de l'Imaginaire.* Brussels: Dessart, 1967.

May, Rollo. *Symbolism in Religion and Literature.* New York: G. Braziller, 1961.

Millet, Louis. *Le symbole.* Paris: Fayard, 1959.

Nataf, Georges. *Symboles, signes et marques.* Paris: Berg, 1973.

Otto, Rudolf. *Le sacré.* Paris: Payot, 1949.

Ourgaud, René. *Le symbolisme et la science antique.* Bordeaux: Imp. H. Alzieu, n.d.

Pareto, Vilfredo, and Giovanni Busino. *Mythes et idéologies.* Geneva: Droz, 1966.

Pépin, Jean. *Mythe et allégorie.* Paris: Aubier, 1958.

Puech, Henri-Charles. *La gnose,* 2 vols. Paris: Gallimard, 1978.

Ricoeur, Paul. *De l'interprétation, essai sur Freud.* Paris: Seuil, 1965.

———. *Le conflit des interprétations.* Paris: Seuil, 1969.

Rivière, Claude. *Anthropologie religieuse des Evé du Togo.* Paris: Nouvelles éditions africaines, 1981.

Rosolato, Guy. *Essais sur le symbolique.* Paris: Gallimard, 1969.

Ruyer, Raymond. *Dieu des religions, Dieu de la science.* Paris: Flammarion, 1970.

———. *Esquisse d'une philosophie de la structure.* Paris: 1930.

———. *La gnose de Princeton.* Paris: Fayard, 1974.

———. *L'animal, l'homme, la fonction symbolique.* Paris: Gallimard, 1962.

———. *Le conflit des interprétations.* Paris: Seuil, 1969.

———. *Le monde des valeurs.* Paris: Aubier, 1947.

———. *Les nourritures psychiques.* Paris: Calmann-Lévy, 1975.

Schlesinger, Max. *Geschichte des Symbols.* Hildesheim: G. Olms, 1967.

Schwaller de Lubicz, R. A. *Symbol and the Symbolic.* Rochester, Vt.: Inner Traditions, 1981.

Scriabine, Marina. *Introduction au langage musical.* Paris: Éd. de Minuit, 1961.

Silberer, Herbert. *Problems of Mysticism and Its Symbolism.* Eastbourne, East Sussex, England: Gardners Books, 2007.

Thom, René. *Mathematical Models of Morphogenesis.* New York: Halsted Press, 1983.

Todorov, Tzvetan. *Symbolism and Interpretation.* Ithaca, N.Y.: Cornell University Press, 1982.

———. *Theories of the Symbol.* Ithaca, N.Y.: Cornell University Press, 1982.

Tuzet, Hélène. *Le Cosmos et l'imagination.* Paris: Corti, 1965.

Verbrugge, Armand Raymond. *La continuité des symboles,* 2 vols. Paris: 1969.

Wheelwright, Philip. *Metaphor and Reality.* Bloomington: Indiana University Press, 1962.

Collective Works

Aenishänslin, Markus. *Systèmes symboliques, sciences et philosophie.* Paris: Éd. du Centre national de la recherche scientifique, 1978.

Alquié, Ferdinand, et al. *Polarité du symbole.* Paris: Desclée de Brouwer, 1960.

Balandier, Georges, et al. *Nouvelles images, nouveau reel.* Paris: Presses Universitaires de France, 1987.

Cazenave, Michel, et al. *Science and Consciousness: Two Views of the Universe.* New York: Pergamon Press, 1984.

Delanglade, Schmalenbach, Godet, and Leuba. *Signe et Symbole.* Neuchâtel: Éd. de la Baconnière, 1946.

Millet, Louis, Marie Madeleine Davy, and Jean Trouillard. *Le symbole.* Paris: Fayard, 1959.

Mouloud, Noël, ed. *Les signes et leur interprétation.* Paris: Éditions Universitaires, 1972.

PSYCHOLOGICAL AND PSYCHOANALYTICAL SYMBOLS

Abraham, Karl. *Oeuvres complètes,* 2 vols. Paris: Payot, 1965–66.

Aeppli, Ernst. *Les rêves et leur interprétation.* Paris: Payot, 2002.

Bachelard, Gaston. *L'air et les songes.* Paris: Corti, 1943.

———. *La terre et les rêveries de la volonté.* Paris: Corti, 1948.

———. *L'eau et les rêves.* Paris: Corti, 1942.

———. *Psychanalyse de feu.* Paris: Gallimard, 1938.

Bastide, Roger. *Le rêve, la transe et la folie.* Paris: Flammarion, 1972.

———. *Le sacré sauvage.* Paris: Payot, 1976.

Baudouin, Charles. *Introduction à l'analyse des rêves.* Geneva: Éd. du Mont-Blanc, 1944.

———. *L'oeuvre de Jung*. Paris: Payot, 1963.

———. *Psychanalyse du symbole religieux*. Paris: Fayard, 1957.

———. *Psychanalyse du symbole religieux*. Paris: Seuil, 1964.

Bonaparte, Marie. *Mythes de guerre*. Paris: P.U.F., 1950.

Chateau, Jean. "Le réel et l'imaginaire dans le jeu de l'enfant, essai sur la genèse de l'imagination." In *Études de philosophie et de psychologie*. Paris: J. Vrin, 1946.

Devereux, Georges. *Essais d'ethnopsychiatrie générale*. Paris: Gallimard, 1969.

Duvignaud, Jean. *La banque des rêves. Essai d'anthropologie du rêveur contemporain*. Paris: Payot, 1979.

Ewer, Mary Anita. *A Survey of Mystical Symbolism*. New York: Macmillan Co., 1933.

Foucault, Michel. *Maladie mentale et psychologie*. Paris: P.U.F., 1965.

Frétigny, Roger, and André Virel. *L'imagerie mentale*. Geneva: Éd. du Mont-Blanc, 1968.

Freud, Sigmund. *The Basic Writings of Sigmund Freud*. Translated by A. A. Brill. New York: Modern Library, 1995.

———. *The Interpretation of Dreams*. Translated by A. A. Brill. New York: Modern Library, 1950.

———. *Introduction à la psychanalyse*. Paris: Payot, 1959.

———. *Le rêve et son interprétation*. Paris: Gallimard, 1969.

———. *Totem and Taboo: Resemblances between the Psychic Lives of Savages and Neurotics*. Translated by A. A. Brill. Amherst, N.Y.: Prometheus Books, 2000.

Girard, René. *Violence and the Sacred*. Baltimore: Johns Hopkins University Press, 1977.

Groddeck, Georg. *La maladie, l'art, le symbole*. Paris: Gallimard, 1976.

———. *Le livre de Ça*. Paris: Gallimard, 1974.

———. *The World of Man*. London: Vision, 1951.

Jacobi, Jolan. *Complex, Archetype, Symbol in the Psychology of C. G. Jung*. New York: Pantheon Books, 1959.

Jones, Ernest. *Papers on Psycho-analysis*. London: Tindall-Cox, 1949.

Jung, C. G. *Alchemical Studies (Collected Works of C. G. Jung)*. Translated by R. F. C. Hull and Gerhard Adler. Princeton, N.J.: Princeton University Press, 1983.

Jung, Emma, and James Hillman. *Anima et animus*. Paris: Seghers, 1981.

Lasswell, Harold D. *The Comparative Study of Symbols: An Introduction*. Stanford, Calif.: Stanford University Press, 1952.

Lopez-Pedraza, Rafael, et al. *Hermès et ses enfants dans la psychothérapie*. Paris: Imago, 1980.

Marcuse, Herbert. *Éros et civilisation, contribution à Freud*. Paris: Éd. de Minuit, 1963.

Mendel, Gérard. *La révolte contre le père.* Paris: Payot, 1968.

Mowrer, O. Hobatt. *Learning Theory and the Symbolic Processes.* New York: Wiley, 1960.

Pages, Robert, et al. "Rêve, rite, conversation: rythmes et tendances d'interactions." *Revue internationale de psychologie sociale,* no. 1 (1988).

Piaget, Jean. *La formation du symbole chez l'enfant.* Paris: Delachaux et Niestlé, 1945.

Robert, Marthe. *Roman des origines et origines du roman.* Paris: Grasset, 1972.

———. *D'Oedipe à Moïse, Freud et la conscience juive.* Paris: Calmann-Lévy, 1975.

Tauber, Edward S. *Prelogical Experience: An Inquiry into Dreams and Other Creative Processes.* New York: Basic Books, 1959.

Valabrega, Jean-Paul. *Phantasme, mythe, corps et sens.* Paris: Payot, 1980.

Winnicott, D. W. *Jeu et réalité.* Paris: Gallimard, 1975.

SYMBOLS AND MYTHS

Abraham, Karl. *Rêve et mythe.* Paris: Payot, 1977.

Andronikoff, Constantin. *Le sens des fêtes.* Éditions du Cerf, 1970.

Bachofen, Johann. *Myth, Religion and Mother Right.* Princeton, N.J.: Princeton University Press, 1967.

Barora, Julio Caro. *Les sorcières et leur monde.* Paris: Gallimard, 1985.

Batfroi, Séverin. *Du chaos à la lumière.* Paris: Éd. de la Maisnie, 1978.

Böhme, Jakob. *De la signature des choses.* Translated by Pierre Deghaye. Paris: Grasset, 1985.

Bounoure, Vincent. "Le mythe." In *Encyclopédie thématique Weber.* Paris: Weber, 1971.

Caillois, Roger. *The Dream and Human Societies.* Berkeley: University of California Press, 1966.

———. *Le mythe et l'homme.* Paris: Gallimard, 1938.

———. *Les jeux et les hommes.* Paris: Gallimard, 1967.

———. *Man and the Sacred.* Westport, Conn.: Greenwood Press, 1980.

Carlyle, Thomas. *On Heroes, Hero-Worship, and the Heroic in History.* Whitefish, Mont.: Kessinger, 2007.

Cope, Gilbert Frederick. *Symbolism in the Bible and Church.* London: SCM Press, 1959.

Corbin, Henry. *Alchimie comme art hiératique.* Paris: L'Herne, 1986.

———. *Avicenna and the Visionary Recital.* Translated by W. R. Trask. New York: HarperCollins, 1981.

———. *Creative Imagination in the Sufism of Ibn 'Arabi.* New York: Routledge, 2007.

———. *En Islam iranien: aspects spirituels et philosophiques,* 4 vols. Paris: Gallimard, 1971–73.

———. *The Man of Light in Iranian Sufism.* Translated by Nancy Pearson. New Lebanon, N.Y.: Omega Publications, 1994.

———. *Spiritual Body and Celestial Earth.* Translated by Nancy Pearson. Princeton, N.J.: Princeton University Press, 1989.

Corbin, Henry, et al. *Trilogie ismaélienne.* Paris: Verdier, 1994.

Creuzer, Georg Friedrich. *Les religions de l'antiquité considérées principalement sous leurs formes symboliques,* 10 vols. Translated by Guigniaut. Paris: 1825–51.

Cumont, Franz-Valery-Marie. *Recherches symbolisme funéraire des Romaines.* Paris: Paul Geuthner, 1942.

Dabezies, André. *Visages de Faust au XXᵉ siècle, littérature, idéologie et mythes.* Paris: P.U.F., 1967.

———. *Le mythe de Faust.* Paris: Armand Colin, 1972.

Danckert, Werner. *Tonreich und Symbolzahl in Hochkulturen und in der Primitivenwelt.* Bonn: Bouvier, 1966.

Daniélou, Alain. *Gods of Love and Ecstasy: The Traditions of Shiva and Dionysus.* Rochester, Vt.: Inner Traditions, 1992.

Daniélou, Jean. *Le signe du Temple.* Paris: Gallimard, 1942.

———. *Primitive Christian Symbols.* Baltimore: Helicon Press, 1964.

Davy, Marie-Madeleine. *Clefs de l'art roman: la symbolique roman.* Paris: Berg, 1973.

———. *Initiation à la symbolique romane.* Paris: Flammarion, 1967.

Détienne, Marcel. *Dionysos à ciel ouverte.* Paris: Hachette, 1986.

———. *Dionysus Slain.* Baltimore: Johns Hopkins University Press, 1979.

———. *Le jardin d'Adonis.* Paris: Gallimard, 1979.

———. *L'invention de la mythologie.* Paris, 1981.

De Diéguez, Manuel. *Le mythe rationnel de l'Occident.* Paris: P.U.F., 1980.

Diel, Paul. *Le symbolisme dans la Bible.* Paris: Payot, 1976.

———. *Le symbolisme dans la mythologie grecque.* Paris: Payot, 1952.

Dontenville, Henri. *La mythologie française.* Paris: Payot, 1948.

Duchesne-Guillemin, Jacques. *Symbols and Values in Zoroastrianism.* New York: Harper and Row, 1966.

Dumézil, Georges. *Apollon sonore et autres essais.* Paris: Gallimard, 1982.

———. *Jupiter, Mars, Quirius, essai sur la conception indo-européenne de la société et sur les origines de Rome.* Paris: Gallimard, 1941.

———. *La courtisane et les seigneurs colorés.* Paris: Gallimard, 1983.

———. *La religion romaine archaïque.* Paris: Payot, 1966.

———. *L'oubli de l'homme et l'honneur des dieux.* Paris: Gallimard, 1985.

———. *Mitra-Varuna, essai sur deux représentations indo-européennes de la souveraineté.* Paris: Gallimard, 1948.

———. *Naissance d'archanges.* Paris: Gallimard, 1946.

———. *Naissance de Rome.* Paris: Gallimard, 1944.

Eliade, Mircea. *Aspects du mythe.* Paris: Gallimard, 1988.

———. *Images and Symbols: Studies in Religious Symbolism.* Translated by Philip Mairet. Princeton, N.J.: Princeton University Press, 1991.

———. *Myths, Dreams, and Mysteries.* Translated by Philip Mairet. New York: Harper and Brothers, 1960.

———. *The Sacred and the Profane: The Nature of Religion.* Translated by Willard R. Trask. San Diego: Harcourt Brace Jovanovich, 1987.

Eliade, Mircea, et al. *Initiation: Contributions to the Theme of the Study.* Conference of the Association for the History of Religions. Leiden: E. J. Brill, 1965.

Evola, Julius. *The Mystery of the Grail.* Rochester, Vt.: Inner Traditions, 1996.

Florensky, Père Paul. *La colonne et le fondement de la vérité.* Translated by C. Andronikoff. Lausanne: L'Âge d'Homme, 1975.

Frazer, James. *The Golden Bough.* Mineola, N.Y.: Dover, 2002.

———. *Myths of the Origin of Fire.* New York: Routledge, 2000.

Goodenough, Erwin. *Jewish Symbols in the Greco-Roman Period.* New York: Pantheon, 1968.

———. *Symbolism in the Dura Synagogue.* New York: Pantheon, 1964.

Granet, Marcel. *La pensée chinoise.* Paris: Renaissance du livre, 1934.

Griffith, Helen Stuart. *The Sign Language of Our Faith.* Grand Rapids, Mich.: Eerdmans, 1966.

Grodecki, Louis. *Symbolisme cosmique et monuments religieux.* Paris: 1953.

Guardini, Abbé Romano. *Les signes sacrées.* Paris: Éditions Spes, 1951.

Guedez, A. "Les mythes vivants du compagnonnage." *Cause commune,* no. 1 (October 18, 1976).

Gusdorf, Georges. *L'expérience humaine de sacrifice.* Paris: P.U.F., 1948.

Hani, Jean. *Le symbolisme du temple chrétien.* Paris: La Colombe, 1962.

Hentze, Carle. *Mythes et symboles lunaires.* Translated by Herbert Kühn. Antwerp: Éd. de Sirrel, 1952.

Hopper, Vincent Foster. *Medieval Number Symbolism.* New York: Columbia University Press, 1938.

Jeanmaire, Henri. *Dionysos.* Paris: Payot, 1970.

Kirchgässner, Alfons. *La puissance des signes, origines, formes et lois du culte.* Tours: Mame, 1962.

Krappe, Alexander Haggerty. *Mythologie universelle.* Paris: Payot, 1930.

———. *La genèse des mythes.* Paris: Payot, 1962.

Lanoë-Villène, Georges. *Les sources de la symbolique chrétienne*. Paris: Fischbacher, 1921.

——. *Principes généraux de la symbolique des religions*. Paris: Jouve, 1915.

Leroi-Gourhan, André. *Technique et langage. Le geste et la parole,* vol. 1. Paris: Albin Michel, 1964.

——. *La mémoire et les rhythmes. Le geste et la parole,* vol 2. Paris: Albin Michel, 1965.

Lévy-Bruhl, Lucien. *L'expérience mystique et les symboles*. Paris: Alcan, 1938.

——. *Primitives and the Supernatural*. New York: E. P. Dutton, 1935.

——. *Primitive Mythology: The Mythic World of the Australian and Papuan Natives*. St. Lucia: University of Queensland Press, 1983.

Marcuse, Herbert. *L'homme unidimensionnel*. Paris: Éd. de Minuit, 1968.

Matsumoto, Yeïchi. *The Astronomical Emblems in the Oriental Fine Arts*. 1927.

Nougayrol, Jean. "La divination babylonienne." In *La divination*. Paris: P.U.F., 1968.

Reinach, Salomon. *Cultes, mythes et religions,* 5 vols. Paris: Leroux, 1905–11.

Roheim, Géza. *Psychanalyse et anthropologie, culture, personnalité, inconscient*. Paris: Gallimard, 1967.

Saunier, Marc. *La légende des symboles philosophiques, religieux et maçonniques*. Paris: E. Sansot, 1911.

Sauvy, Alfred. *La mythologie de notre temps*. Paris: Payot, 1965.

Siblot, Joseph. *Signes de Dieu*. Paris: Éditions Ouvrières, 1953.

Solé, Jacques. *Les mythes chrétiens de la Renaissance aux Lumières*. Paris: Albin Michel, 1979.

Stables, Pierre. *Deux clefs initiatiques de la légende dorée: La Kabbale et le Yi-King*. Paris: Dervy, 1975.

Steiner, George. *Les Antigones*. Paris: Gallimard, 1992.

Vernant, Jean Pierre. *La mort dans les yeux*. Paris: Hachette, 1985.

——. *Myth and Thought among the Greeks*. Boston: Routledge and Kegan Paul, 1983.

Vernant, Jean Pierre, and Marcel Détienne. *The Cuisine of Sacrifice among the Greeks*. Chicago: University of Chicago Press, 1989.

Veynes, Paul. *Les Grecs croyaient-ils à leur mythes?* Paris: Seuil, 1983.

von Schelling, Friedrich Wilhelm Joseph. *Introduction à la philosophie de la mythologie*. Paris: Aubier, 1945.

Zimmer, Heinrich Robert. *Mythes et symboles dans l'art et la civilisation de l'Inde*. Paris: Payot, 1951.

SYMBOLISM IN CONNECTION WITH ICONOLOGY, LANGUAGE, AND PHILOSOPHY

Abellio, Raymond. *La structure absolue.* Paris: Gallimard, 1965.

Alciati, Andrea. *Emblemata.* Paris: 1580.

Aratus, Paulus. *Emblemas sacras y profanas, seguidas de un discurso . . .* Rome: 1589.

Artin, Yacoub. *Contribution à l'étude du blason en Orient.* London: B. Quaritch, 1902.

Atlan, Henri. *A tort et à raison. Intercritique de la science et du mythe.* Paris: Seuil, 1986.

Baczko, Bronislaw. *Les imaginaires sociaux. Mémoires et espoirs collectifs.* Paris: Payot, 1984.

Baltrusaitis, Jurgis. *Aberrations: 4 essais sur la légende des formes.* Paris: O. Perrin, 1957.

———. *Art sumérien, art roman.* Paris: E. Leroux, 1934.

———. *Essai sur la légende d'un mythe: la quête d'Isis.* Paris: O. Perrin, 1967.

———. *Le Moyen Age fantastique.* Paris: 1955.

———. *Réveils et prodiges, le gothique fantastique.* Paris: O. Perrin, 1960.

Baudouin, Jean. *Recueil d'emblèmes divers.* Hildesheim, Germany: Olms, 1977.

Benveniste, Émile. *Problèmes de linguistique générale.* Paris: Gallimard, 1975.

Berger, Peter, and T. Luckmann. *La construction sociale de la réalité.* Paris: Armand Colin, 2006.

Bianchini, Francesco. *Historia universale provata con monumenti e figuri con simboli degli antichi.* Rome: 1747.

Black, Max. *Language and Philosophy: Studies and Method.* Ithaca, N.Y.: Cornell University Press, 1949.

Bloch, Ernst. *Le principe espérance.* Paris: Gallimard, 1982.

Bocchio, Achille. *Symbolicarum quaestionum de universo genere.* Bologna: 1555.

Bochart, Samuel. *Hierozoicon, sive bipartitum opus de Animalibus S. Scripturae.* London: 1663.

Boissaer, Jean-Jacques. *Emblematum Liber.* Frankfurt: 1593.

Bornitus, Jacobus. *Emblemata ethico-politica.* Mainz: 1669.

Boulanger, Nic. Ant. *L'antiquité dévoilée par ses usages.* Amsterdam: 1766.

Bréhier, Louis. *L'art chrétien, son développement iconographique des origines à nos jours.* Paris: Librairie Renouard, 1928.

Breton, André. *L'art magique.* Paris: Club français de l'Art, 1957.

Bruck Angermunt, Jacobus. *Emblemata politica.* Köln: 1618.

Buren, E. Douglas van. *Symbols of the Gods in Mesopotamian Art.* Rome: Analecta Orientalia, 1945.

Camerarius, Joachinus. *Symbolorum et emblematum centuriae.* Mainz: 1668.

Carnac, Pierre. *Architecture sacrée. Le symbolisme des premières formes.* Paris: Dangles, 1978.

Carnap, Rudolf. *Introduction to Semantics and Formalization of Logic.* Cambridge, Mass.: Harvard University Press, 1959.

———. *Introduction to Symbolic Logic and Its Applications.* New York: Dover, 1958.

Cartari, Vincenzo. *Le imagine delli Dei delle antichi.* Venice: 1625.

Cassirer, Ernst. *The Philosophy of the Symbolic Forms.* New Haven, Conn.: Yale University Press, 1953–57.

Chenique, François. *Éléments de logique classique.* Paris: Dunod, 1975.

Colonna, Francesco. *Hypnerotomachia Poliphili.* Venice: 1499.

Condon, John C. *Semantics and Communication.* New York: Macmillan, 1985.

Coomaraswamy, Ananda Kentish. *Elements of Buddhist Iconography.* Cambridge, Mass.: Harvard University Press, 1935.

———. "The Inverted Tree." *The Quarterly Journal of the Mythic Society* 24, no. 2 (1938).

———. "Symbolism of the Dome." *Indian Historical Quarterly* 14, no. 1 (1935).

Dagognet, François. *Philosophie de l'image.* Paris: J. Vrin, 1984.

d'Espagnat, Bernard, et al. *En busco de lo real, la vision de un fisico.* Madrid: Alianza, 1983.

de Fleury, Charles Rohault. *L'Évangile; études iconographiques.* Tours: Alfred Mame, 1874.

de Gissey, Odo. *Les emblesmes et devises du roy, des princes.* Paris: 1657.

de Horrozco y Covvarrubias, Juan. *Emblemas morales.* Segovia: 1604.

Deken, Joseph. *Les images du futur. L'informatique graphique.* Paris: Mazarine, 1984.

de Ledesma, Alfonso. *Epigramas y hieroglyficos.* 1623.

de Marneffe, Alphonse. *Les combinaisons s de la croix et du triangle divin dans les blasons et les marques des Marchands.* Charleroi: La Table Ronde, 1939.

de Montfaucon, Bernard. *Antiquity Explained and Represented in Sculptures: London 1721–1722.* New York: Garland, 1976.

de Saussure, Ferdinand. *Course in General Linguistics.* Translated by Roy Harris. Chicago: Open Court, 1986.

de Sorval, Gérard. *Le langue secret du blason.* Paris: Dervy, 2003.

Didron, Adolphe-Napoléon. *Christian Iconography.* New York: F. Ungar, 1965.

Evans, Edward Payson. *Animal Symbolism in Ecclesiastical Architecture.* Detroit: Gail Research Co., 1969.

Ferrero, Guglielmo. *I Simboli in rapporto alla storia a filosofia del diritto.* Turin: 1893.

Focillon, Henri. *Vie des formes.* Paris: P.U.F., 1981.

Francastel, P. *L'image, la vision et l'imagination. De la peinture au cinéma.* Paris: Denoël-Gonthier, 1983.

Francisco de Holanda. *De Aetatibus Mundi Imagines.* Lisbon: 1545.

Gerlach, Martin. *Allegorien und Embleme.* Vienna: 1900.

Gevaert, Émile. *L'héraldique; son esprit, son langage, et ses applications.* Brussels: Vromant, 1923.

Gilles, René. *Le symbolisme dans l'art religieux.* Paris: Éd. de la Maisnie, 1979.

Girard, René. *Things Hidden Since the Foundation of the World.* Stanford, Calif.: Stanford University Press, 1987.

Gravelot, Hubert-François, and Charles Nicolas Cochin. *Iconologie par figures ou traité complet des allégories, emblèmes, etc.* Geneva: Minkoff, 1972.

Green, Henry. *Andrea and His Books of Emblems.* London: 1872.

Greimas, Agirdas Julien. *Sémantique structurale.* Paris: Larousse, 1966.

Guilhot, Jean. *La dynamique de l'expression et de la communication.* Paris: La Haye, Mouton, 1962.

Guiraud, Pierre. *La sémantique.* Paris: P.U.F., 1955.

Hautecoeur, Louis. *Mystique et architecture, symbolisme du cercle et de la coupole.* Paris: 1954.

Hinks, Roger. *Myth and Allegory in Ancient Art.* Nendeln, Lichtenstein: Krauss Reprint, 1976.

Holz-Bonneau, F. *L'image et l'ordinateur.* Paris: Aubier, I.N.A., 1986.

Hyginus, C. Julius. *Hygini quae hodie extant, etc., accedunt Thomae Munckeri in fabulas Hygini annotationes.* Hamburg: 1674.

———. *Iconologia, of Uytbeeldingen des Verstands van Cesare Ripa van Perugien. . . .* Amsterdam: 1644.

———. *Iconologie, ou explication nouvelle de plusieurs images, emblèmes, et autres figures hiéroglyphiques, des Vertus, des Vices, des Arts, des Sciences, des Causes naturelles, des Humeurs différentes, et des Passions humaines . . . , tirée des Recherches et des Figures de Cesar Ripa, moralisées par I. Baudouin.* Paris: 1643.

Jakobson, Roman. *Essais de linguistique générale.* Paris: Éd. de Minuit, 1970.

Junius, Adrianus. *Emblemata.* Antwerp: 1565.

Kircher, A. *Aedipus aegyptiacus, hoc est universalis hieroglyphicae veterum doctrinae instauratio.* Rome: 1652.

Langer, Susanne K. *Feeling and Form: A Theory of Art.* New York: Scribner, 1953.

———. *An Introduction to Symbolic Logic.* New York: Dover Publications, 1953.

———. *Philosophy in a New Key: A Study in Symbolism of Reason, Rite and Art.* Cambridge, Mass.: Harvard University Press, 1957.

Leclerq, Henri, and Fernand Cabrol. *Dictionnaire d'archéologie chrétienne et de liturgie.* Paris: Letouzey, 1907–27.

Le Doeuf, Michèle. *L'imaginaire philosophique.* Paris: Payot, 1980.

Lefebvre, Henri. *Le langage et la société.* Paris: Gallimard, 1964.

———. *La présence et l'absence. Contribution à la théorie des représentations.* Paris: Casterman, 1980.

Le Forestier, R. *Maçonnerie féminine et loges académiques.* Milan: Arche, 1979.

MacClatchie, Thomas R. H. *Japanese Heraldry.* Yokohama: 1877.

Male, Émile. *Religious Art in France: The Late-Middle Ages—a Study of Medieval Iconography and Its Sources.* Princeton, N.J.: Princeton University Press, 1986.

———. *L'art religieux après le concile de Trente.* Paris: Armand Colin, 1932.

Mannhardt, Wilhelm. *Germanische Mythen.* Berlin: F. Schneider, 1858.

Menestrier, Claude-François. *La philosophie des images; Paris 1682.* New York: Garland, 1979.

Merleau-Ponty, Maurice. *Signes.* Paris: Gallimard, 1960.

Mills, C. Wright. *Images of Man: The Classic Tradition in Sociological Thinking.* New York: George Braziller, 1960.

———. *The Sociological Imagination.* New York: Oxford University Press, 1959.

Moles, Abraham A. *L'image, communication fonctionelle.* Tournai: Casterman, 1981.

Morris, Charles. *Signs, Language and Behavior.* New York: Prentice Hall, 1946.

Muntz, Eugène. *Études iconographiques et archéologiques sur le Moyen Age.* Paris: Leroux, 1887.

Noel, Fr. *Dictionnaire de la fable.* Paris: Le Normant, 1823.

Nuñez de Cépeda, Francisco. *Emblemas sacras.* Leon: 1682.

Oehler, Gustav Friedrich. *Lehrbuch der Symbolik.* Stuttgart: 1891.

Panofsky, Erwin. *Essais d'iconologie; les thèmes humanistes dans l'art de la Renaissance.* Paris: Gallimard, 1967.

———. *L'oeuvre d'art et ses significations; essais sur les arts visuels.* Paris: Gallimard, 1969.

Perdrizet, Paul. *L'art symbolique du Moyen Age.* Leipzig: 1907.

Picinelli, D. Filippo. *Mondo Simbolico ampliato.* Venice: 1670.

Pierius Valerianus, J. *Commentaires hiéroglyphiques ou images des choses.* Translated by Gabriel Chappuis. Lyon: 1576.

Przywara. E., et al. *Filosofia e simbolismo.* Rome: Bocca, 1956.

Queau, Philippe. *Éloge de la simulation.* Seyssel, France: Champ Vallon, 1986.

Quere, Louis. *Des miroirs équivoques, aux origines de la communication moderne.* Paris: Aubier Montaigne, 1982.

Reusens, Edmond. *Éléments d'archéologie chrétienne.* Aix-la-Chapelle: Rudolf Barth, 1885–86.

Richardson, George. *Iconology: or a Collection of Emblematical Figures, Moral and Instructive*. London: 1778.

Rihs, Charles. *Les philosophes utopistes. Le mythe de la cité communautaire en France au XVIIe siècle*. Paris: Marcel Rivière, 1970.

Robin, Léon. *La théorie platonicienne des idées et des nombres*. Hildesheim: Olms, 1984.

Rossignol, Jean-Pierre. *Des services que peut rendre l'archéologie aux études classiques*. Paris: A. Labitte, 1878.

Rousset, Jean-Paul. *Forme et signification*. Paris: Corti, 1964.

Saison, Maryvonne. *Imaginaire, imaginable*. Paris: Klincksieck, 1981.

Sambucus, Johannes. *Emblemata cum aliquot nummis antiqui operis*. Antwerp: 1564.

Sartre, Jean-Paul. *L'imaginaire*. Paris: Gallimard, 1940.

———. *L'imagination*. Paris: P.U.F., 1950.

Schenck, Georg. *Monstrorum historia memorabilis*. Frankfurt: 1609.

Schipper, Kristofer Marinus. *The Taoist Body*. Berkeley: University of California Press, 1993.

Schuhl, Pierre-Maxime. *Études sur la fabulation platonicienne*. Paris: P.U.F., 1947.

———. *L'imagination et le merveilleux, la pensée et l'action*. Paris: Flammarion, 1969.

Sèchehaye, Marguerite. *Symbolic Realization: A New Method of Psychotherapy Applied to a Case of Schizophrenia*. New York: International Universities Press, 1960.

Siganos, André. *Les mythologies de l'insecte*. Paris: Librairie des Méridiens, 1985.

Soldi-Colbert de Beaulieu, Émile. *La langue sacrée*. Paris: A. Heymann, 1897.

Solorzanopereira, Ioannes. *Emblemata. . . .* Madrid: 1651.

Springer, Anton. *Ikonographische Studien*. Vienna: 1860.

Starobinski, Jean. *Jean-Jacques Rousseau: Tranparency and Obstruction*. Chicago: University of Chicago Press, 1988.

Typotius, Jacobus. *Symbola varia diversorum principum*. Arnheim: 1679.

Urban, Wilbur Marshall. *Language and Reality: The Philosophy of Language and the Principles of Symbolism*. London: Allen and Unwin, 1939.

van Marle, Raymond. *Iconographie de l'art profane au Moyen Age et à la Renaissance*. New York: Hacker Art Books, 1971.

Viel, Robert. *Les origines symboliques du blason, l'hermétisme dans l'art héraldique*. Paris: Berg International, 1971.

Westerhovius, A. H. *Hieroglyphica oder Denkbilder der alten Völken*. Amsterdam: 1741.

Wheelwright, Philip. *The Burning Fountain: A Study in the Language of Symbolism*. Bloomington: Indiana University Press, 1954.

Yates, Frances Amelia. *Giordano Bruno and the Hermetic Tradition*. London: Routledge, 2002.

SYMBOLISM AND THE IMAGINARY IN
EVERYDAY URBAN MODERNITY

Agel, Henri. *Cinéma et nouvelle naissance*. Paris: Albin Michel, 1981.

Augoyard, Jean-François. *Step by Step: Everyday Walks in a French Urban Housing Project*. Minneapolis: University of Minnesota Press, 2007.

Baudrillard, Jean. *Symbolic Exchange and Death*. London: Sage Publications, 1993.

Brun, Jean. *Le retour de Dionysos*. Paris: Desclée, 1969.

Cauquelin, Anne. *Court traité du fragment. Usages de l'oeuvre d'art*. Paris: Aubier, 1986.

Chalas, Y. "Raison technique et 'phantaisie' quotidienne." In *Informatique et société. Des chercheurs s'interrogent*. Grenoble: P.U.G., 1988.

Dorfles, Gillo. *Mythes et rites d'aujourd'hui*. Paris: Klincksieck, 1975.

Ferrarotti, Franco. *Une théologie pour athées*. Paris: Librairie des Méridiens, 1984.

Gouvion, Colette, and François van de Mert. *Le symbolisme des rues et des cités*. Paris: Berg International, 1974.

Ledrut, Raymond. *La forme et le sens dans la société*. Paris: Librairie des Méridiens, 1984.

Letoublon, Françoise, et al. *Fonder une cité*. Grenoble: ELLUG, 1987.

Lévy, Françoise P. *La ville en croix*. Paris: Librairie des Méridiens, 1984.

Maffesoli, Michel. *La connaissance ordinaire*. Paris: Librairie des Méridiens, 1985.

———. *Le temps des tribus*. Paris: Librairie des Méridiens, 1988.

Medam, Alain. *La cité des noms Jérusalem*. Paris: Galilée, 1980.

———. *New York Terminal*. Paris: Galilée, 1977.

Moles, Abraham. *Labyrinthe du vécu*. Paris: Librairie des Méridiens, 1982.

———. *Psychologie de l'espace*. Paris: Casterman, 1978.

Morin, Edgar. *Le cinéma ou l'homme imaginaire. Essai d'anthropologie*. Paris: Éd. de Minuit, 1956.

———. *Rumour in Orleans*. London: Blond, 1971.

Mucchielli, Roger. *Le mythe de la cité idéale*. Paris: P.U.F., 1960.

Noschis, Kaj. *Signification affective du quartier*. Paris: Librairie des Méridiens, 1984.

Ostrowetsky, Sylvia. *L'imaginaire bâtisseur, les villes nouvelles françaises*. Paris: Librairie des Méridiens, 1984.

Pessin, Alain, and Henri Skoff Torgue. *Villes imaginaires*. Paris: Champ Urbain, 1980.

Sansot, Pierre. *Les formes sensibles de la vie sociale*. Paris: P.U.F., 1986.

———. *Poétique de la ville*. Paris: Klincksieck, 1984.

Thomas, Louis-Vincent. *Anthropologie de la mort.* Paris: Payot, 1988.

———. *Civilisations et divagation. Mort, fantasmes, science-fiction.* Paris: Payot, 1979.

———. *Fantasmes au quotidien.* Paris: Librairie des Méridiens, 1984.

GENERAL SYMBOLOGY IN CONNECTION
WITH MYTHOPOLITICS

Alleau, René. *Epistémologie du mythique et du symbolique dans les discours politiques de la Terreur.* Paris: P.U.F., 1989.

———. *Hitler et les sociétés secrètes.* Paris: Grasset, 1969.

Ansart, Pierre. *Idéologies, conflits et pouvoir.* Paris: P.U.F., 1977.

———. *La gestion des passions politiques.* Lausanne: L'Âge d'Homme, 1983.

Balandier, Georges. *Le détour. Pouvoir et modernité.* Paris: Fayard, 1985.

———. *Political Anthropology.* New York: Pantheon, 1970.

Barel, Yves. *La quête du sens. Comment l'esprit vient à la cité.* Paris: Seuil, 1987.

Chalas, Yves. *Vichy et l'imaginaire totalitaire.* Arles: Actes Sud, 1985.

Cohn, Norman. *Histoire d'un mythe. La conspiration juive et les protocoles des sages de Lion.* Paris: Gallimard, 1967.

Girardet, Raoul. *Mythes et mythologies politiques.* Paris: Seuil, 1986.

Maffesoli, Michel. *La violence totalitaire.* Paris: P.U.F., 1979.

Pelassy, Dominique. *Le signe nazi.* Paris: Fayard, 1983.

Pessin, Alain. *La rêverie anarchiste 1848–1914.* Paris: Méridiens, 1982.

Pessin, Alain, and Michel Maffesoli. *La violence fondatrice.* Paris: Champ Urbain, 1978.

Poliakov, Léon. *The Aryan Myth: A History of Racist and Nationalist Ideas in Europe.* Paris: Calmann-Lévy, 1971.

Reszler, André. *Mythes politiques modernes.* Paris: P.U.F., 1981.

Rivière, Claude. *Les liturgies politiques.* Paris: P.U.F., 1988.

Sfez, Lucien. *La symbolique politique.* Paris: P.U.F., 1996.

———. *L'enfer et le paradis.* Paris: P.U.F., 1978.

Sironneau, Jean-Pierre. *Sécularisation et religions politiques.* Paris: La Haye, 1982.

Tulard, Jean. *Le mythe de Napoléon.* Paris: A. Colin, 1971.

PRINCIPAL JOURNALS ON SYMBOLISM

Cahiers internationaux de symbolisme. Mons, Belgium: C.I.E.P.H.U.M.

Eranos Jahrbuch. Zurich: Rhein-Verlag.

Cahiers de l'hermétisme. Paris: Albin Michel.

Cahiers de l'Université Saint-Jean de Jérusalem. Paris: Berg International.

Hermès. Paris: Éd. Hermès.

INDEX

292